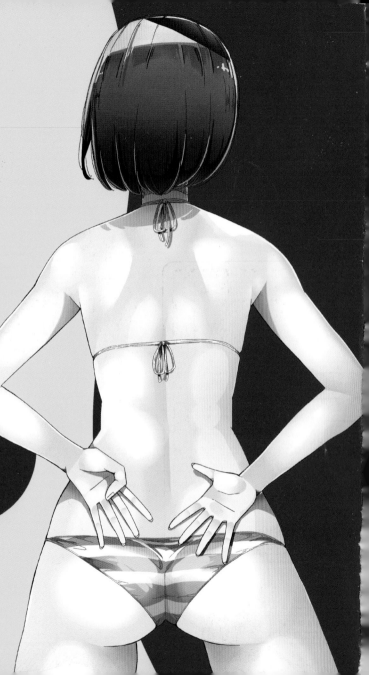

HARUKANA RECEIVE

09

Volume Nine

story & art by
NYOIJIZAI

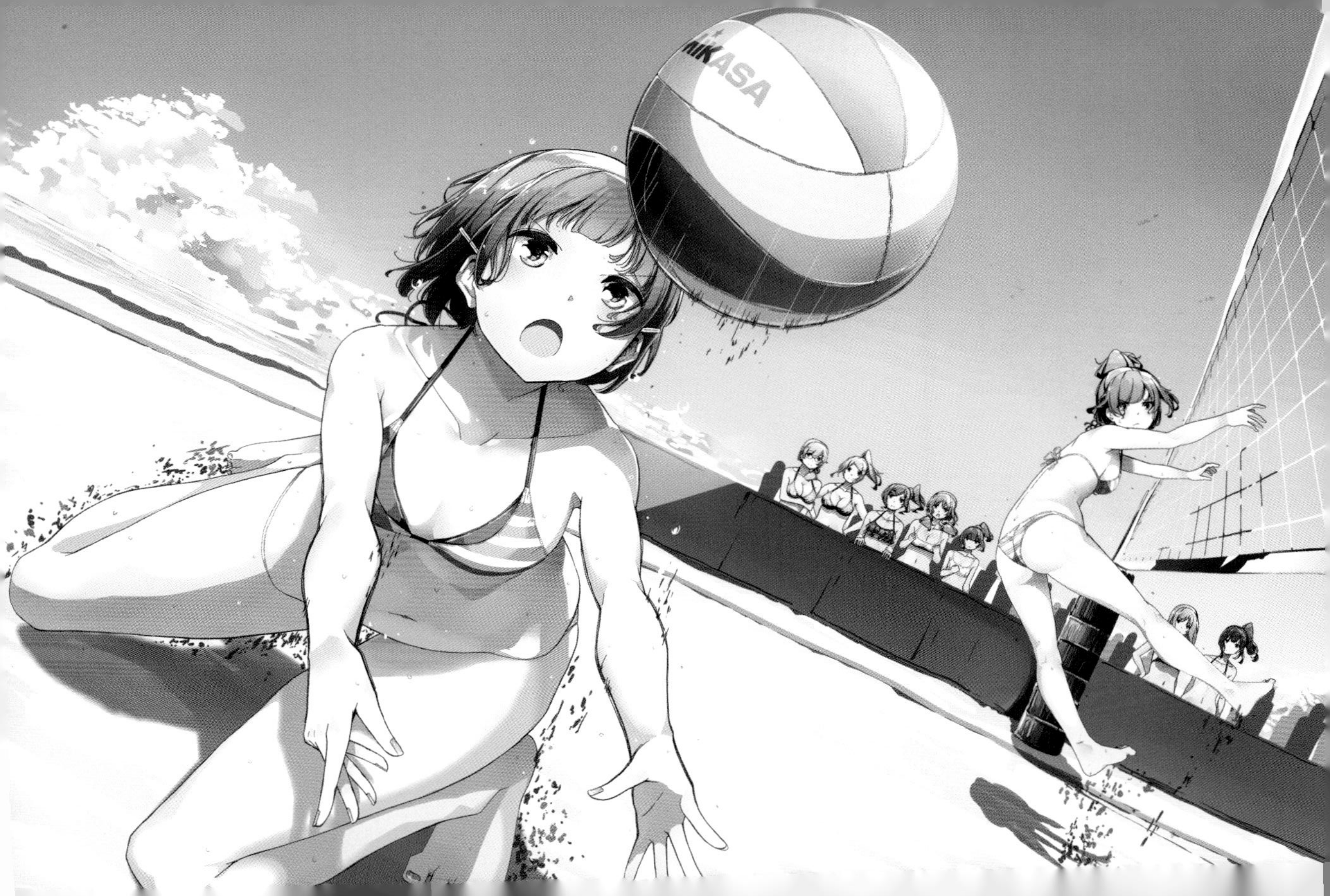
MIKASA

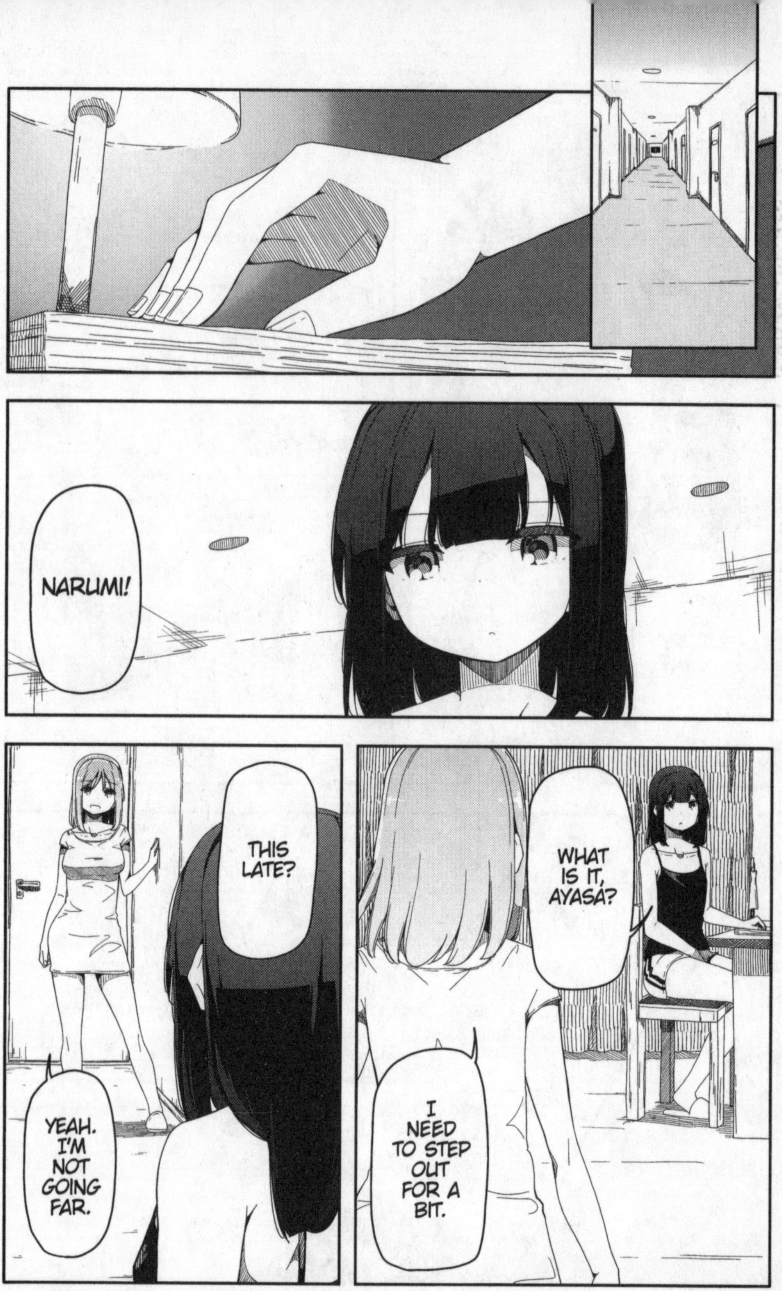
NARUMI!
WHAT IS IT, AYASA?
I NEED TO STEP OUT FOR A BIT.
THIS LATE?
YEAH. I'M NOT GOING FAR.

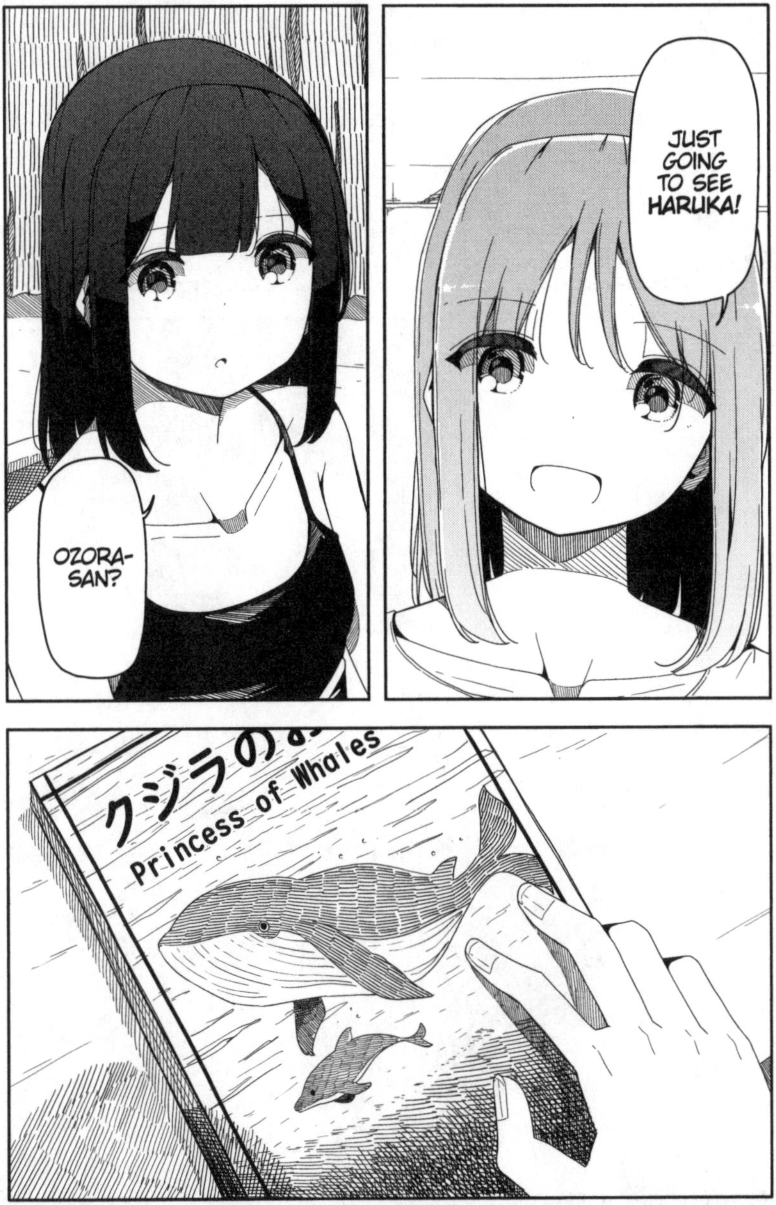
JUST GOING TO SEE HARUKA!
OZORA-SAN?
クジラの
Princess of Whales

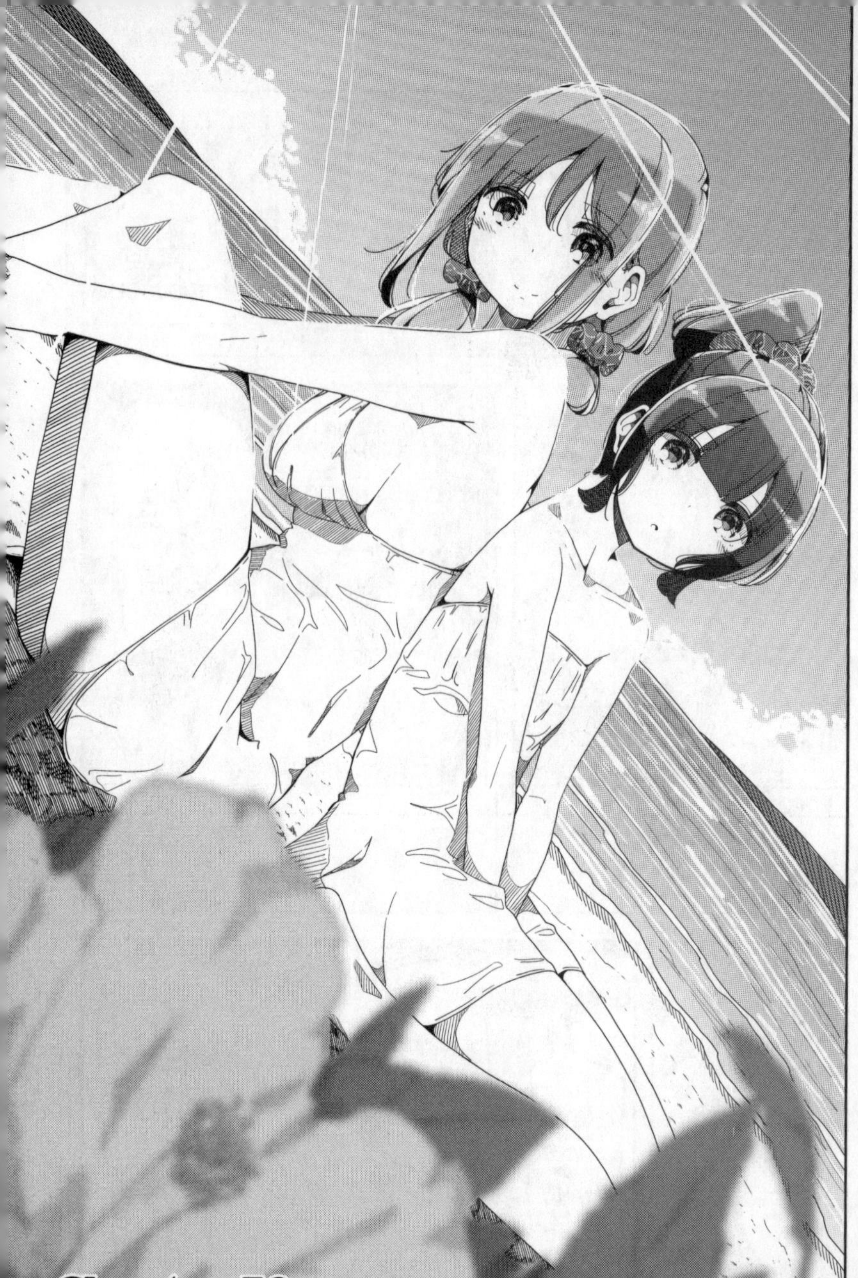

## Chapter 50: The Night Before the Semifinals

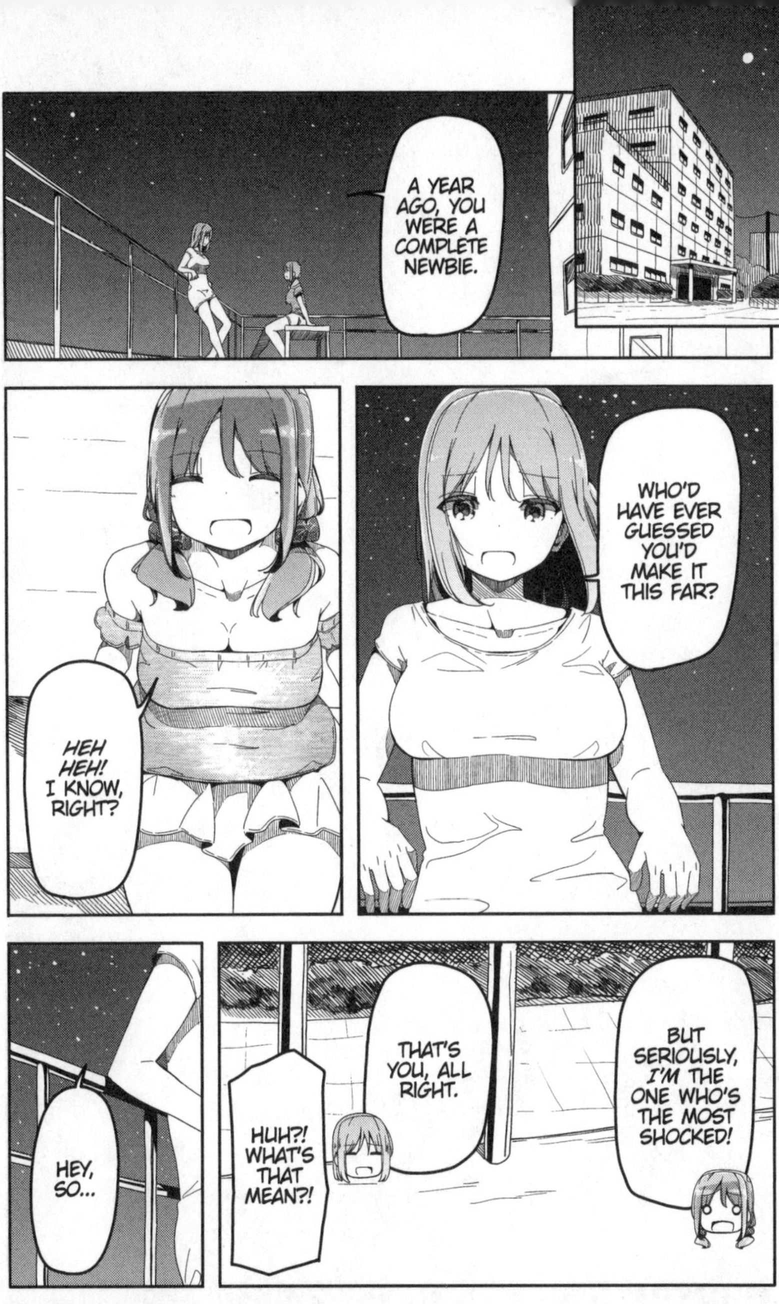
A YEAR AGO, YOU WERE A COMPLETE NEWBIE.
WHO'D HAVE EVER GUESSED YOU'D MAKE IT THIS FAR?
HEH HEH! I KNOW, RIGHT?
BUT SERIOUSLY, *I'M* THE ONE WHO'S THE MOST SHOCKED!
THAT'S YOU, ALL RIGHT.
HUH?! WHAT'S THAT MEAN?!
HEY, SO...

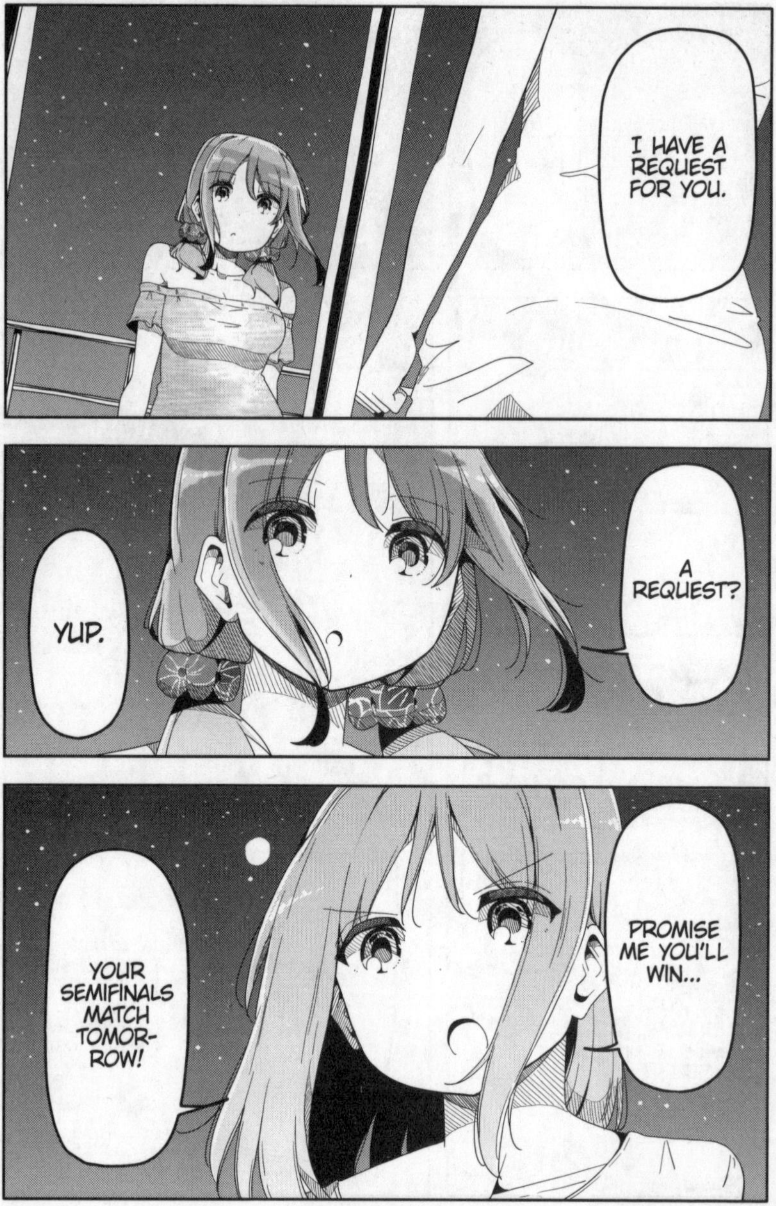
I HAVE A REQUEST FOR YOU.
A REQUEST?
YUP.
PROMISE ME YOU'LL WIN...
YOUR SEMIFINALS MATCH TOMOR-ROW!

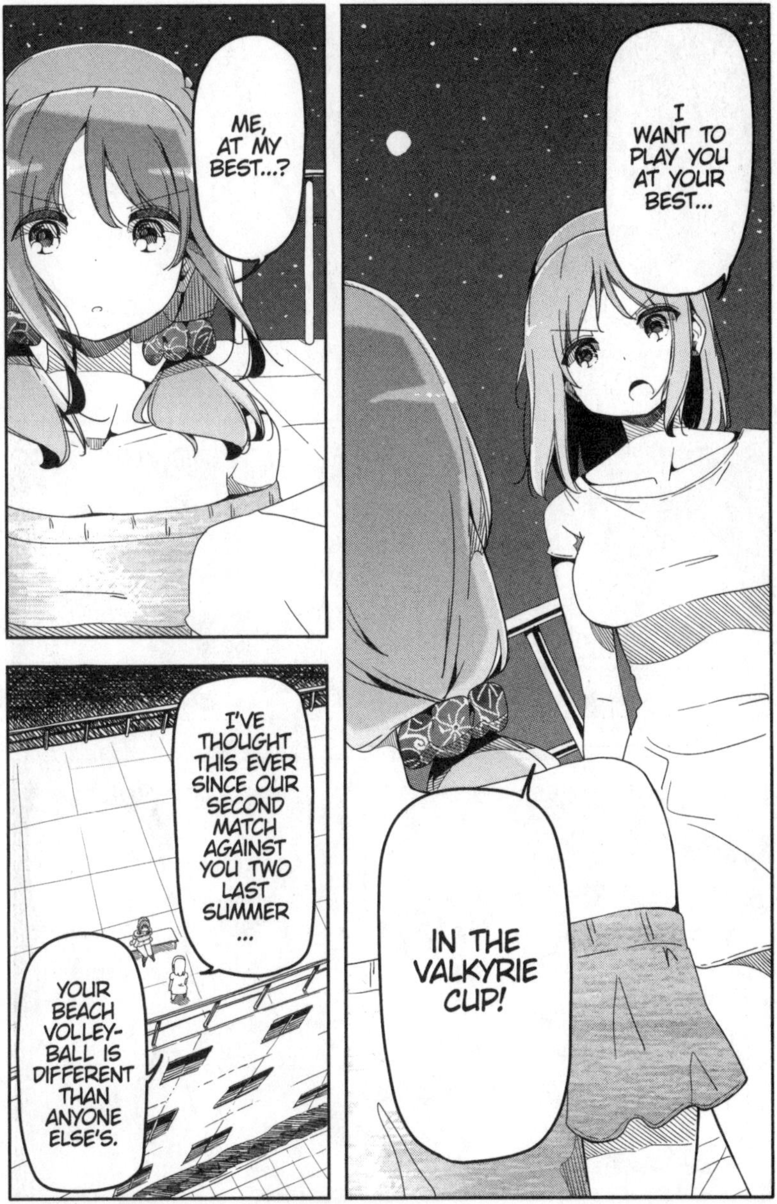
I WANT TO PLAY YOU AT YOUR BEST...
ME, AT MY BEST...?
I'VE THOUGHT THIS EVER SINCE OUR SECOND MATCH AGAINST YOU TWO LAST SUMMER ...
YOUR BEACH VOLLEY-BALL IS DIFFERENT THAN ANYONE ELSE'S.
IN THE VALKYRIE CUP!

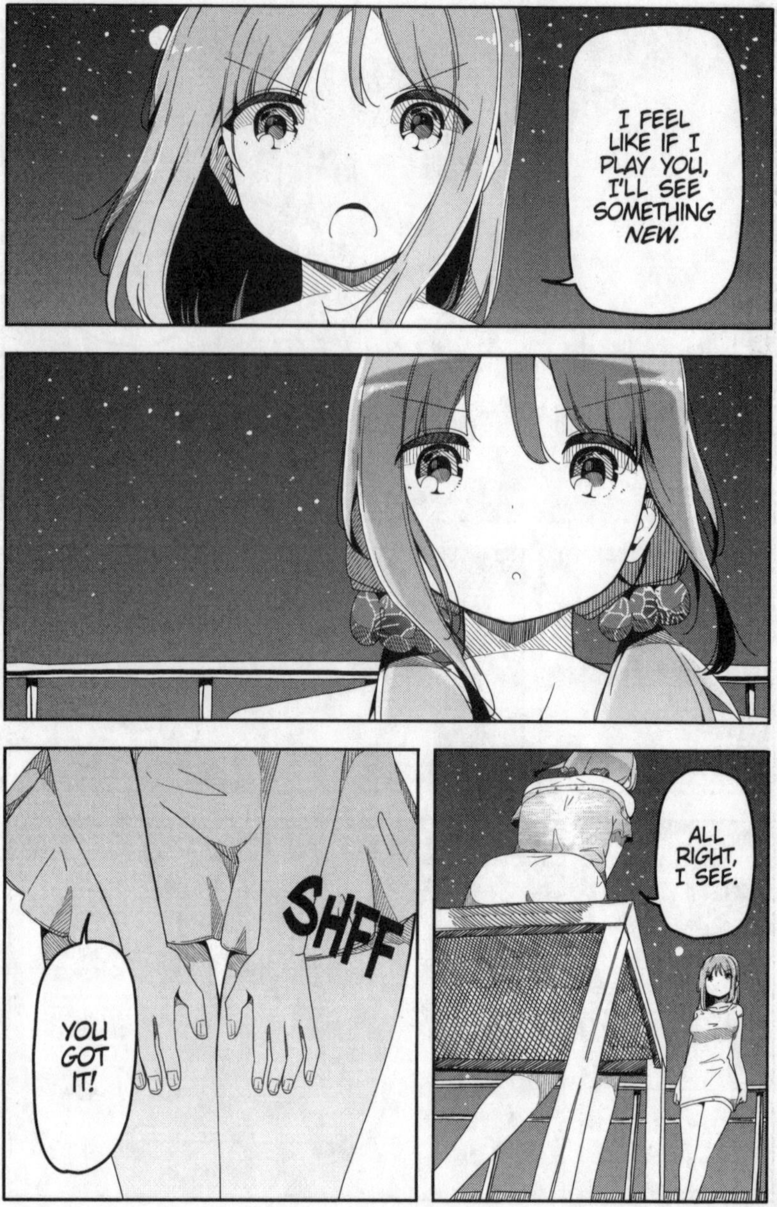
I FEEL LIKE IF I PLAY YOU, I'LL SEE SOMETHING *NEW.*
ALL RIGHT, I SEE.
SHFF
YOU GOT IT!

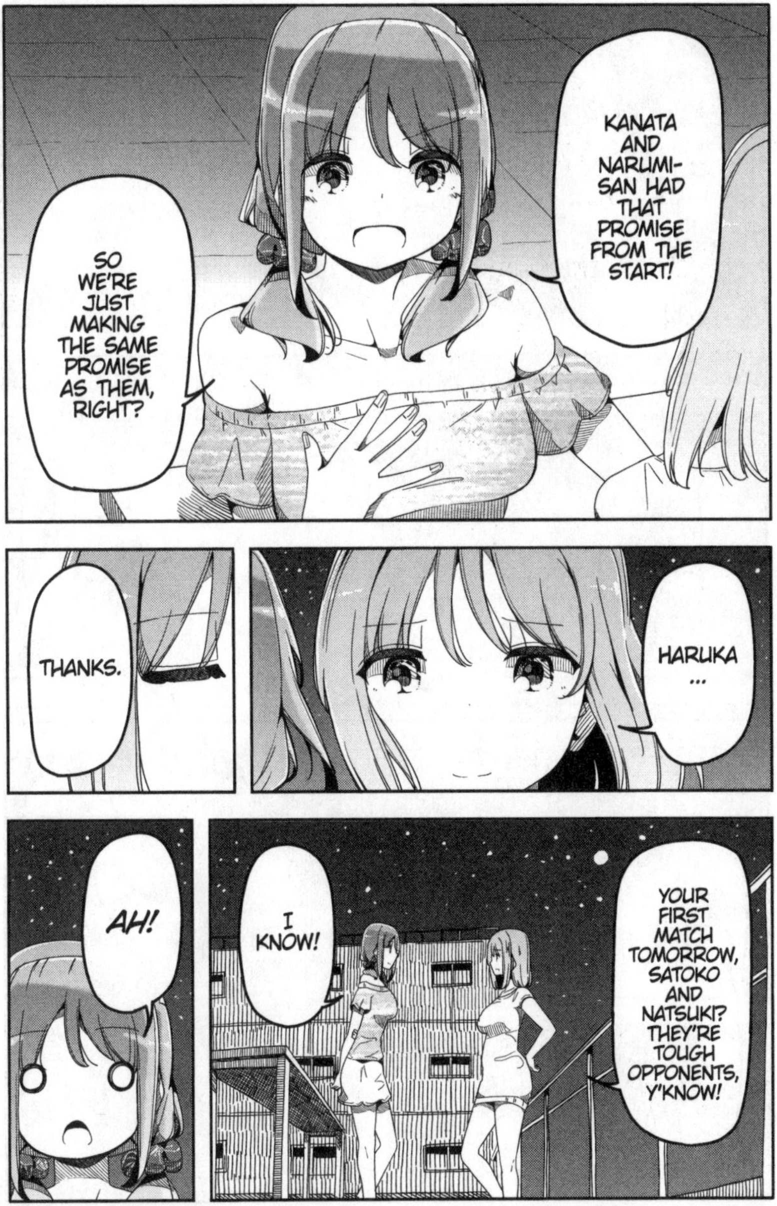
KANATA AND NARUMI-SAN HAD THAT PROMISE FROM THE START!
SO WE'RE JUST MAKING THE SAME PROMISE AS THEM, RIGHT?
HARUKA ...
THANKS.
YOUR FIRST MATCH TOMORROW, SATOKO AND NATSUKI? THEY'RE TOUGH OPPONENTS, Y'KNOW!
I KNOW!
AH!

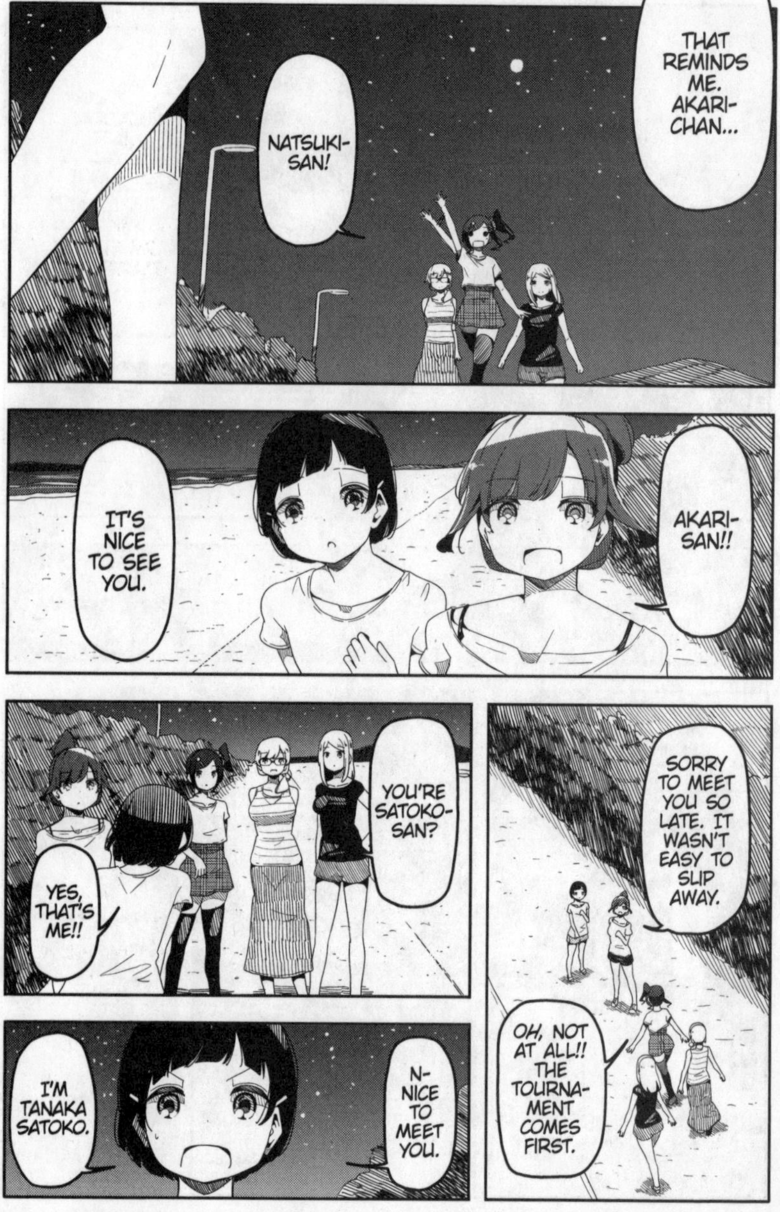
THAT REMINDS ME. AKARI-CHAN...
NATSUKI-SAN!
AKARI-SAN!!
IT'S NICE TO SEE YOU.
SORRY TO MEET YOU SO LATE. IT WASN'T EASY TO SLIP AWAY.
OH, NOT AT ALL!! THE TOURNAMENT COMES FIRST.
YOU'RE SATOKO-SAN?
YES, THAT'S ME!!
N-NICE TO MEET YOU.
I'M TANAKA SATOKO.

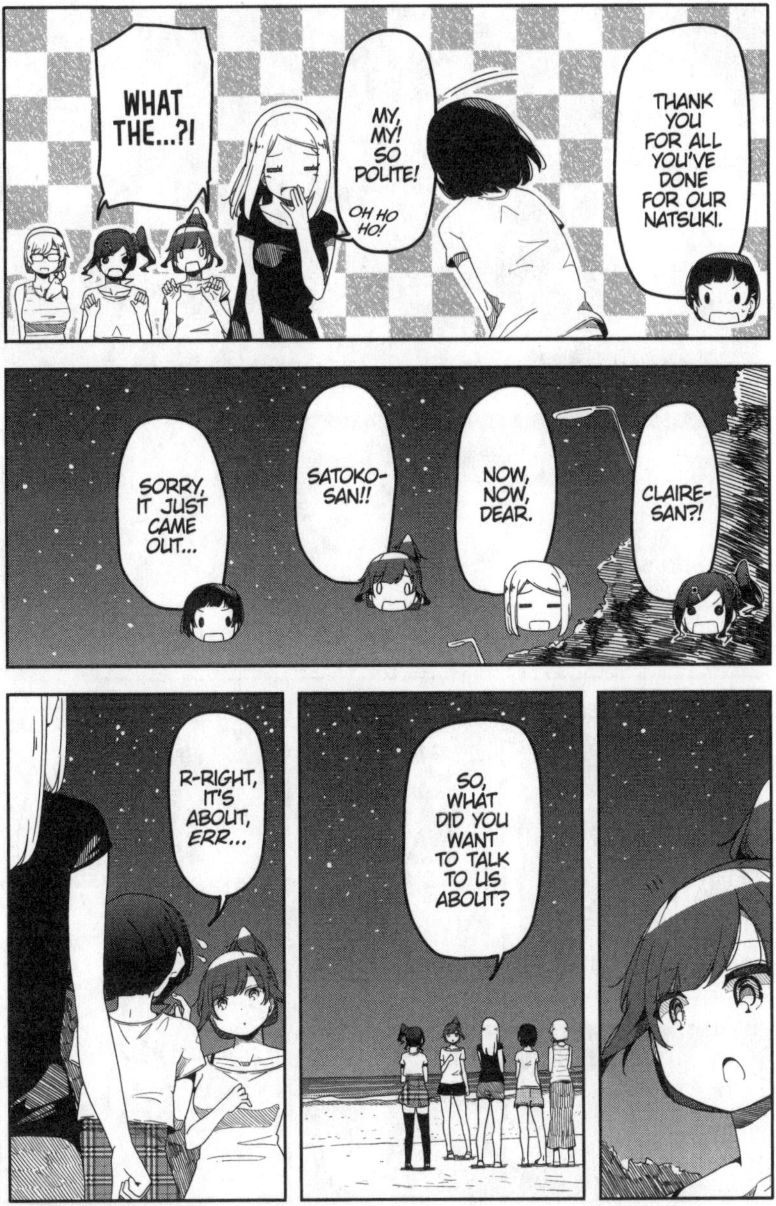
THANK YOU FOR ALL YOU'VE DONE FOR OUR NATSUKI.
MY, MY! SO POLITE!
OH HO HO!
WHAT THE...?!
CLAIRE-SAN?!
NOW, NOW, DEAR.
SATOKO-SAN!!
SORRY, IT JUST CAME OUT...
SO, WHAT DID YOU WANT TO TALK TO US ABOUT?
R-RIGHT, IT'S ABOUT, ERR...

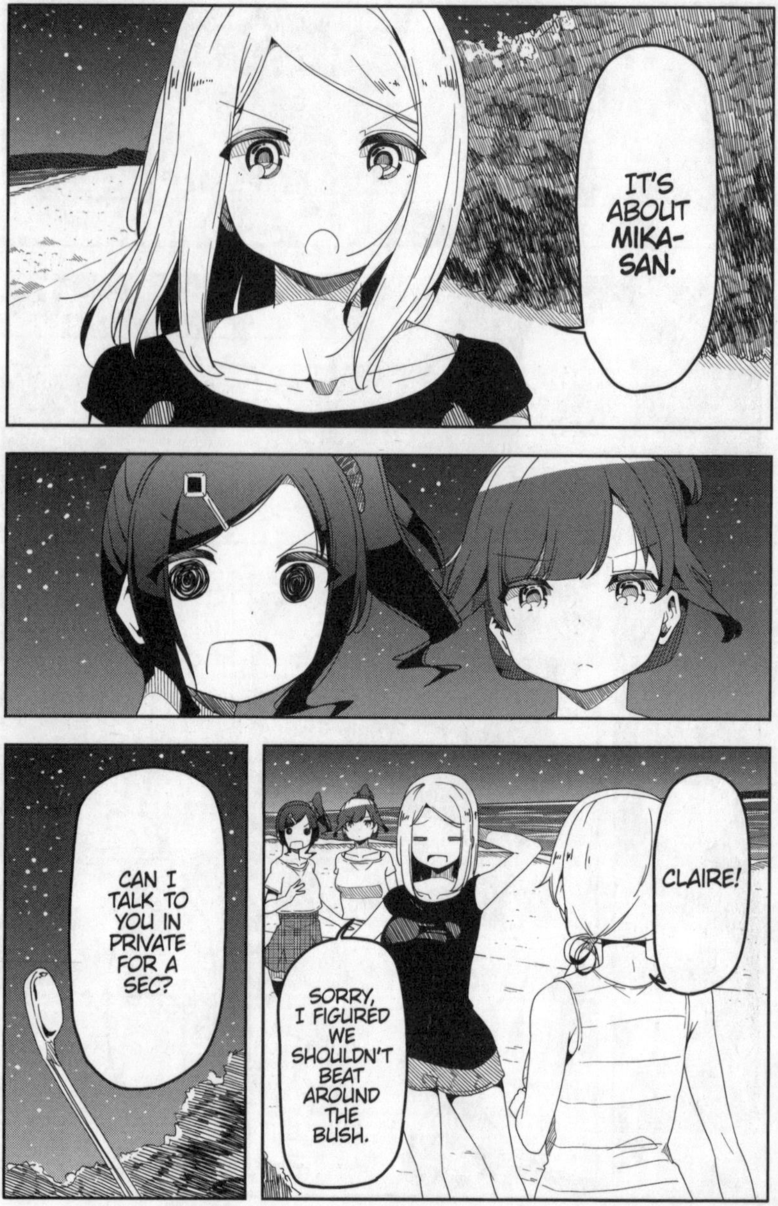
IT'S ABOUT MIKA-SAN.
CLAIRE!
SORRY, I FIGURED WE SHOULDN'T BEAT AROUND THE BUSH.
CAN I TALK TO YOU IN PRIVATE FOR A SEC?

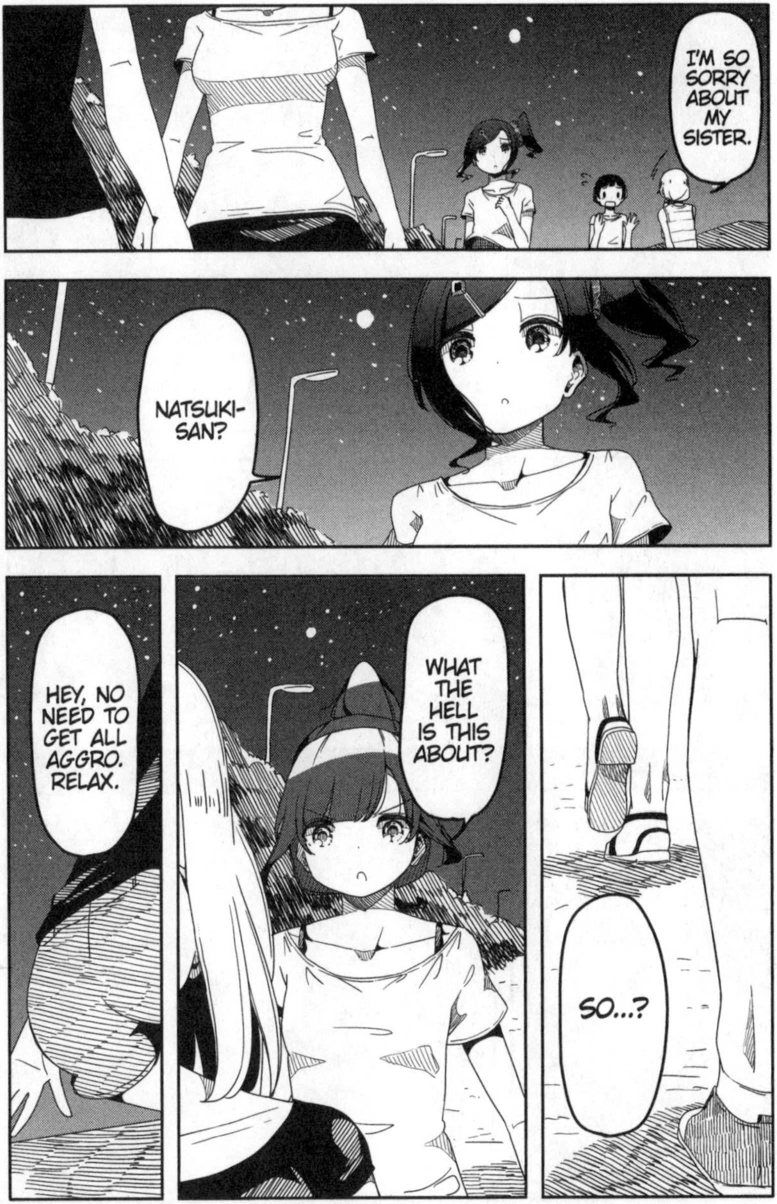
I'M SO SORRY ABOUT MY SISTER.
NATSUKI-SAN?
SO...?
WHAT THE HELL IS THIS ABOUT?
HEY, NO NEED TO GET ALL AGGRO. RELAX.

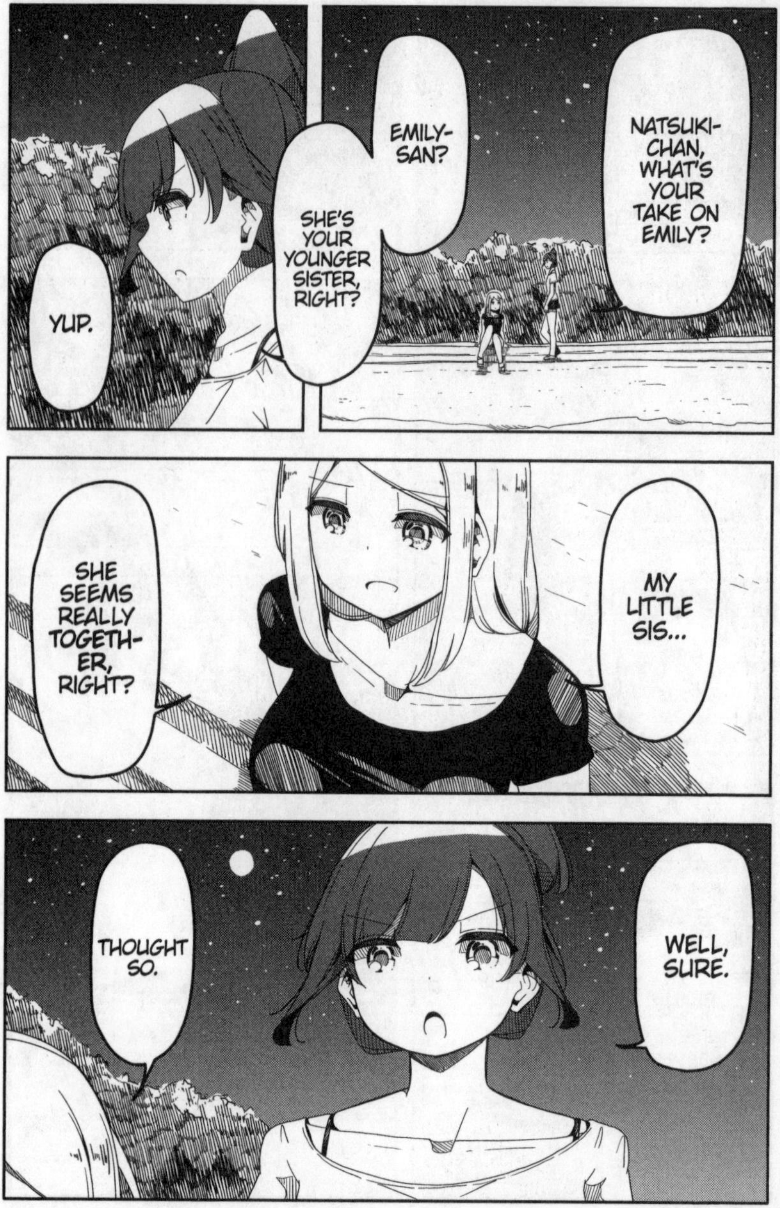
NATSUKI-CHAN, WHAT'S YOUR TAKE ON EMILY?
EMILY-SAN?
SHE'S YOUR YOUNGER SISTER, RIGHT?
YUP.
MY LITTLE SIS...
SHE SEEMS REALLY TOGETH-ER, RIGHT?
WELL, SURE.
THOUGHT SO.

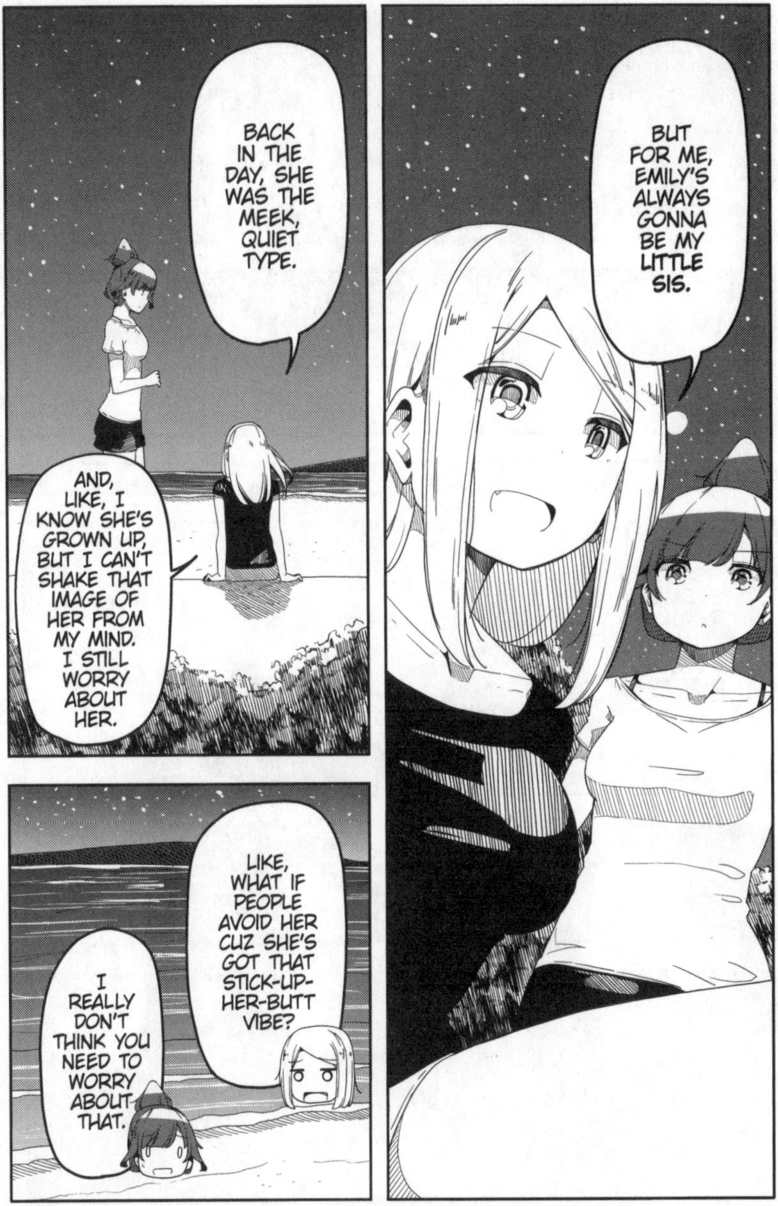
BACK IN THE DAY, SHE WAS THE MEEK, QUIET TYPE.
AND, LIKE, I KNOW SHE'S GROWN UP, BUT I CAN'T SHAKE THAT IMAGE OF HER FROM MY MIND. I STILL WORRY ABOUT HER.
LIKE, WHAT IF PEOPLE AVOID HER CUZ SHE'S GOT THAT STICK-UP-HER-BUTT VIBE?
I REALLY DON'T THINK YOU NEED TO WORRY ABOUT THAT.
BUT FOR ME, EMILY'S ALWAYS GONNA BE MY LITTLE SIS.

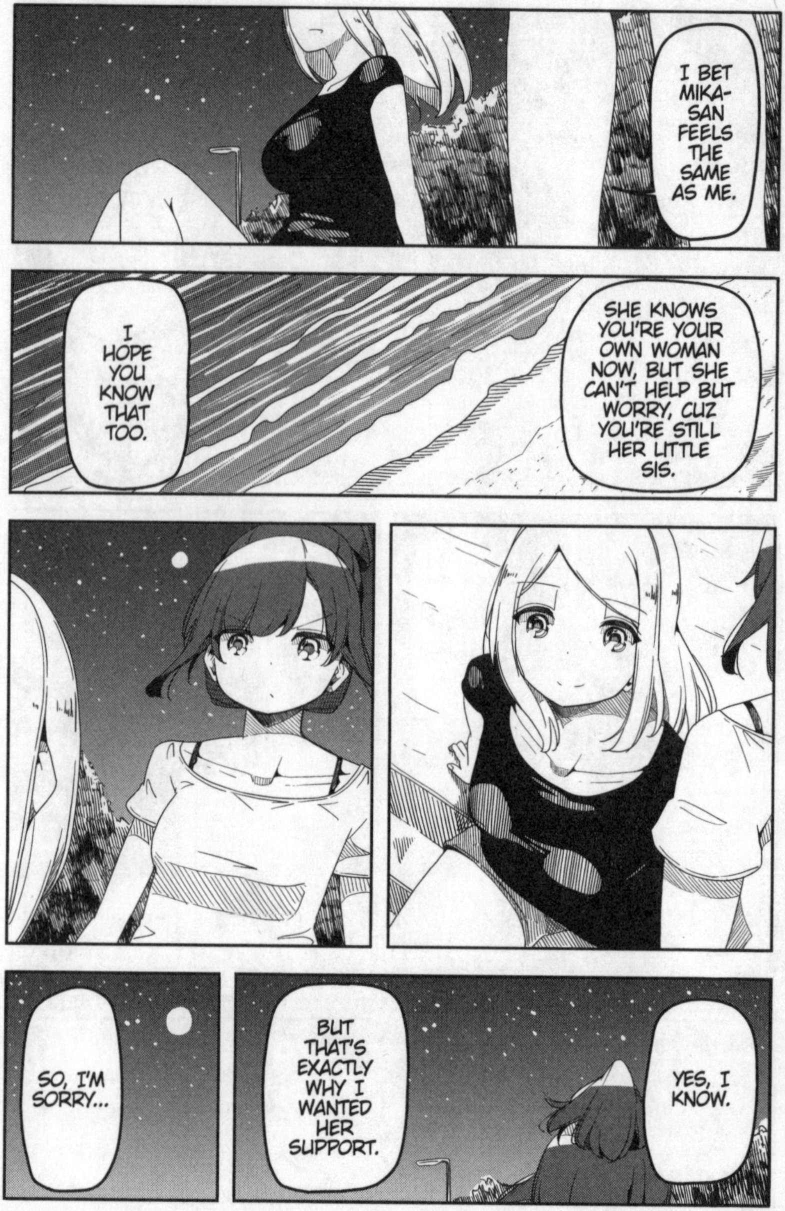
I BET MIKA-SAN FEELS THE SAME AS ME.
SHE KNOWS YOU'RE YOUR OWN WOMAN NOW, BUT SHE CAN'T HELP BUT WORRY, CUZ YOU'RE STILL HER LITTLE SIS.
I HOPE YOU KNOW THAT TOO.
YES, I KNOW.
BUT THAT'S EXACTLY WHY I WANTED HER SUPPORT.
SO, I'M SORRY...

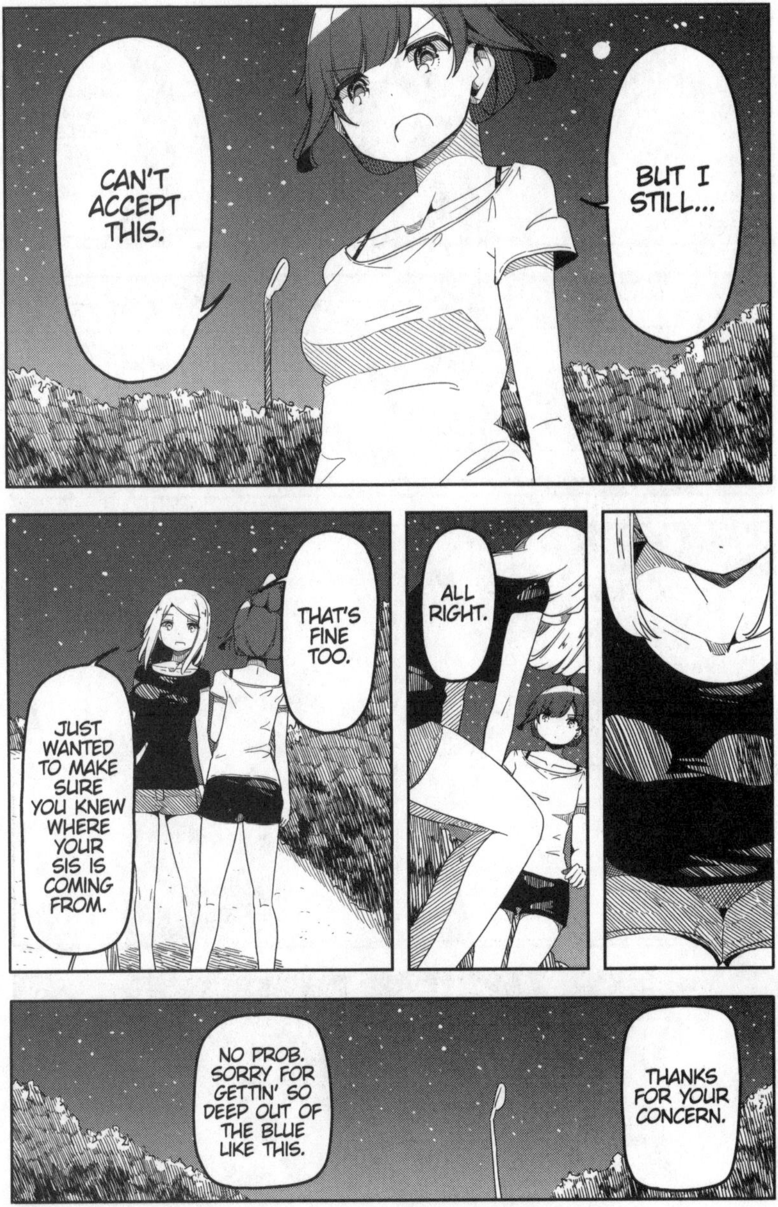
BUT I STILL...
CAN'T ACCEPT THIS.
ALL RIGHT.
THAT'S FINE TOO.
JUST WANTED TO MAKE SURE YOU KNEW WHERE YOUR SIS IS COMING FROM.
THANKS FOR YOUR CONCERN.
NO PROB. SORRY FOR GETTIN' SO DEEP OUT OF THE BLUE LIKE THIS.

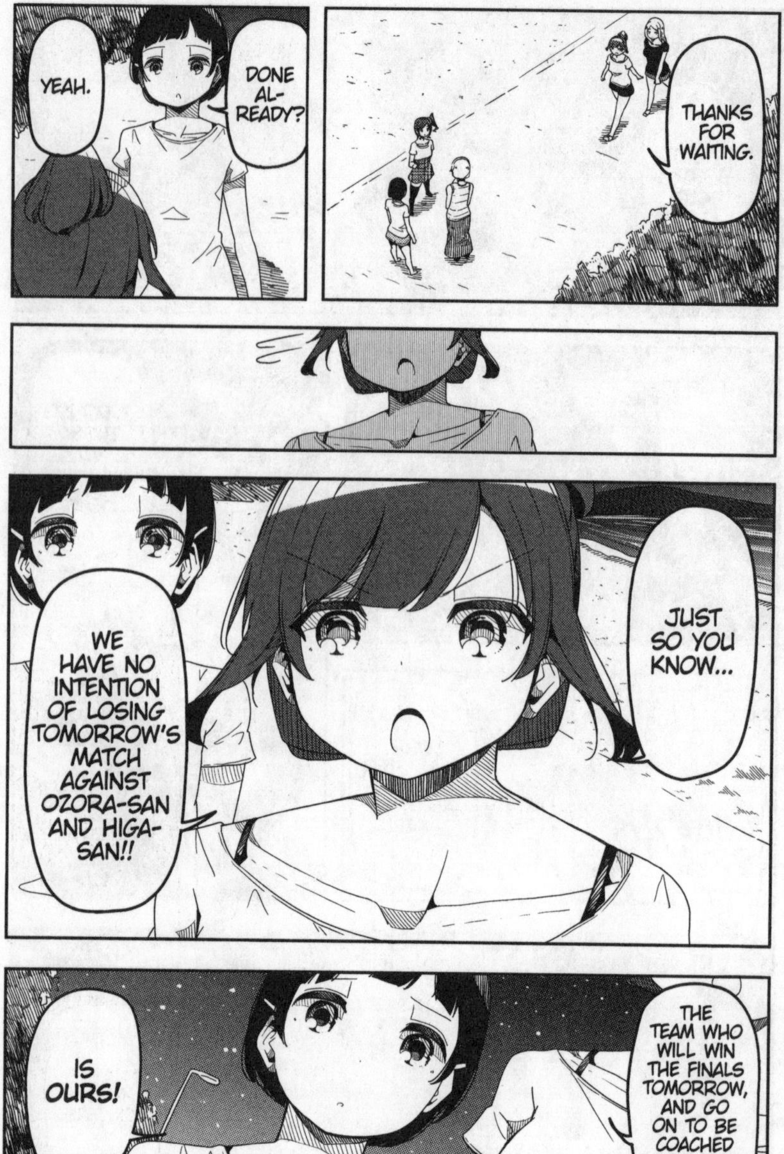
THANKS FOR WAITING.
DONE AL-READY?
YEAH.
JUST SO YOU KNOW...
WE HAVE NO INTENTION OF LOSING TOMORROW'S MATCH AGAINST OZORA-SAN AND HIGA-SAN!!
THE TEAM WHO WILL WIN THE FINALS TOMORROW, AND GO ON TO BE COACHED BY MY SISTER...
IS OURS!

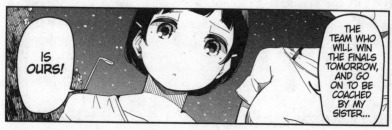

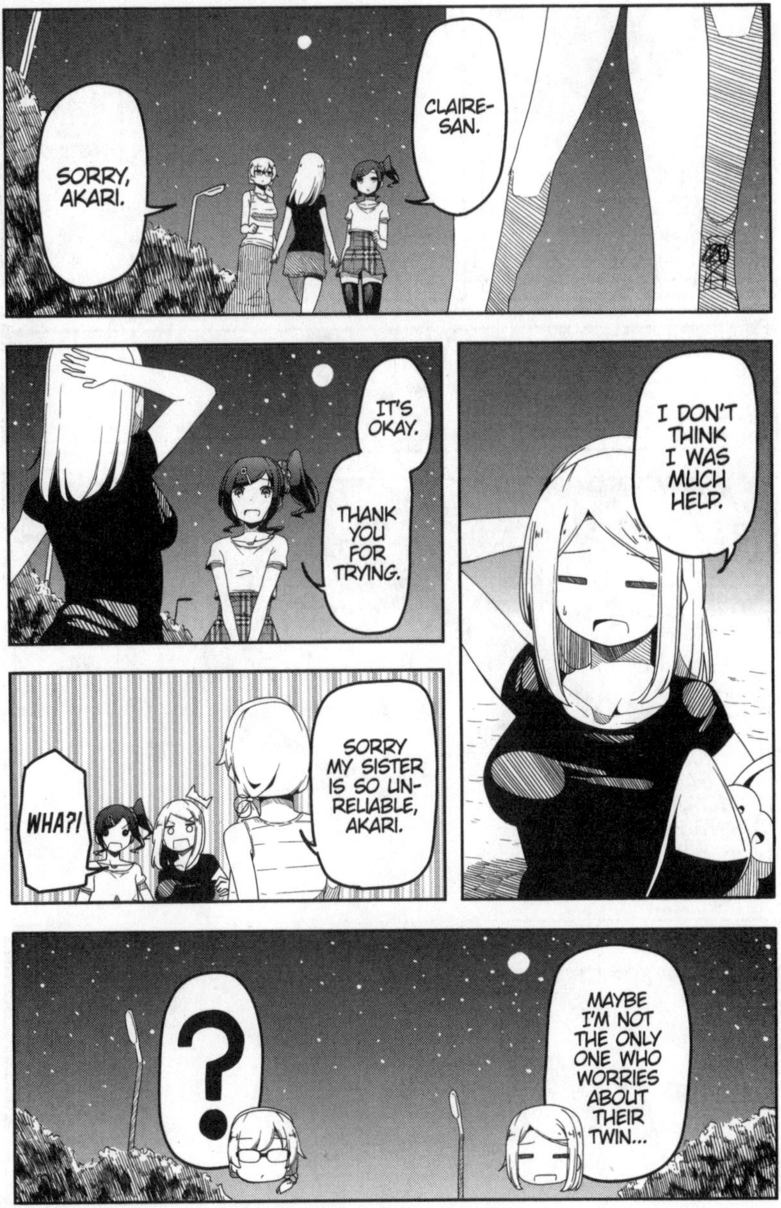
CLAIRE-SAN.
SORRY, AKARI.
I DON'T THINK I WAS MUCH HELP.
IT'S OKAY.
THANK YOU FOR TRYING.
SORRY MY SISTER IS SO UN-RELIABLE, AKARI.
WHA?!
MAYBE I'M NOT THE ONLY ONE WHO WORRIES ABOUT THEIR TWIN...
?

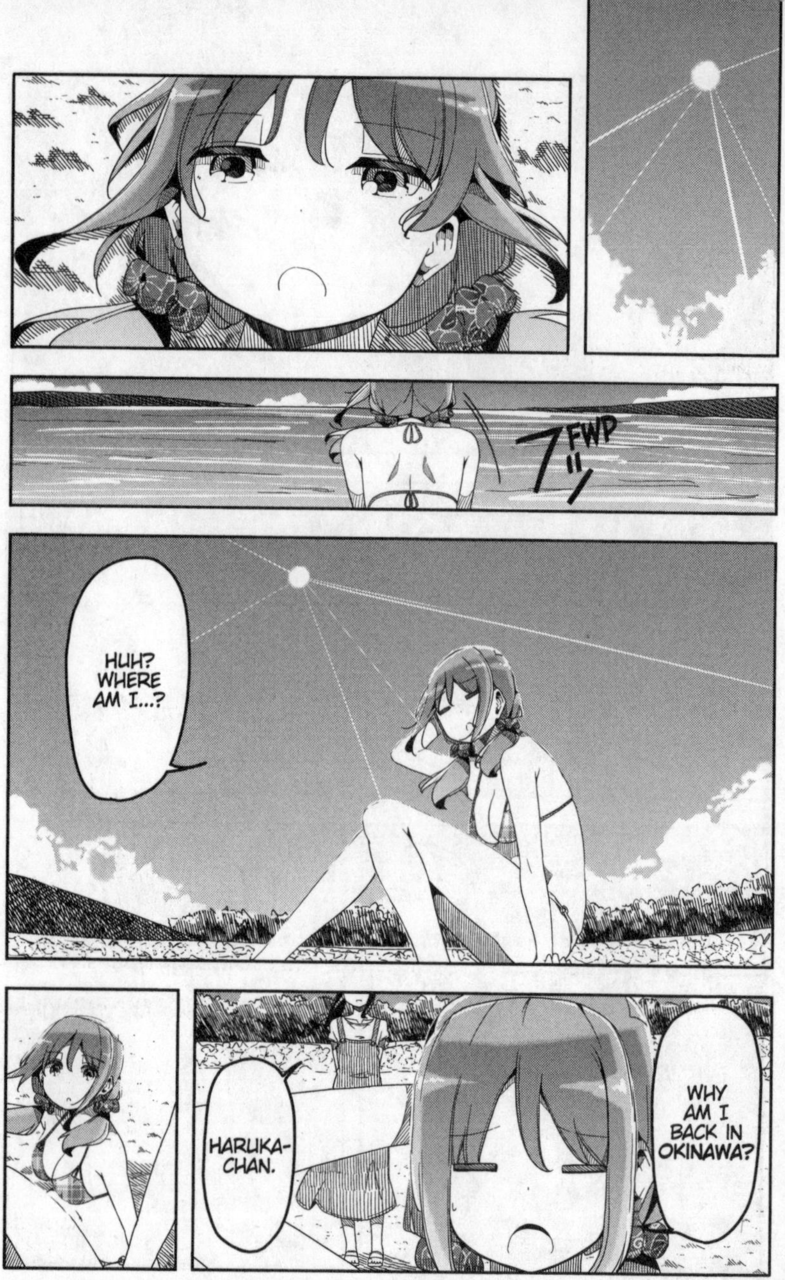
FWP
HUH? WHERE AM I...?
WHY AM I BACK IN OKINAWA?
HARUKA-CHAN.

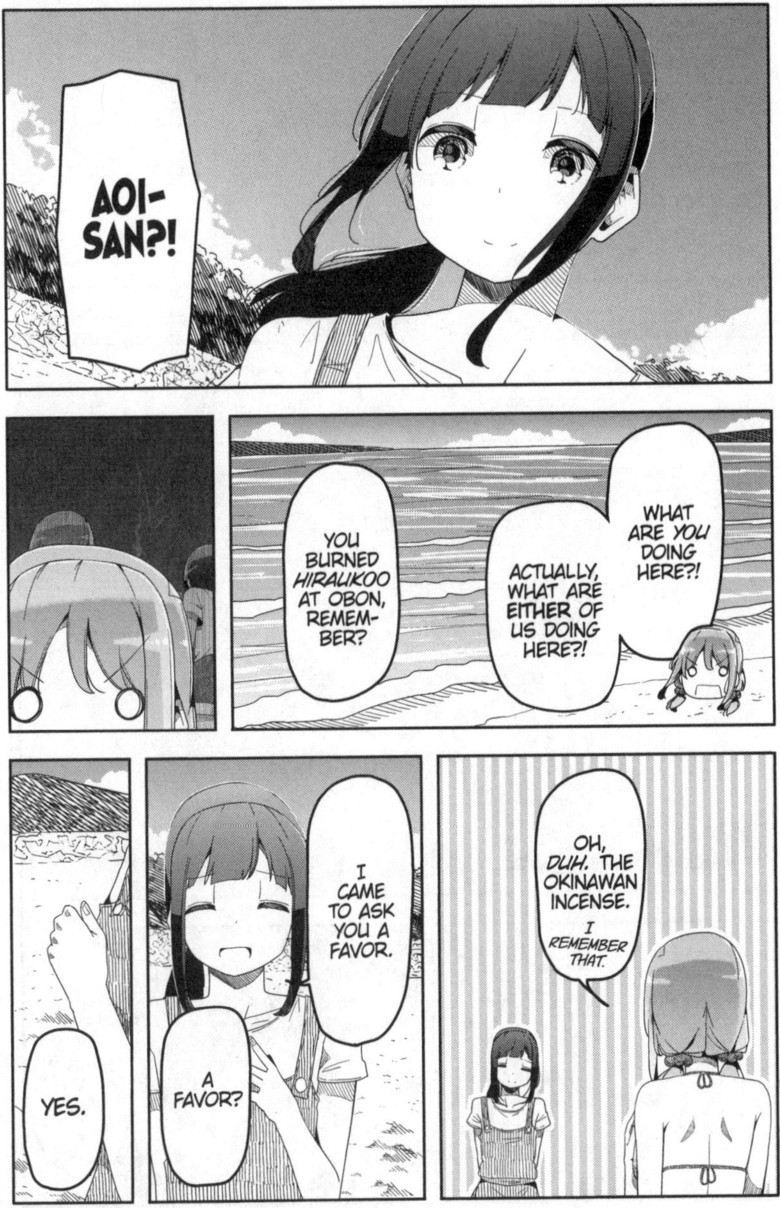
AOI-SAN?!
WHAT ARE YOU DOING HERE?!
ACTUALLY, WHAT ARE EITHER OF US DOING HERE?!
YOU BURNED HIRAUKOO AT OBON, REMEMBER?
OH, DUH. THE OKINAWAN INCENSE.
I REMEMBER THAT.
I CAME TO ASK YOU A FAVOR.
A FAVOR?
YES.

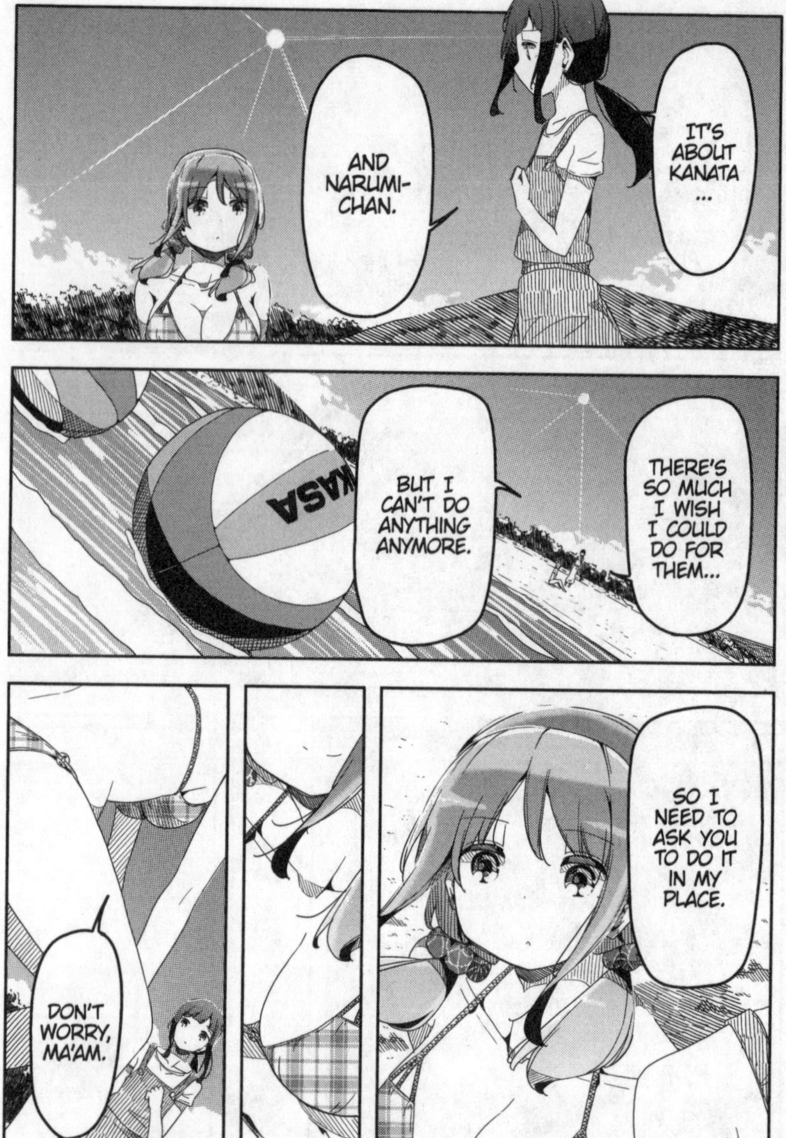
IT'S ABOUT KANATA...
AND NARUMI-CHAN.
THERE'S SO MUCH I WISH I COULD DO FOR THEM...
BUT I CAN'T DO ANYTHING ANYMORE.
SO I NEED TO ASK YOU TO DO IT IN MY PLACE.
DON'T WORRY, MA'AM.

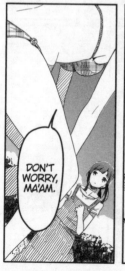

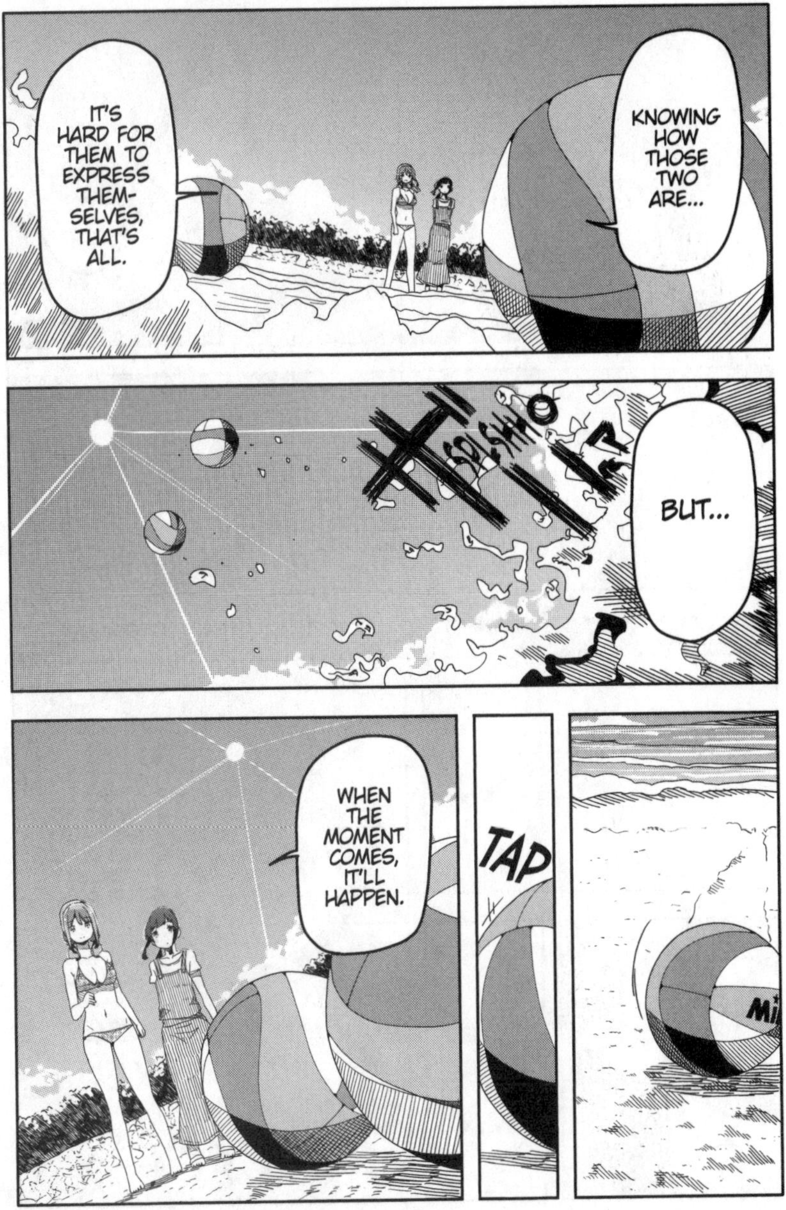
KNOWING HOW THOSE TWO ARE...
IT'S HARD FOR THEM TO EXPRESS THEM-SELVES, THAT'S ALL.
BUT...
TAP
WHEN THE MOMENT COMES, IT'LL HAPPEN.

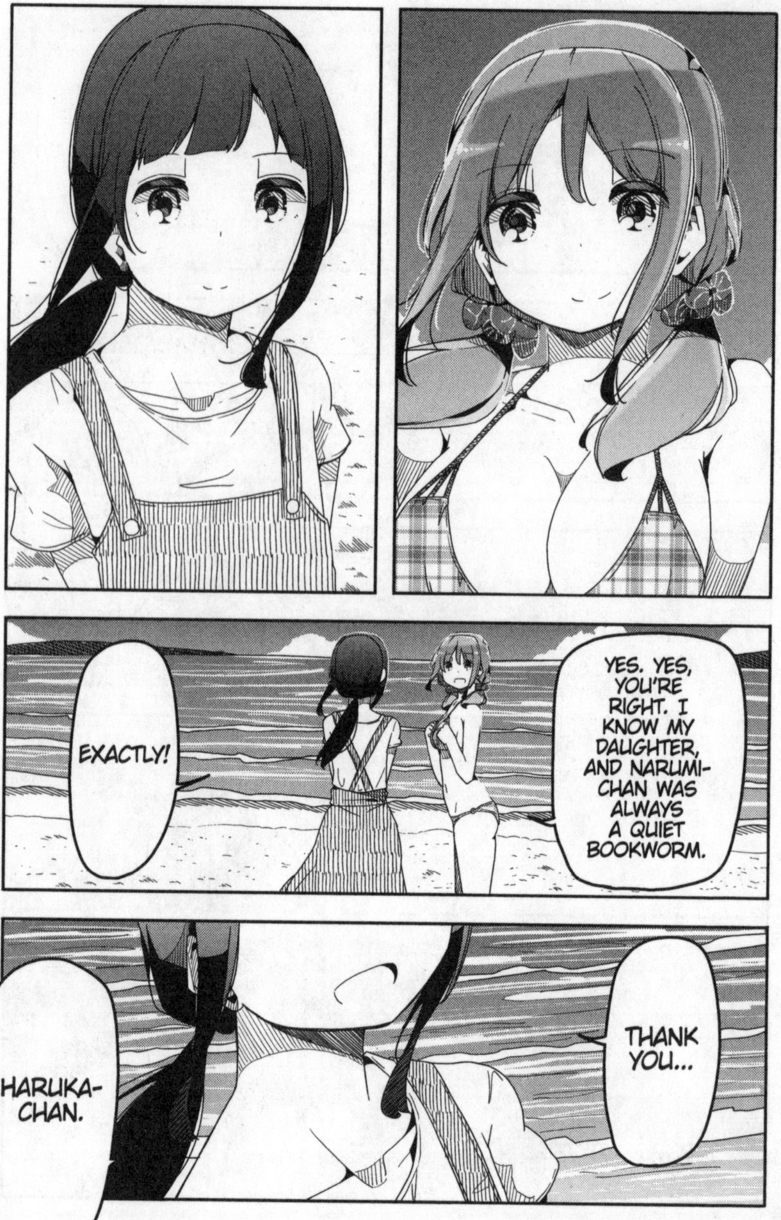
YES. YES, YOU'RE RIGHT. I KNOW MY DAUGHTER, AND NARUMI-CHAN WAS ALWAYS A QUIET BOOKWORM.
EXACTLY!
THANK YOU...
HARUKA-CHAN.

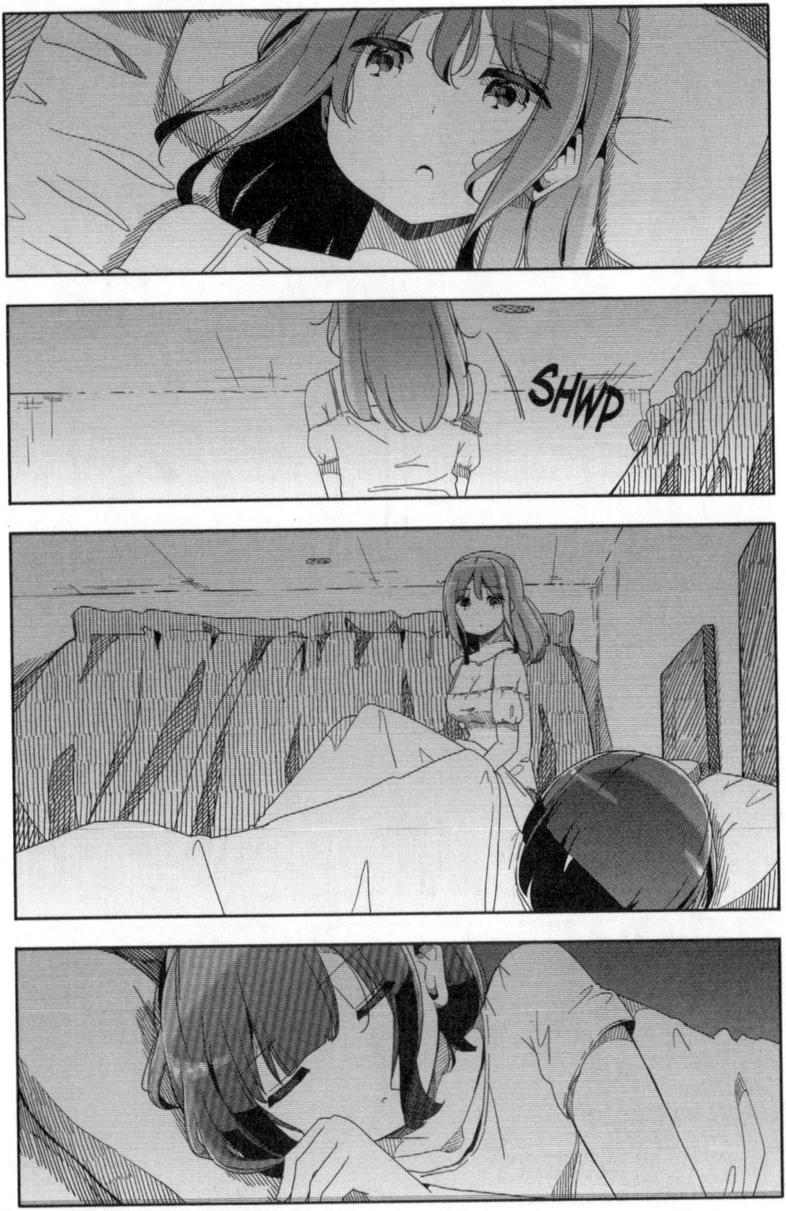
SHWP

Harukana★Receive

Presented by Nyoijizai

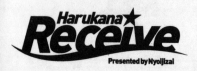

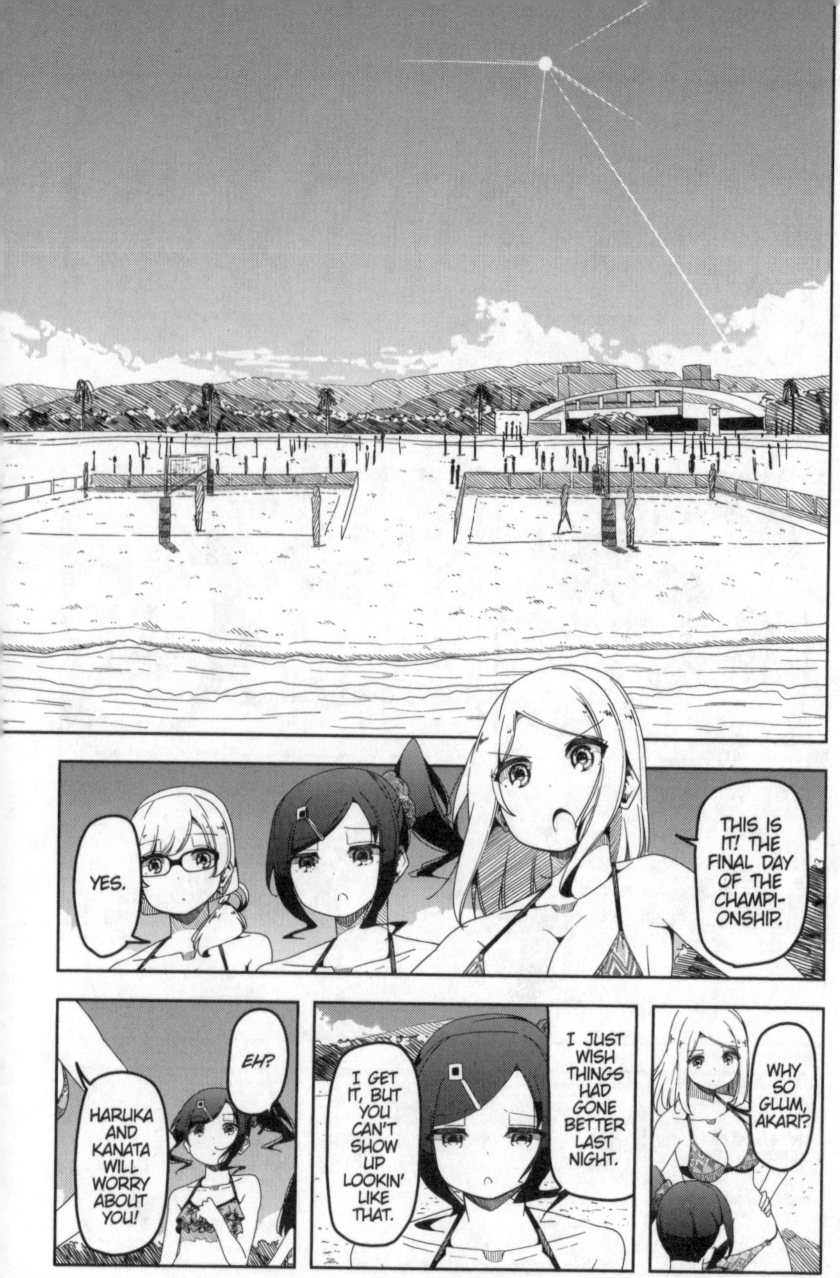
THIS IS IT! THE FINAL DAY OF THE CHAMPIONSHIP.
YES.
WHY SO GLUM, AKARI?
I JUST WISH THINGS HAD GONE BETTER LAST NIGHT.
I GET IT, BUT YOU CAN'T SHOW UP LOOKIN' LIKE THAT.
EH?
HARUKA AND KANATA WILL WORRY ABOUT YOU!

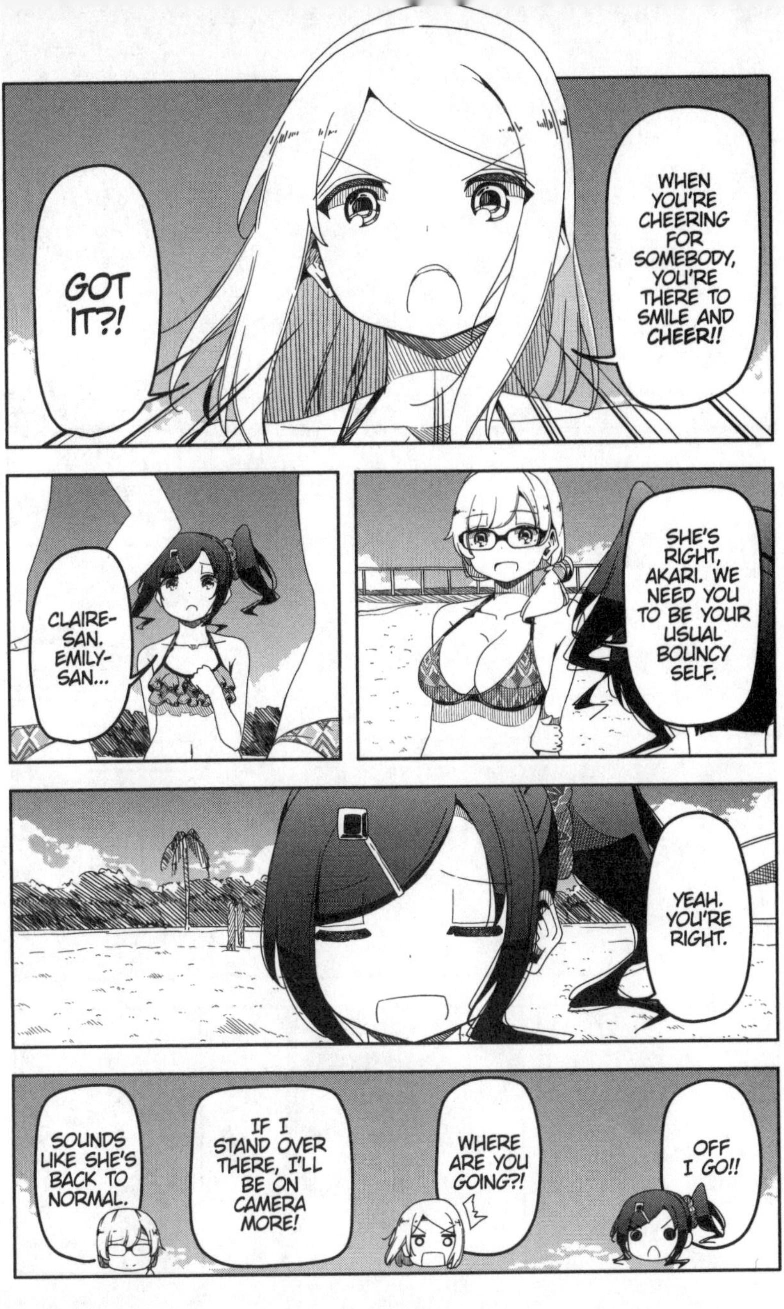
WHEN YOU'RE CHEERING FOR SOMEBODY, YOU'RE THERE TO SMILE AND CHEER!!
GOT IT?!
SHE'S RIGHT, AKARI. WE NEED YOU TO BE YOUR USUAL BOUNCY SELF.
CLAIRE-SAN. EMILY-SAN...
YEAH. YOU'RE RIGHT.
OFF I GO!!
WHERE ARE YOU GOING?!
IF I STAND OVER THERE, I'LL BE ON CAMERA MORE!
SOUNDS LIKE SHE'S BACK TO NORMAL.

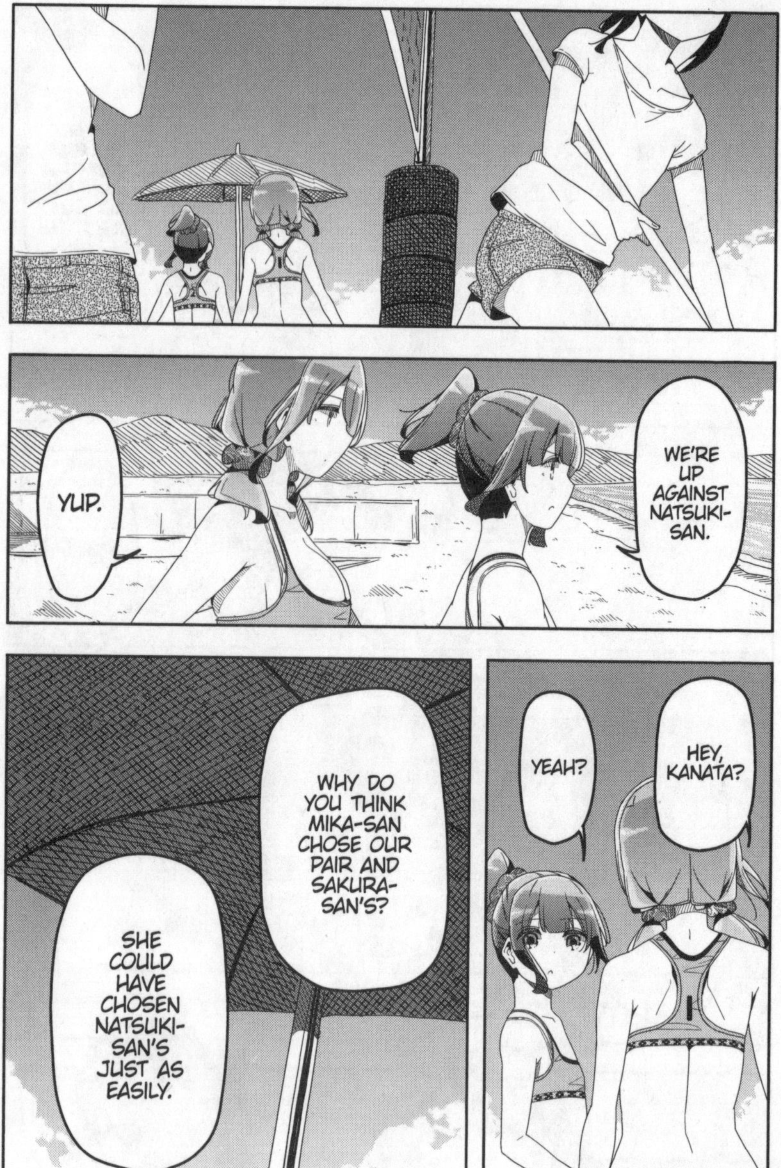
WE'RE UP AGAINST NATSUKI-SAN.
YUP.
HEY, KANATA?
YEAH?
WHY DO YOU THINK MIKA-SAN CHOSE OUR PAIR AND SAKURA-SAN'S?
SHE COULD HAVE CHOSEN NATSUKI-SAN'S JUST AS EASILY.

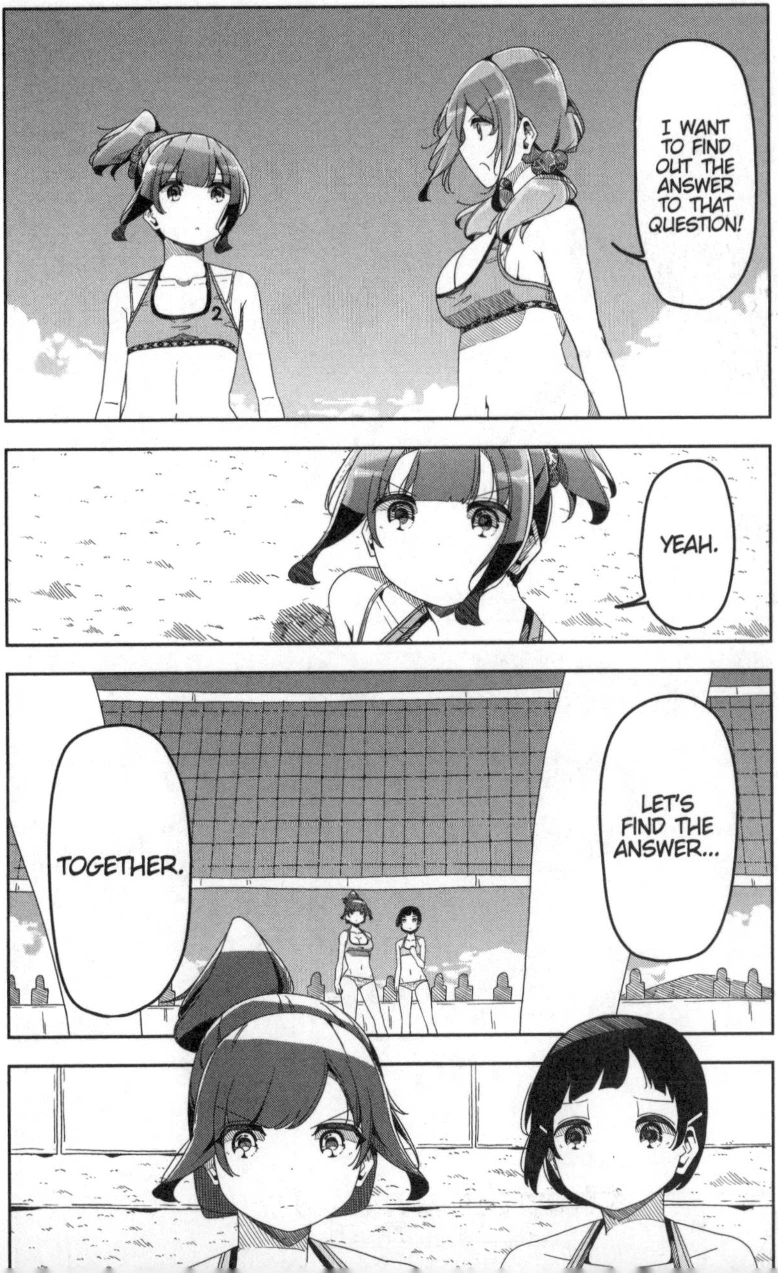
I WANT TO FIND OUT THE ANSWER TO THAT QUESTION!
YEAH.
LET'S FIND THE ANSWER...
TOGETHER.

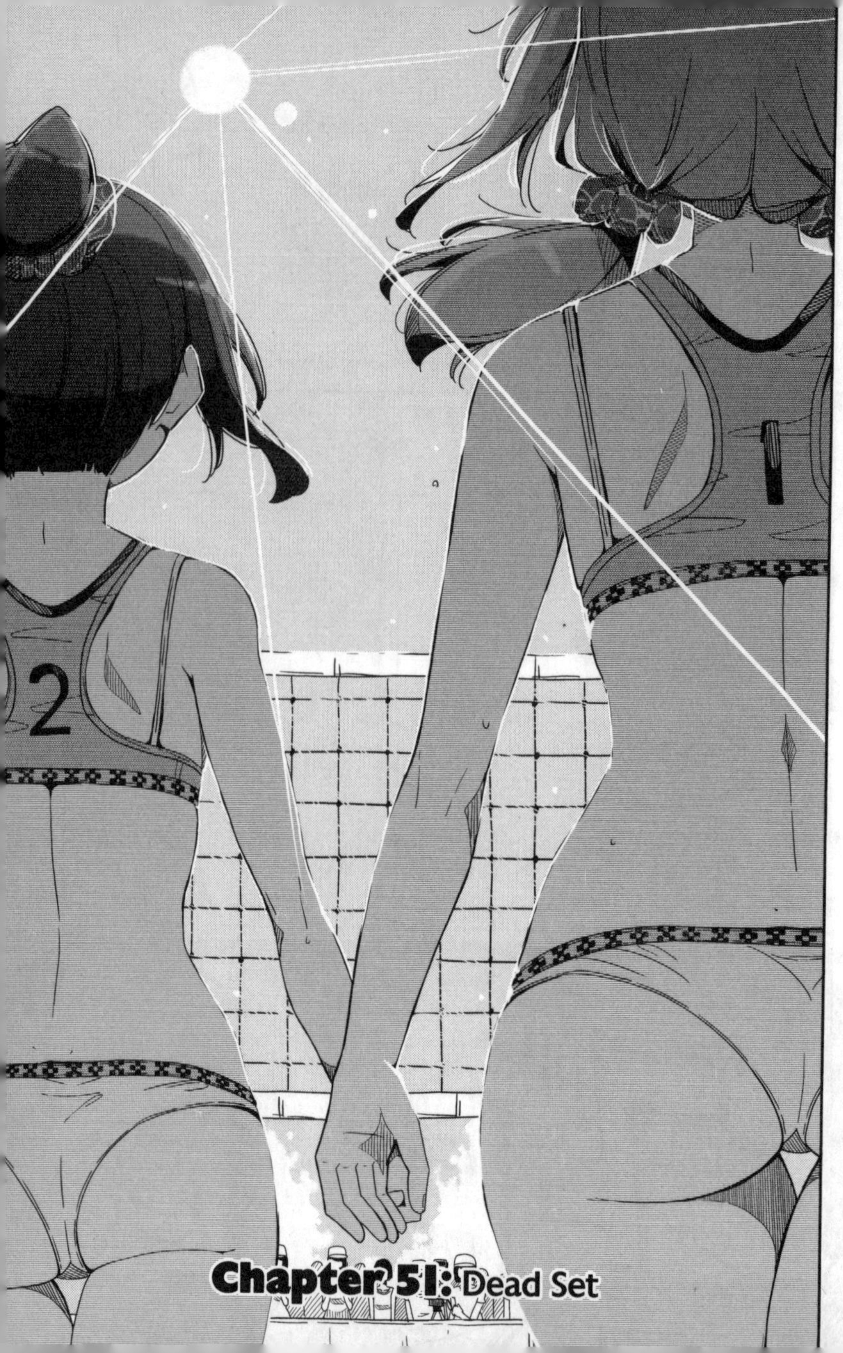
Chapter 51: Dead Set

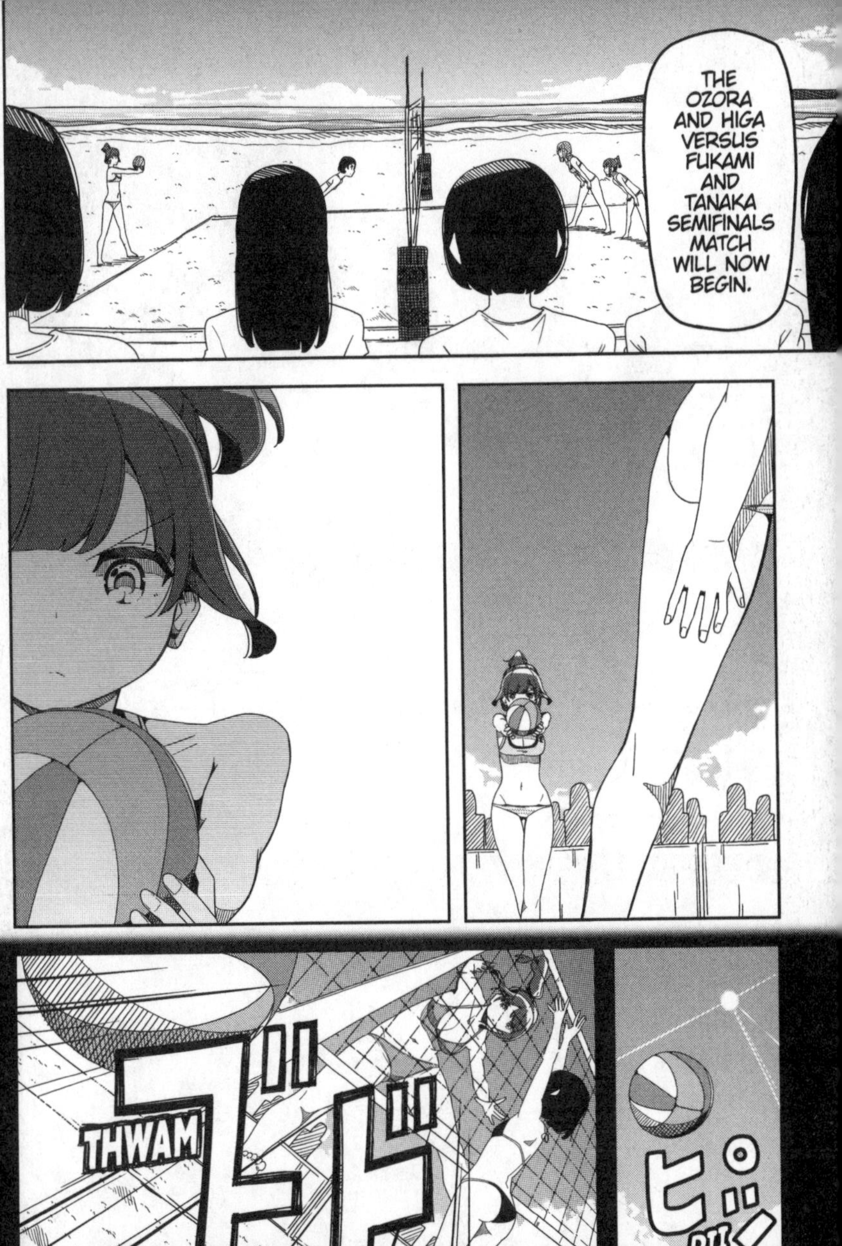
THE OZORA AND HIGA VERSUS FUKAMI AND TANAKA SEMIFINALS MATCH WILL NOW BEGIN.
PII
THWAM

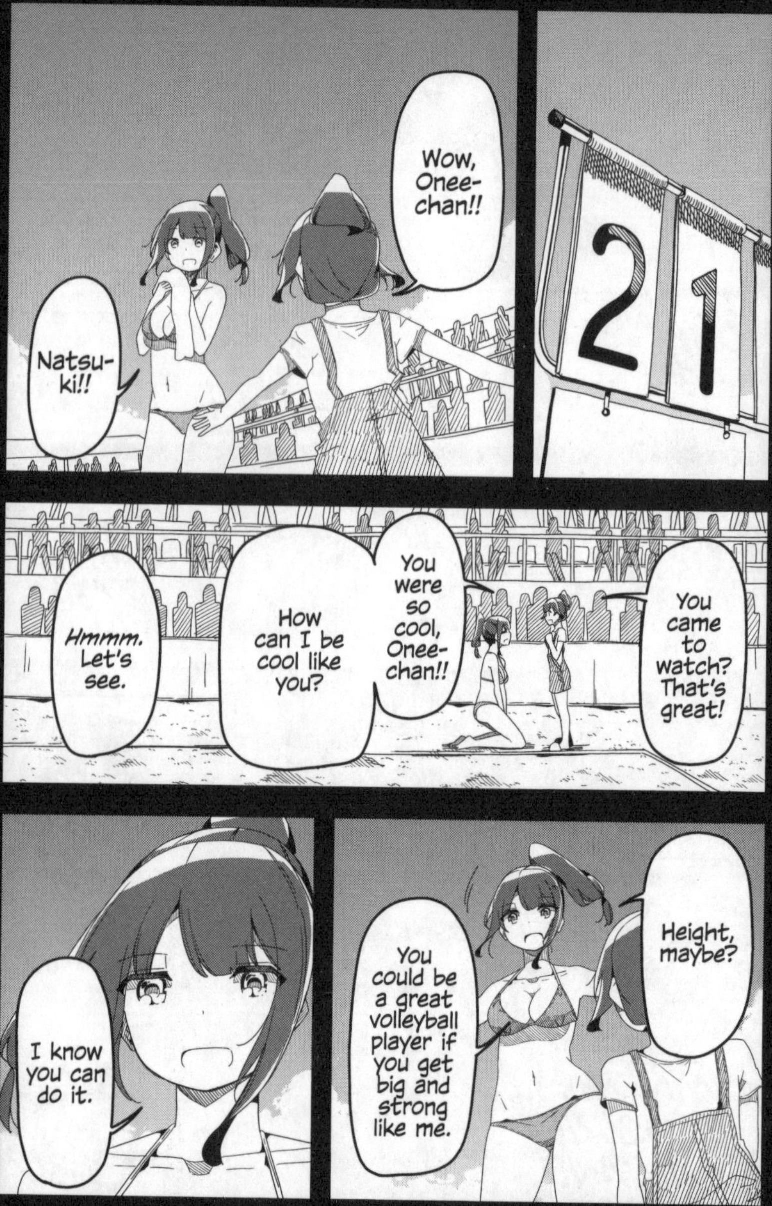
Wow, Onee-chan!!
Natsuki!!
You came to watch? That's great!
You were so cool, Onee-chan!!
How can I be cool like you?
*Hmmm.* Let's see.
Height, maybe?
You could be a great volleyball player if you get big and strong like me.
I know you can do it.

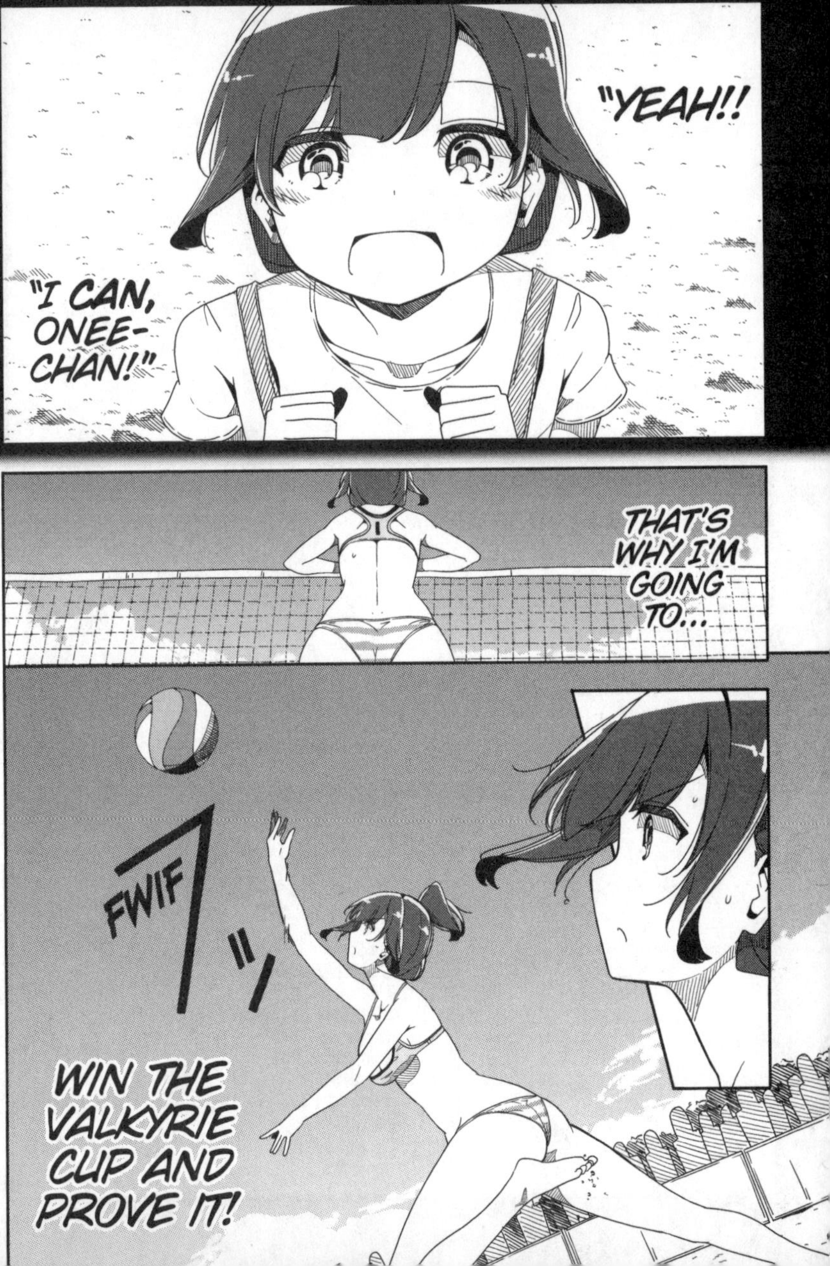
"YEAH!!
"I CAN, ONEE-CHAN!"
THAT'S WHY I'M GOING TO...
FWIF
WIN THE VALKYRIE CUP AND PROVE IT!

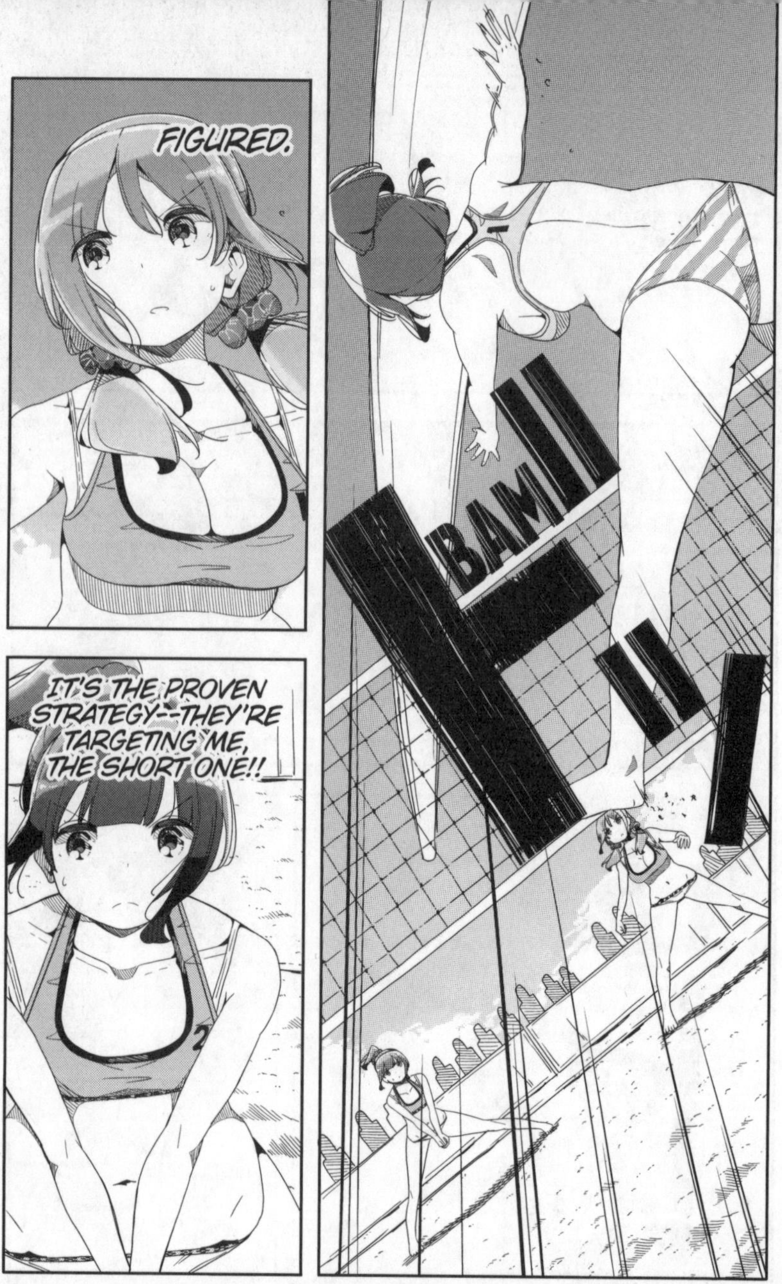
BAM!!
FIGURED.
IT'S THE PROVEN STRATEGY--THEY'RE TARGETING ME, THE SHORT ONE!!

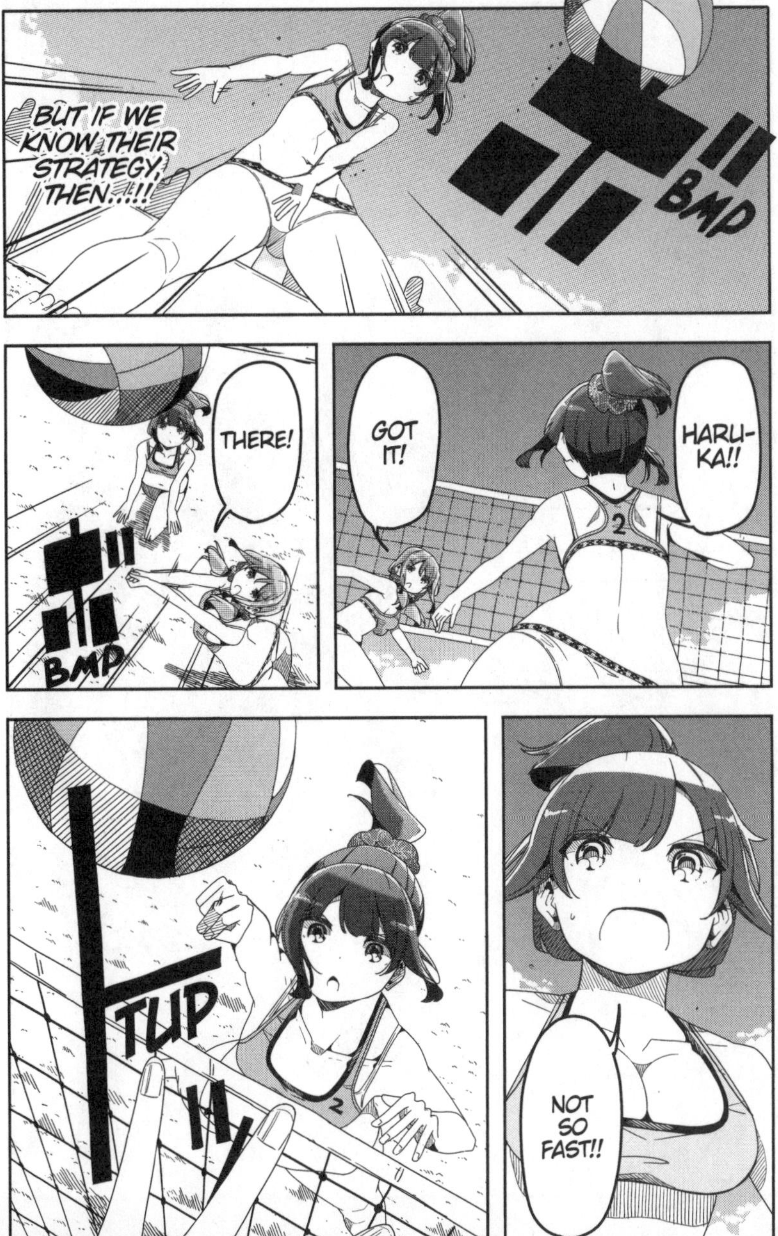
BUT IF WE KNOW THEIR STRATEGY, THEN...!!
BMP
HARU-KA!!
GOT IT!
THERE!
BMP
NOT SO FAST!!
TUP

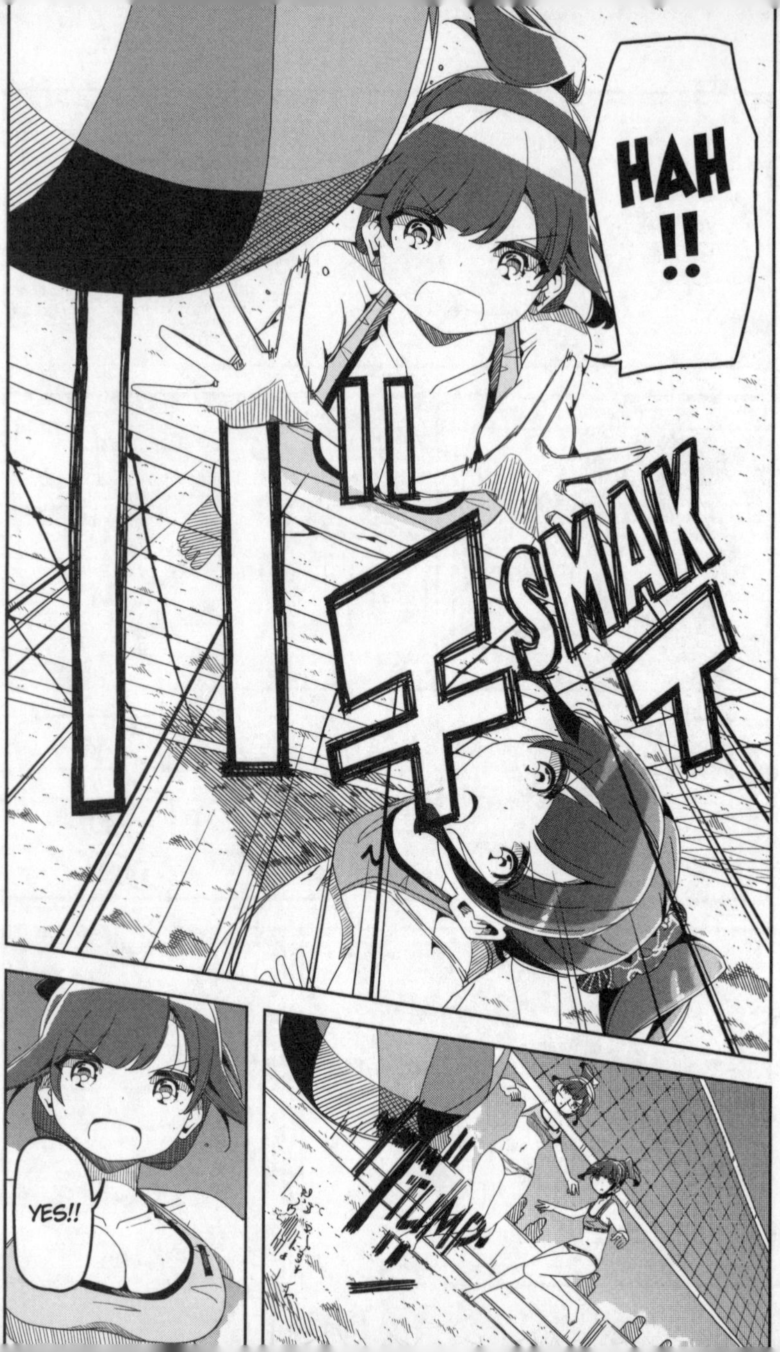
HAH!!
SMAK
THUMP!
YES!!

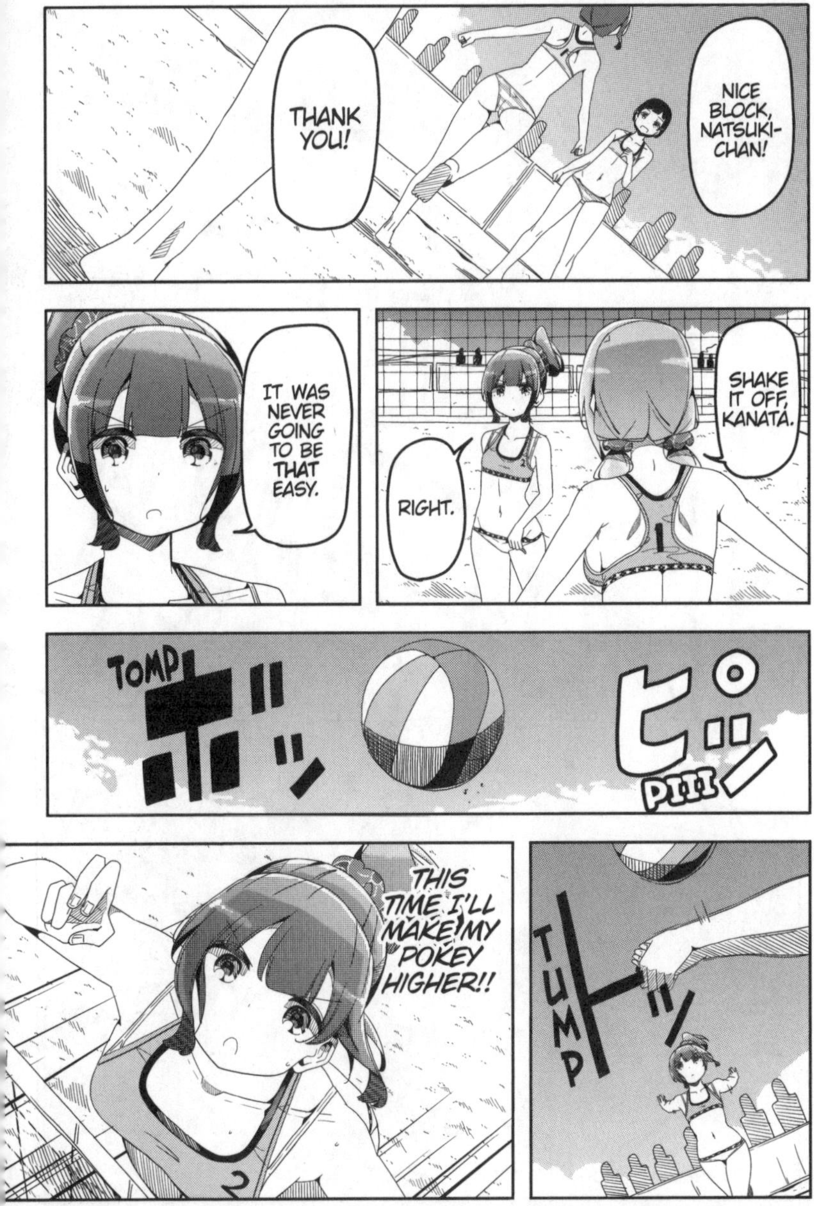
NICE BLOCK, NATSUKI-CHAN!
THANK YOU!
SHAKE IT OFF, KANATA.
RIGHT.
IT WAS NEVER GOING TO BE THAT EASY.
ピッ
PIII
ボッ
TOMP
トッ
TUMP
THIS TIME I'LL MAKE MY POKEY HIGHER!!

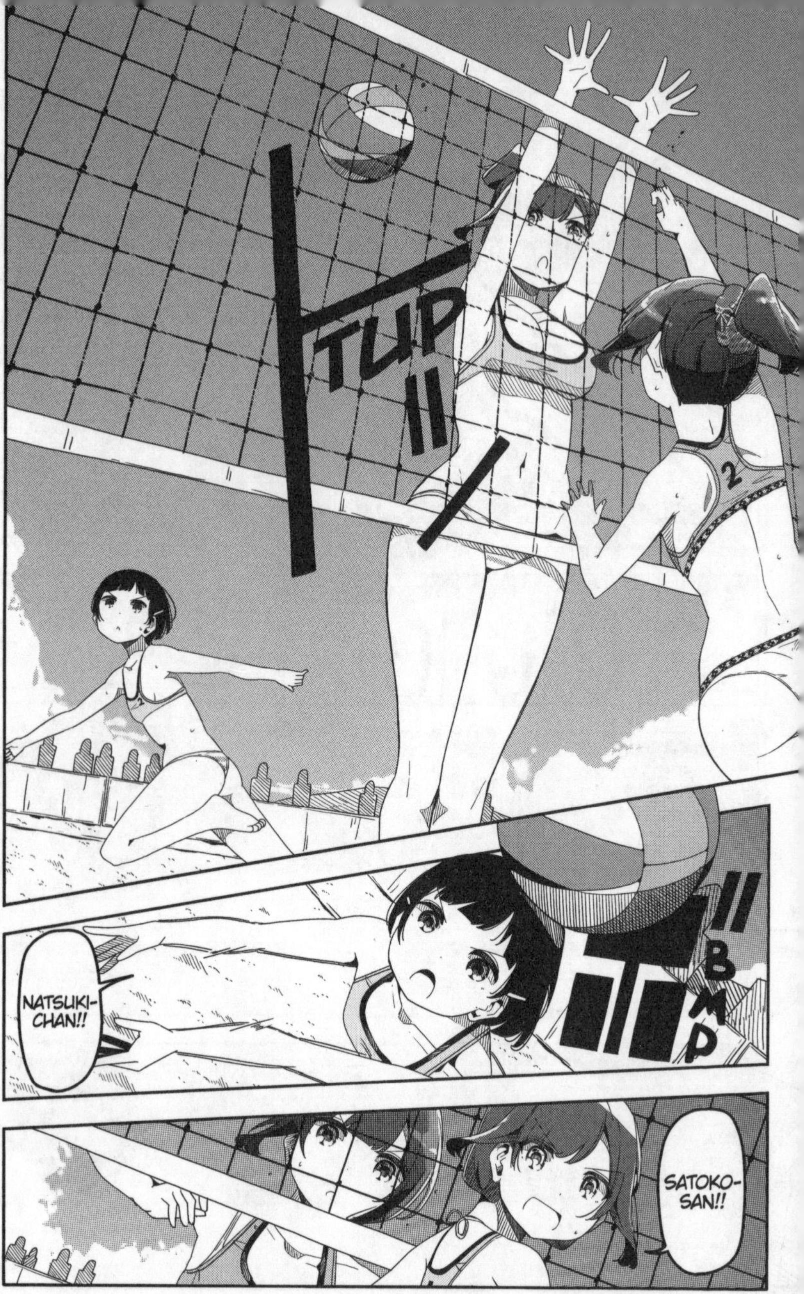
TUP!!
BUMP!!
NATSUKI-CHAN!!
SATOKO-SAN!!

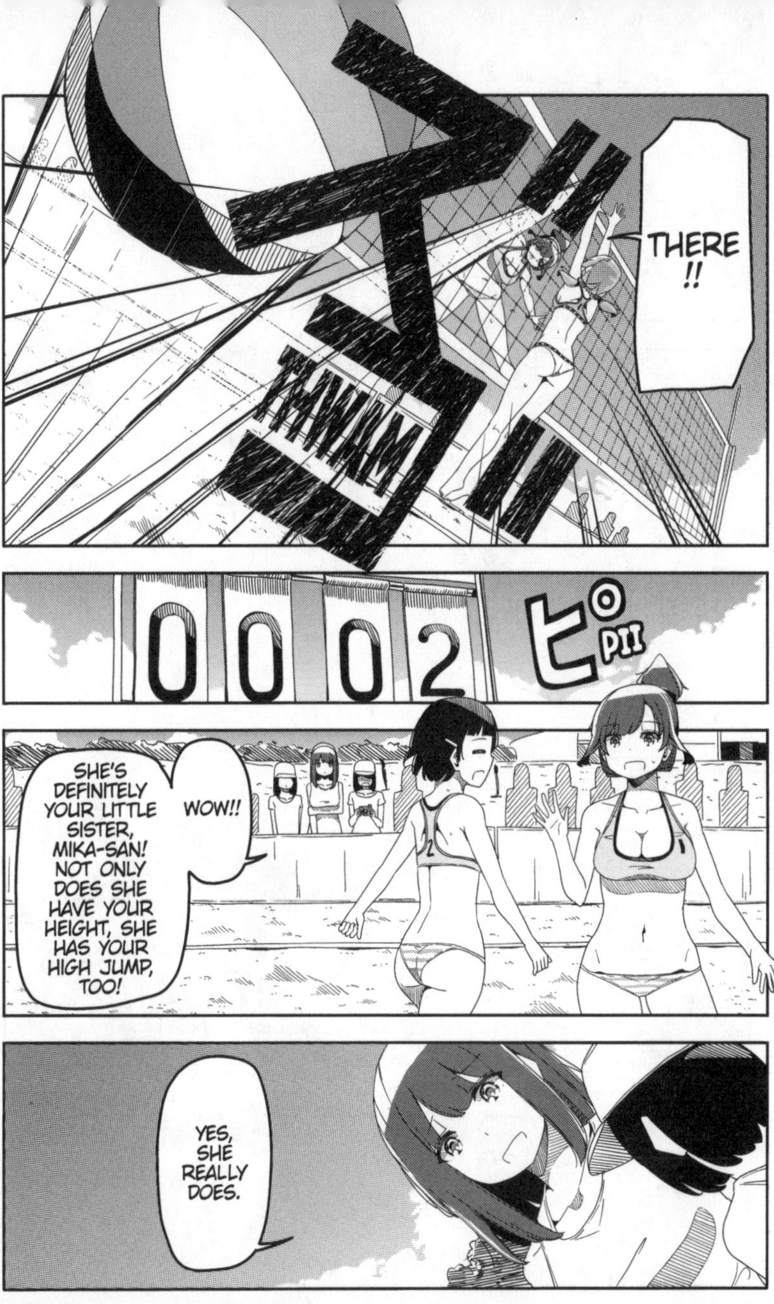
THERE!!
0002
PII
WOW!!
SHE'S DEFINITELY YOUR LITTLE SISTER, MIKA-SAN! NOT ONLY DOES SHE HAVE YOUR HEIGHT, SHE HAS YOUR HIGH JUMP, TOO!
YES, SHE REALLY DOES.

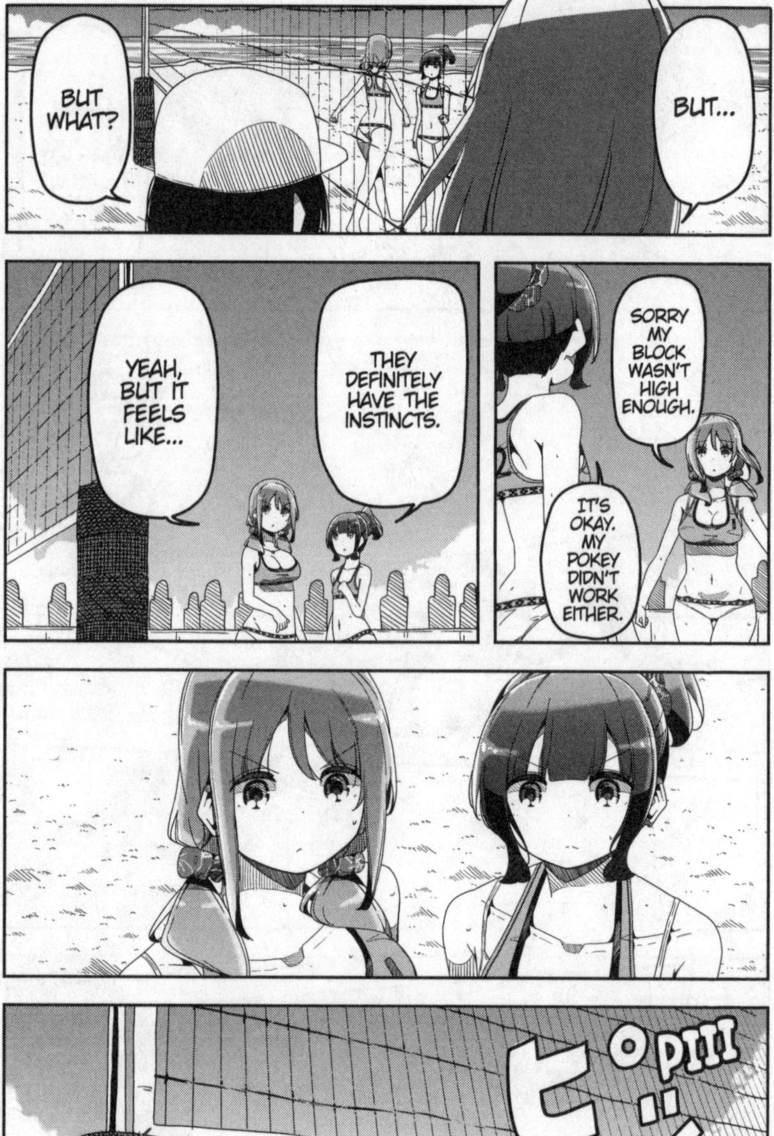
BUT...
BUT WHAT?
SORRY MY BLOCK WASN'T HIGH ENOUGH.
IT'S OKAY. MY POKEY DIDN'T WORK EITHER.
THEY DEFINITELY HAVE THE INSTINCTS.
YEAH, BUT IT FEELS LIKE...
PIII

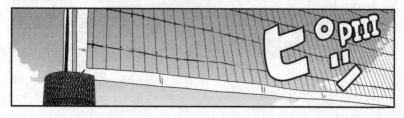

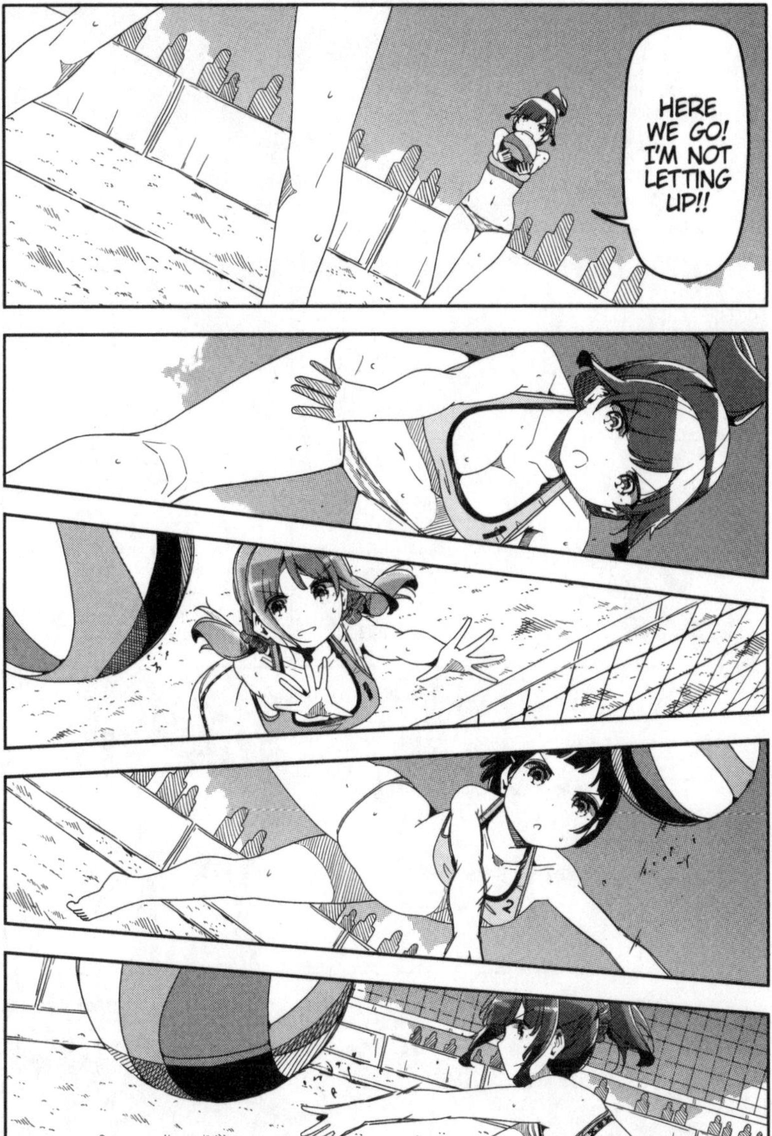
HERE WE GO! I'M NOT LETTING UP!!

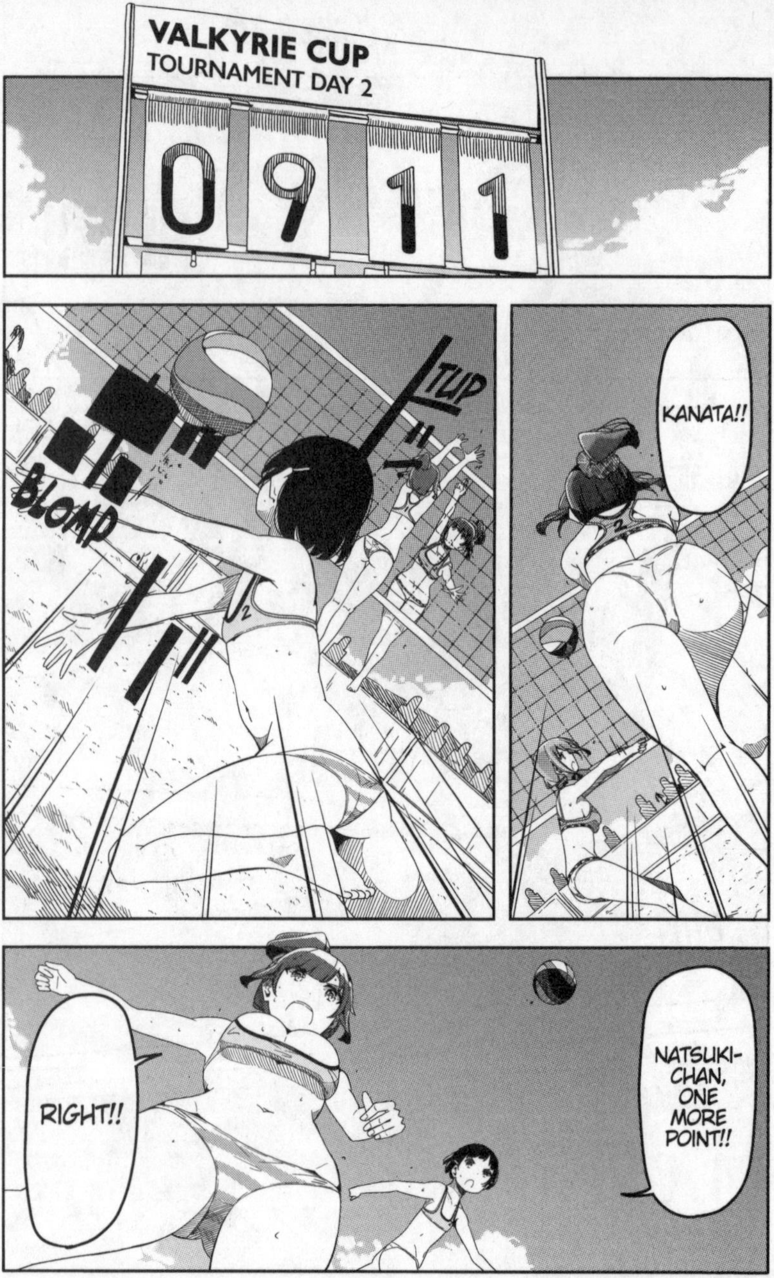
VALKYRIE CUP
TOURNAMENT DAY 2
0911
KANATA!!
TUP
BLOMP
NATSUKI-CHAN, ONE MORE POINT!!
RIGHT!!

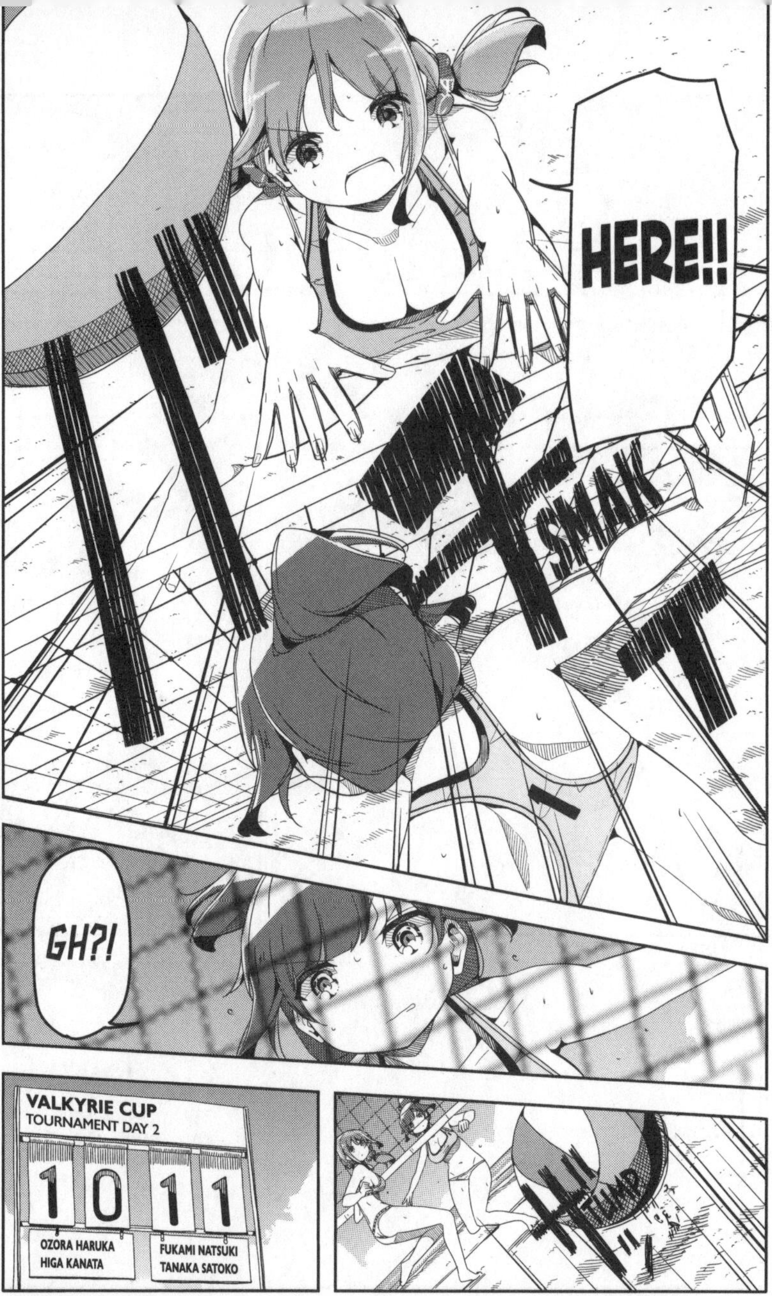
HERE!!
SMAK
GH?!
THUMP
VALKYRIE CUP
TOURNAMENT DAY 2
10 11
OZORA HARUKA
HIGA KANATA
FUKAMI NATSUKI
TANAKA SATOKO

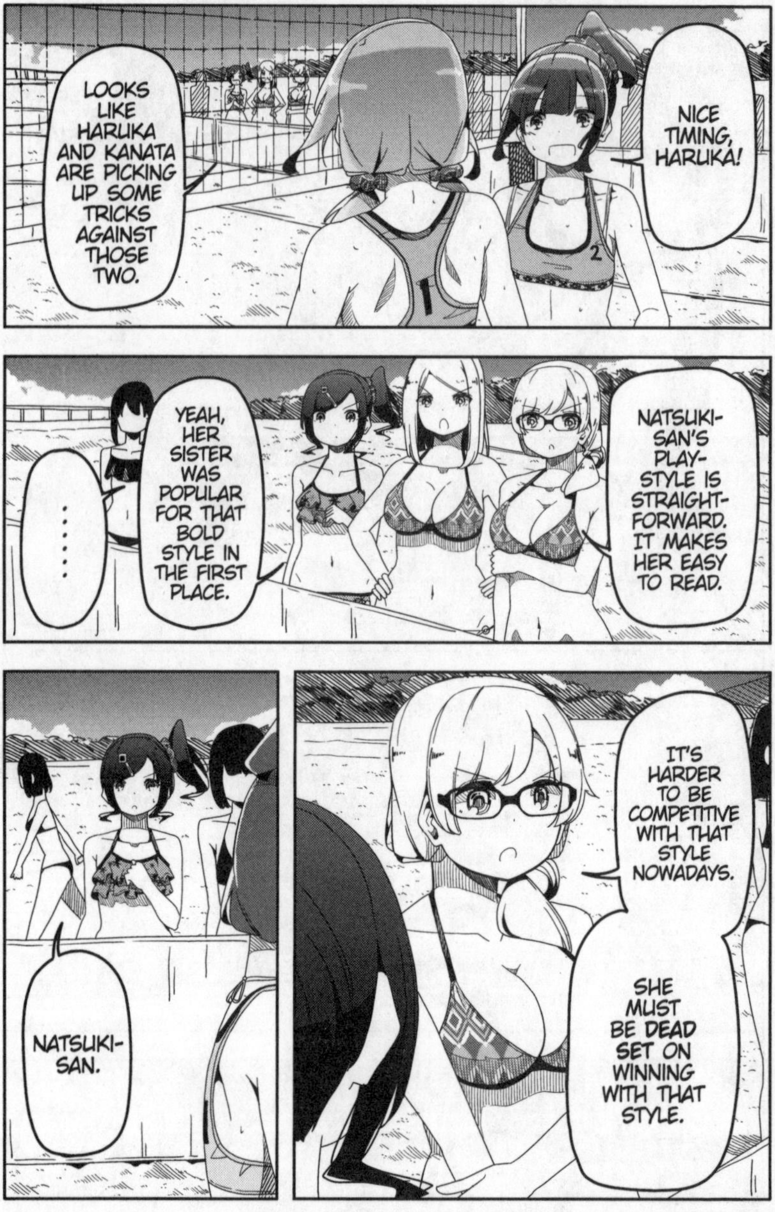
NICE TIMING, HARUKA!
LOOKS LIKE HARUKA AND KANATA ARE PICKING UP SOME TRICKS AGAINST THOSE TWO.
NATSUKI-SAN'S PLAY-STYLE IS STRAIGHT-FORWARD. IT MAKES HER EASY TO READ.
YEAH, HER SISTER WAS POPULAR FOR THAT BOLD STYLE IN THE FIRST PLACE.
......
IT'S HARDER TO BE COMPETITIVE WITH THAT STYLE NOWADAYS.
SHE MUST BE DEAD SET ON WINNING WITH THAT STYLE.
NATSUKI-SAN.

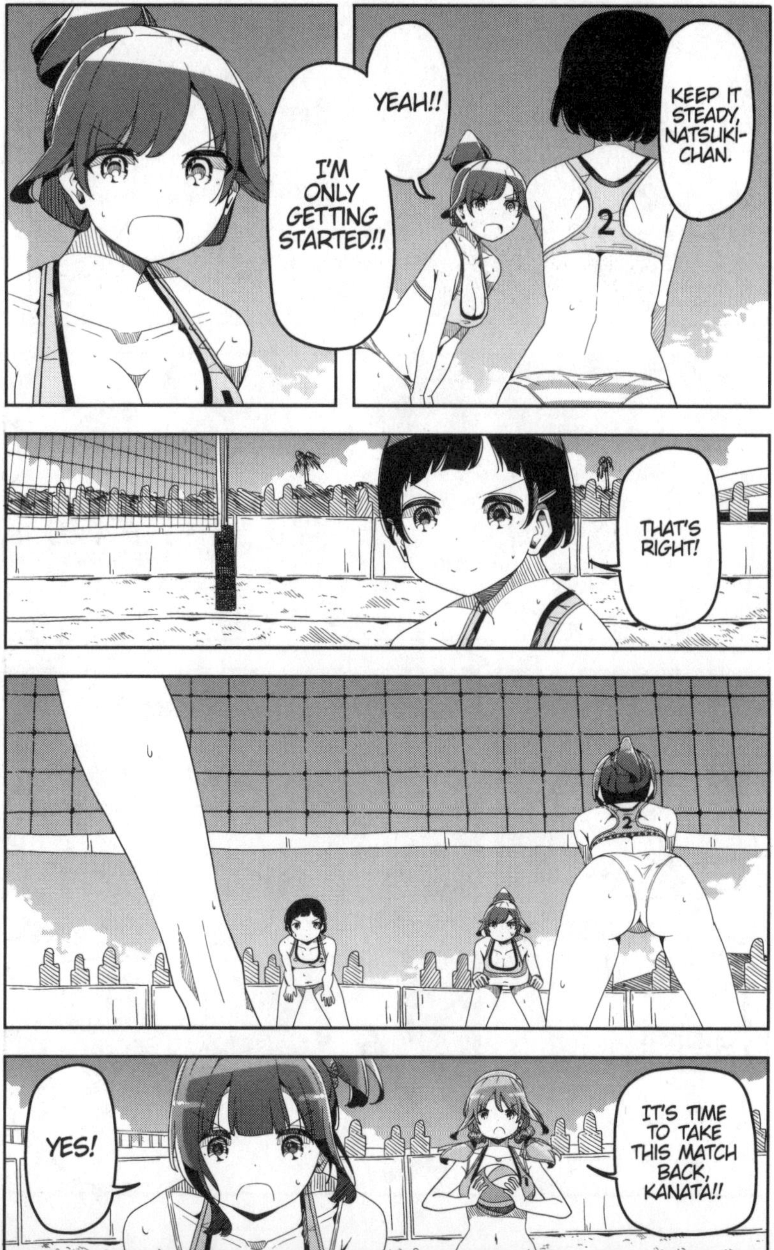
KEEP IT STEADY, NATSUKI-CHAN.
YEAH!! I'M ONLY GETTING STARTED!!
THAT'S RIGHT!
IT'S TIME TO TAKE THIS MATCH BACK, KANATA!!
YES!

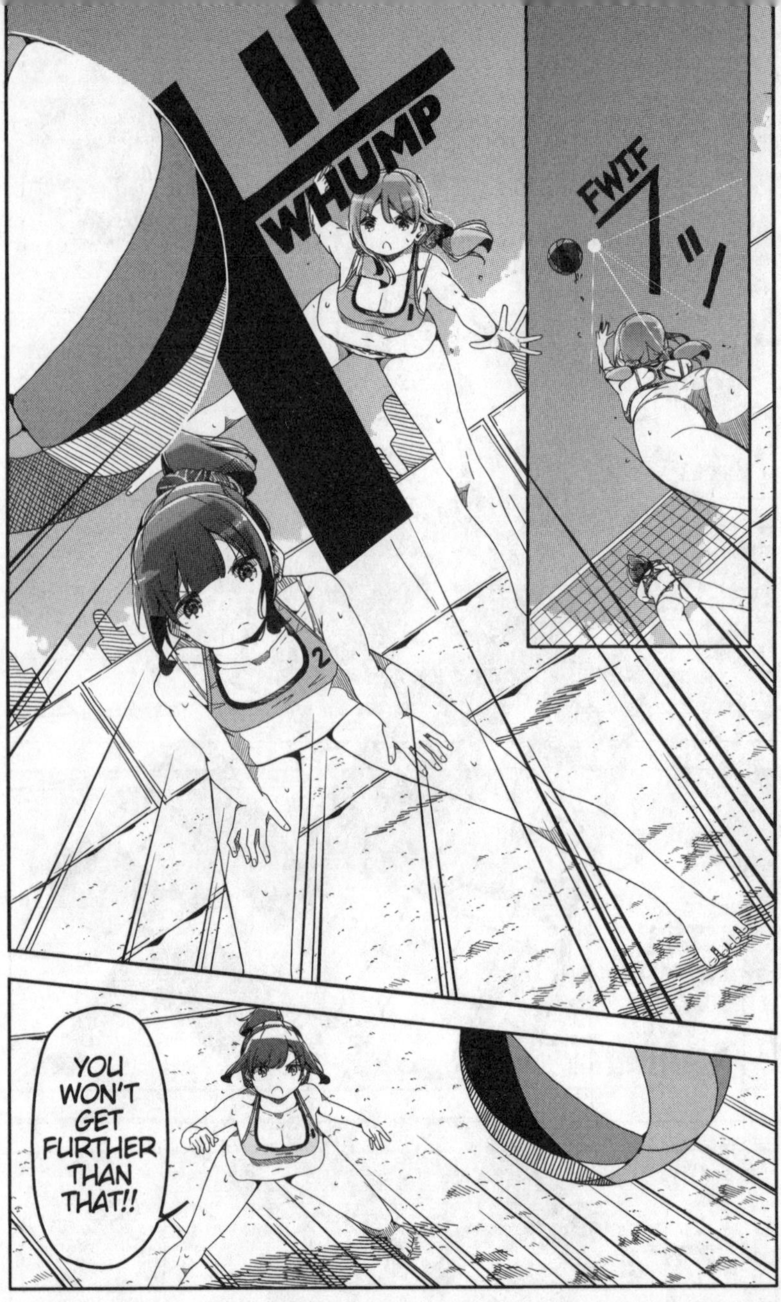
FWIF
WHUMP
YOU WON'T GET FURTHER THAN THAT!!

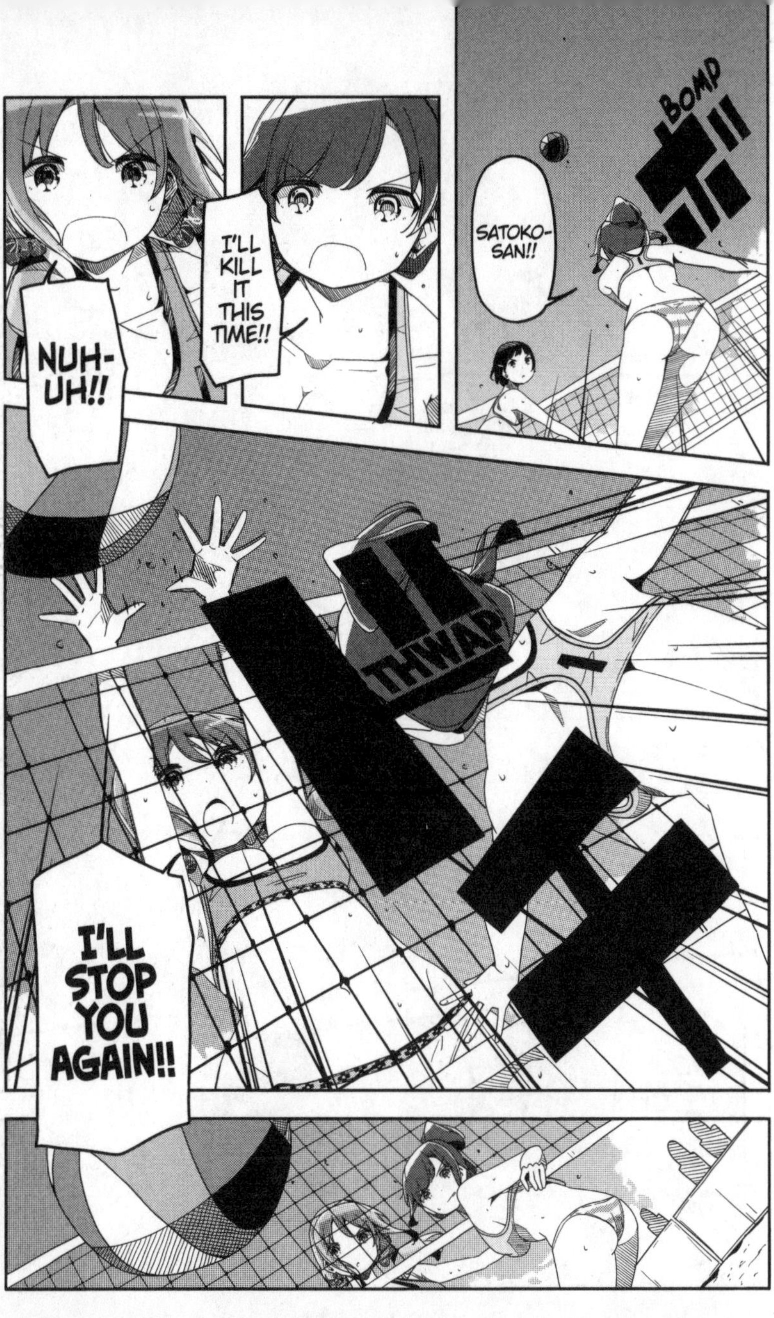
BOMP
SATOKO-SAN!!
I'LL KILL IT THIS TIME!!
NUH-UH!!
THWAP
I'LL STOP YOU AGAIN!!

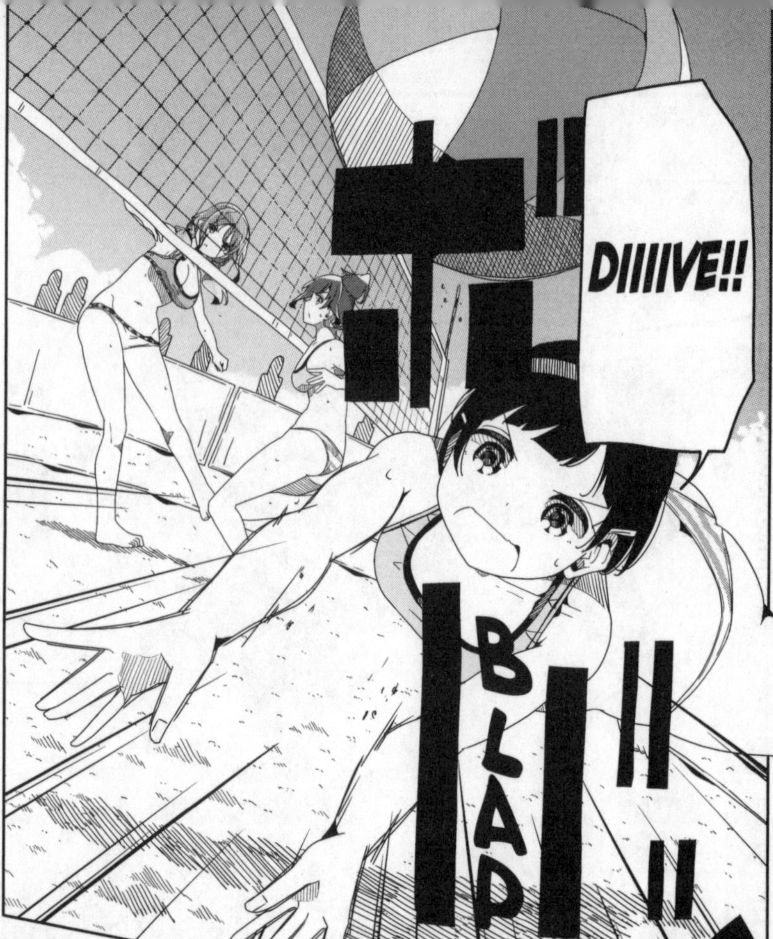
DIIIIVE!!
BLAP

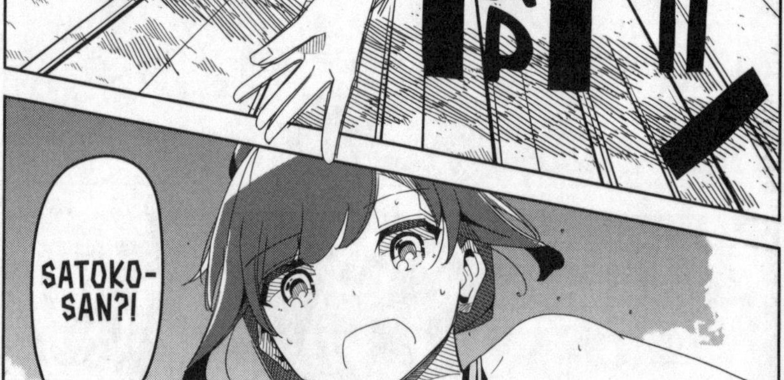
SATOKO-SAN?!

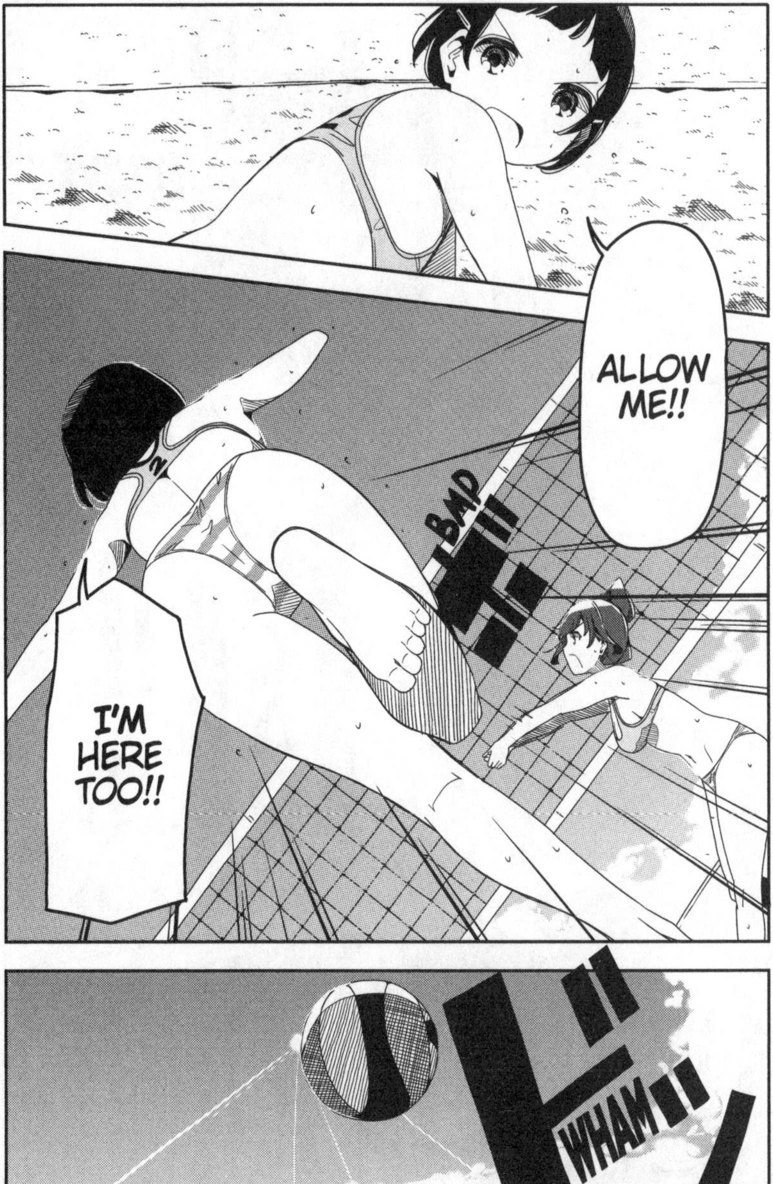
ALLOW ME!!
BAP!!
I'M HERE TOO!!
WHAM!!

Harukana Receive

Presented by Nyoijizai

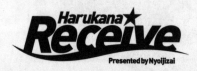

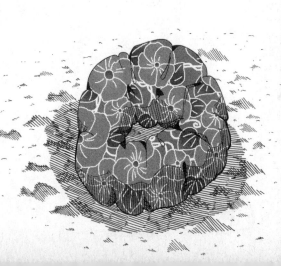

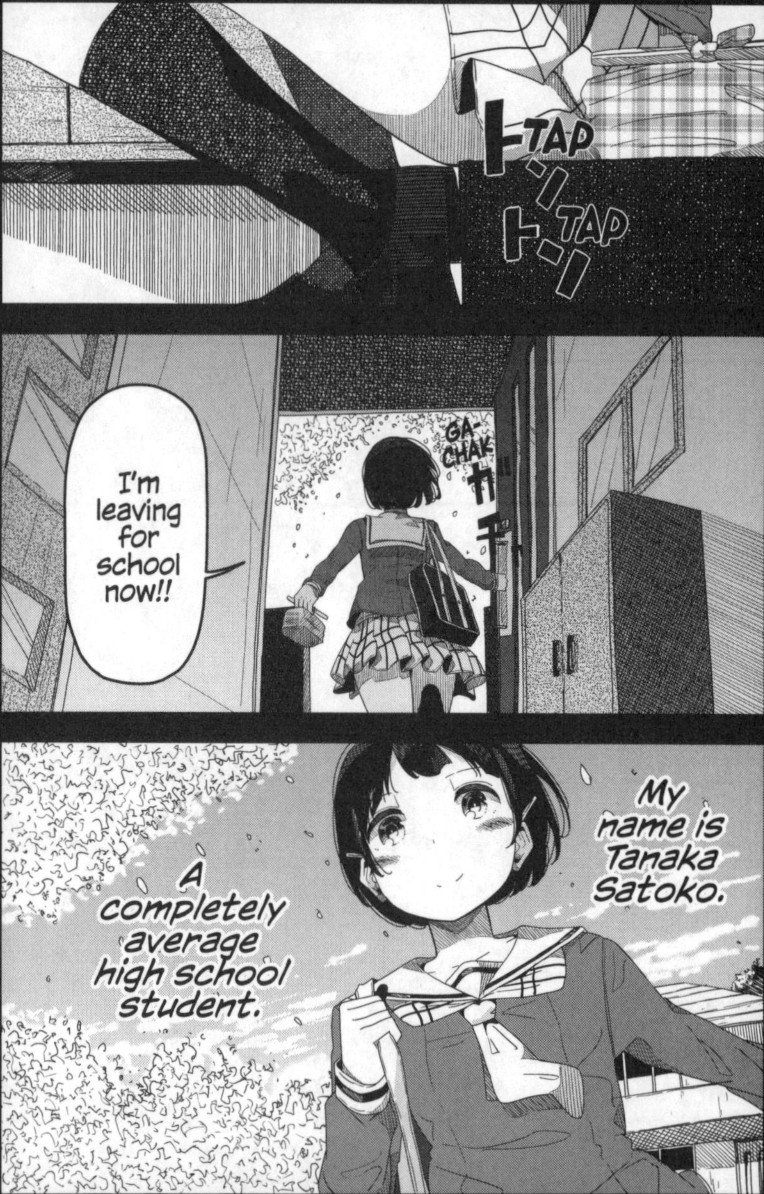
TAP
TAP
GA-CHAK
I'm leaving for school now!!
My name is Tanaka Satoko.
A completely average high school student.

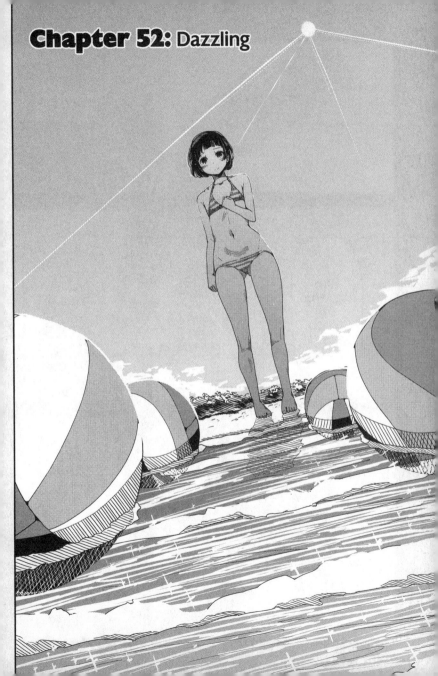

# Chapter 52: Dazzling

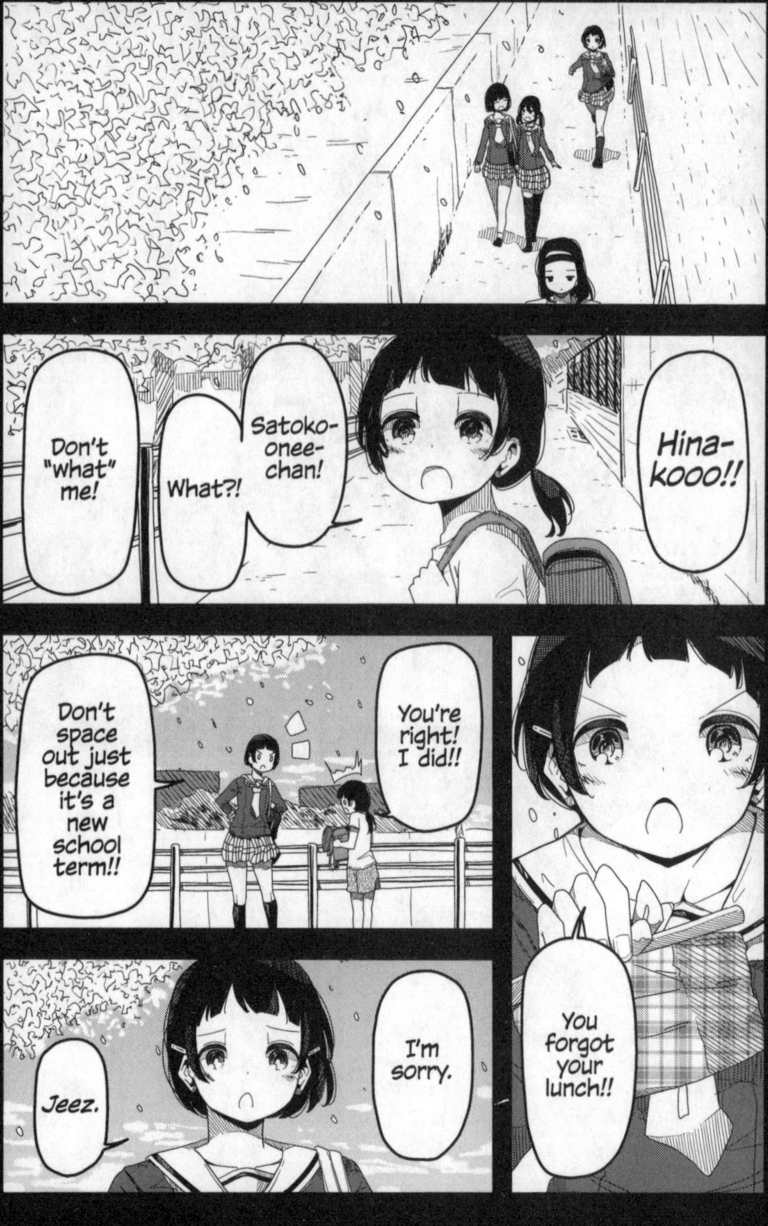
Hina-kooo!!
Satoko-onee-chan!
What?!
Don't "what" me!
You forgot your lunch!!
You're right! I did!!
Don't space out just because it's a new school term!!
I'm sorry.
Jeez.

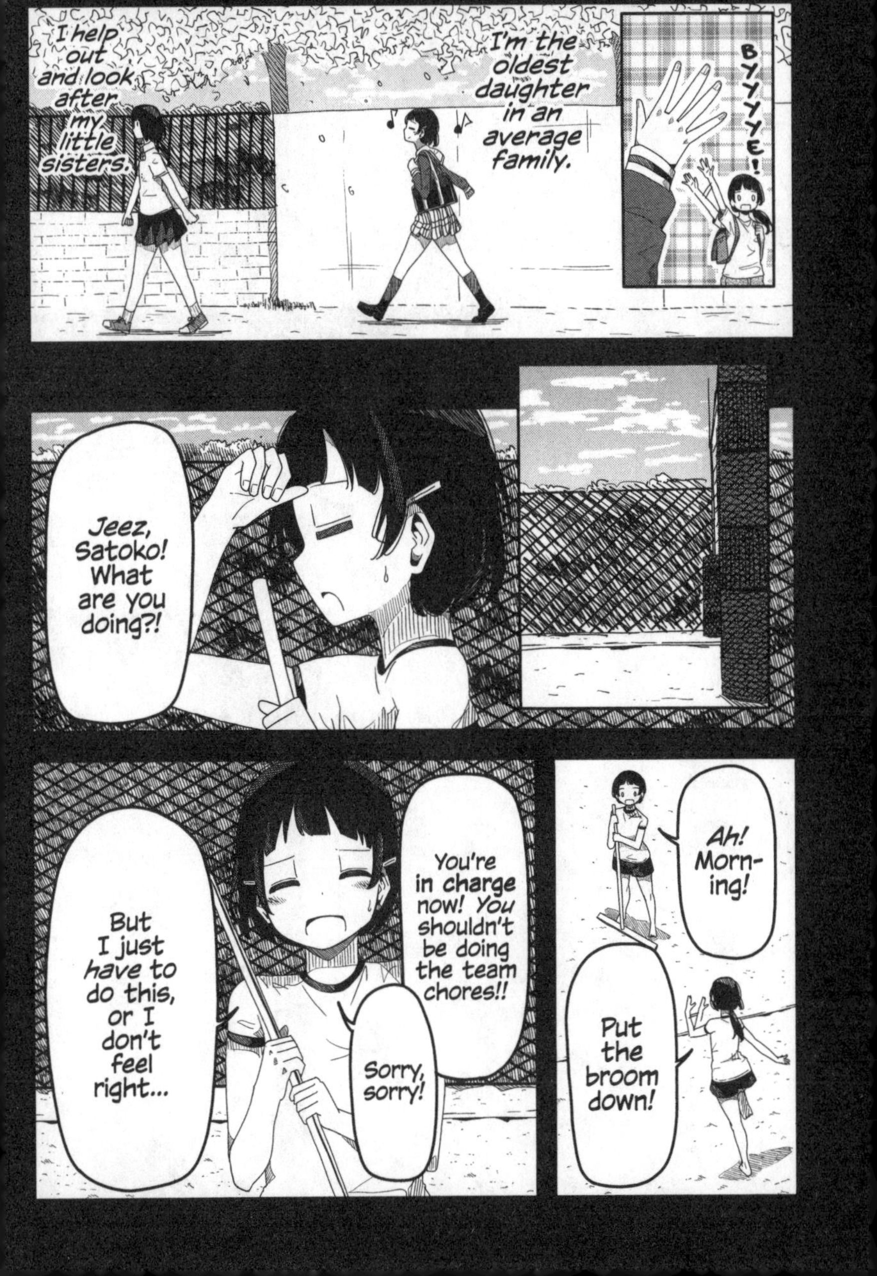
BYYYYE!
I'm the oldest daughter in an average family.
I help out and look after my little sisters.
Jeez, Satoko! What are you doing?!
Ah! Morning!
Put the broom down!
You're in charge now! You shouldn't be doing the team chores!!
Sorry, sorry!
But I just have to do this, or I don't feel right...

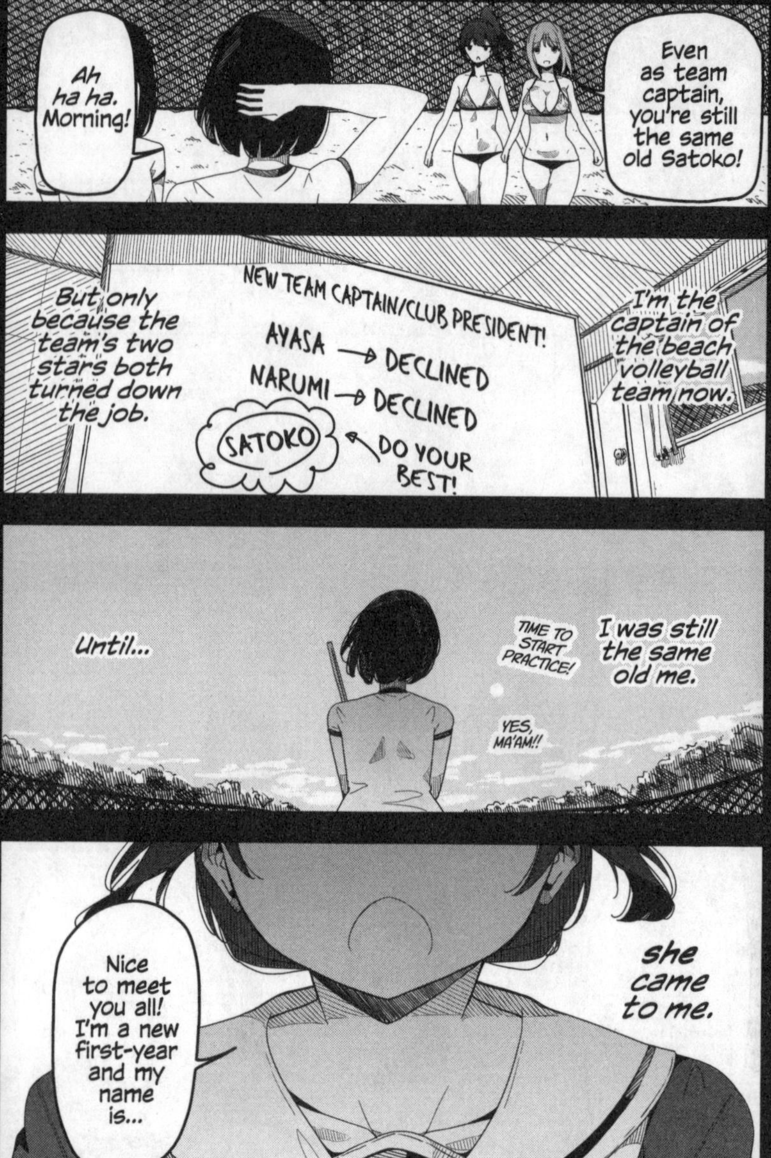
Even as team captain, you're still the same old Satoko!
Ah ha ha. Morning!
I'm the captain of the beach volleyball team now.
NEW TEAM CAPTAIN/CLUB PRESIDENT!
AYASA → DECLINED
NARUMI → DECLINED
SATOKO ← DO YOUR BEST!
But only because the team's two stars both turned down the job.
I was still the same old me.
TIME TO START PRACTICE!
YES, MA'AM!!
Until...
she came to me.
Nice to meet you all! I'm a new first-year and my name is...

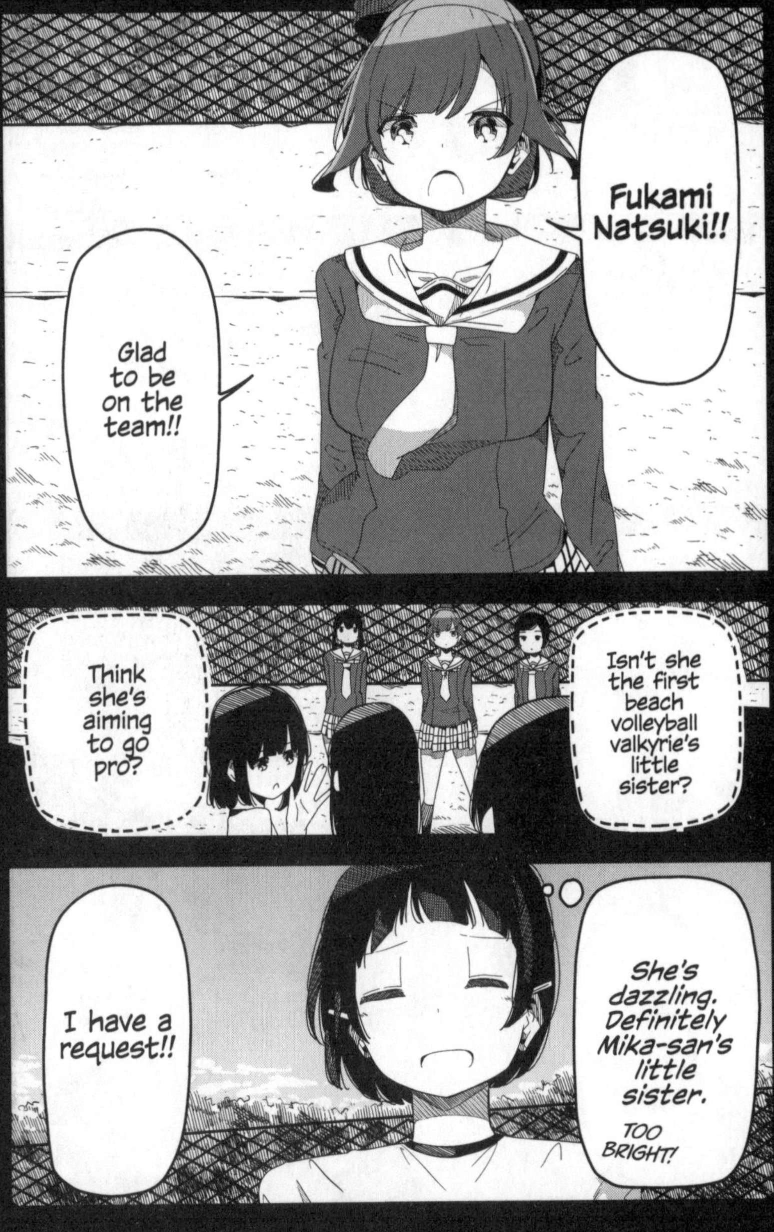
Fukami Natsuki!!
Glad to be on the team!!
Isn't she the first beach volleyball valkyrie's little sister?
Think she's aiming to go pro?
She's dazzling. Definitely Mika-san's little sister.
TOO BRIGHT!
I have a request!!

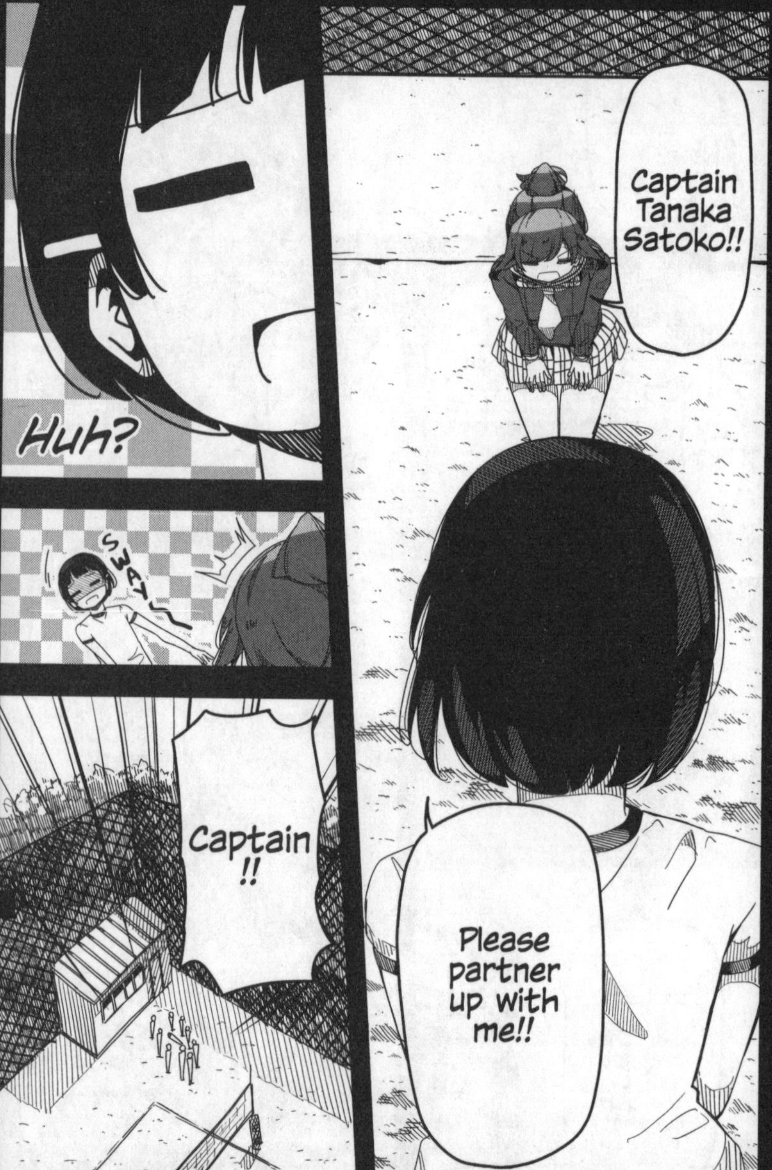
Captain Tanaka Satoko!!
Please partner up with me!!
Huh?
SWAY
Captain !!

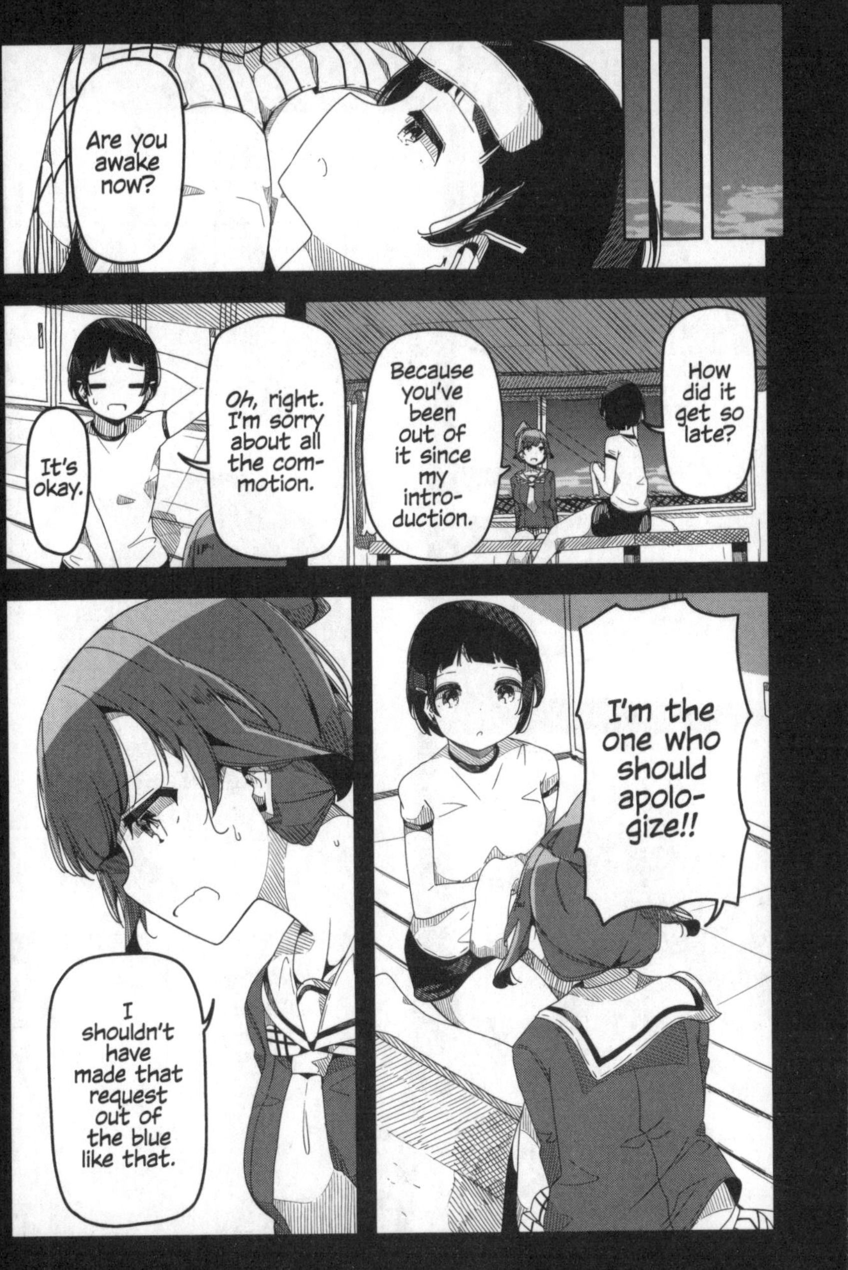
Are you awake now?
How did it get so late?
Because you've been out of it since my intro-duction.
Oh, right. I'm sorry about all the com-motion.
It's okay.
I'm the one who should apolo-gize!!
I shouldn't have made that request out of the blue like that.

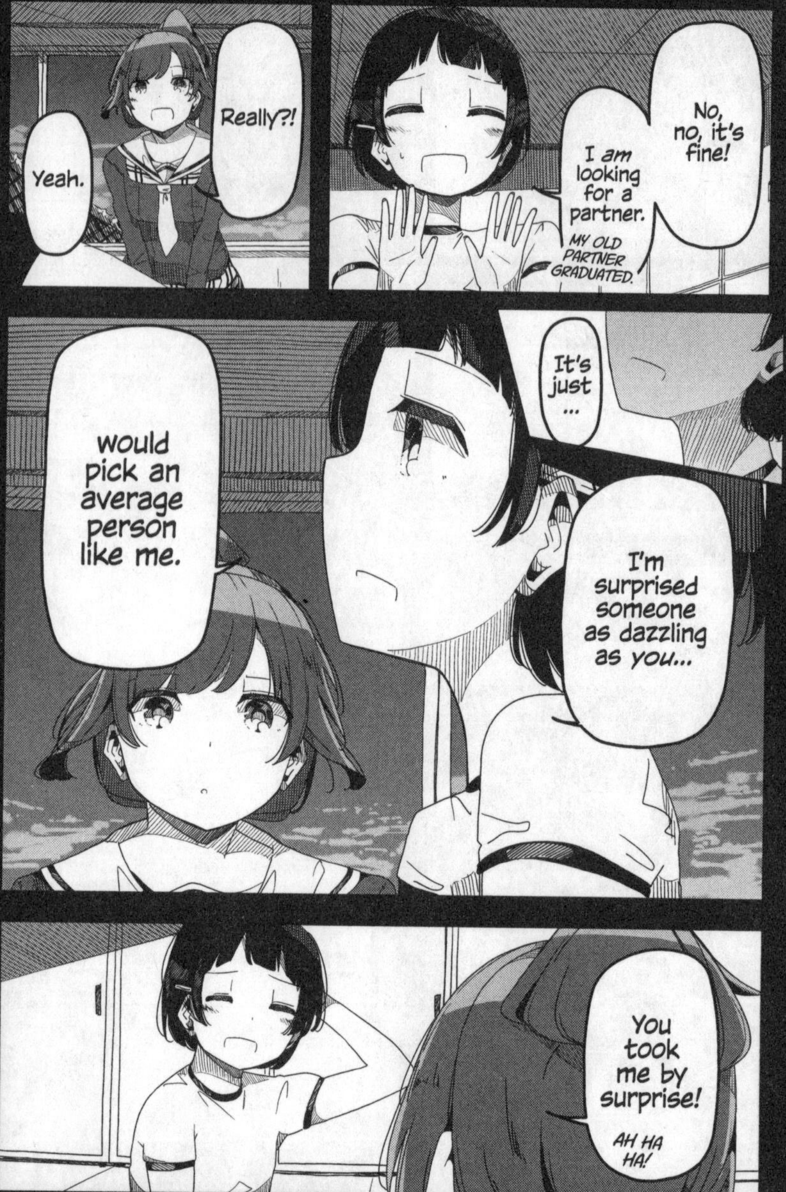
No, no, it's fine!
I *am* looking for a partner.
MY OLD PARTNER GRADUATED.
Really?!
Yeah.
It's just ...
I'm surprised someone as dazzling as *you*...
would pick an average person like me.
You took me by surprise!
AH HA HA!

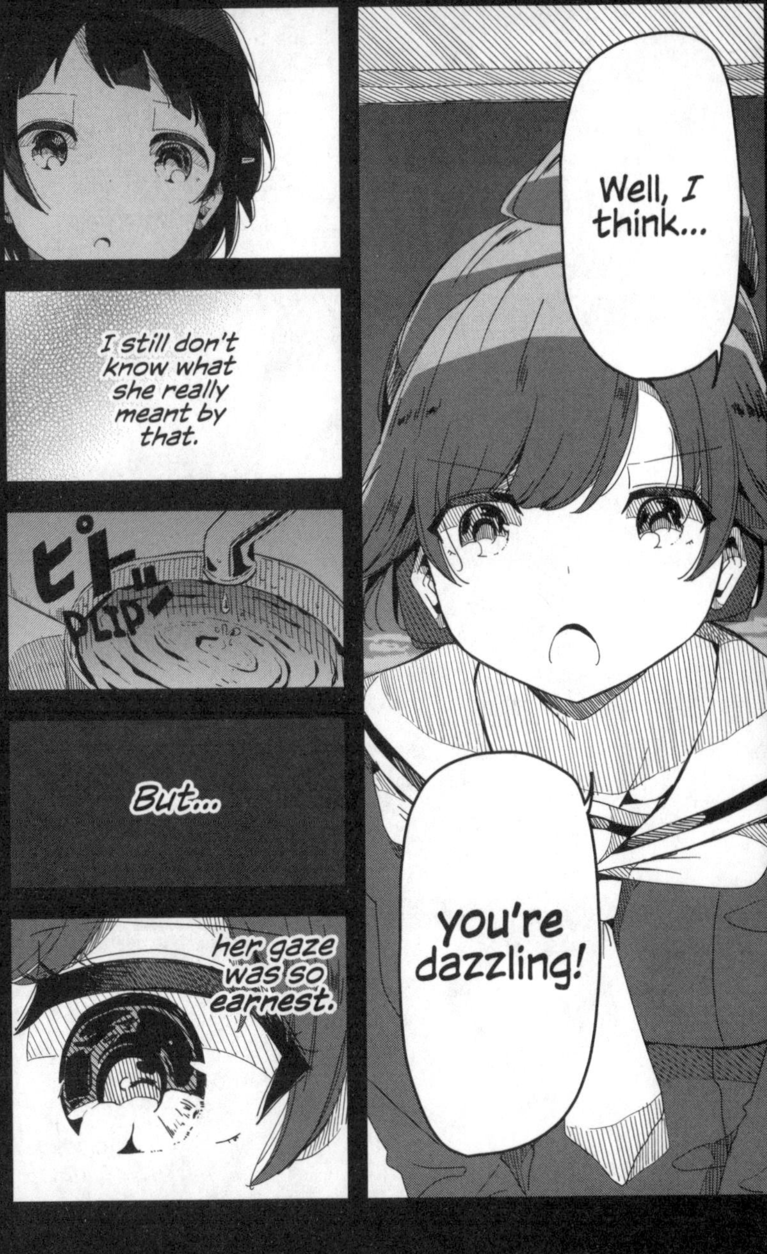
Well, I think...
you're dazzling!
I still don't know what she really meant by that.
PLIP
But...
her gaze was so earnest.

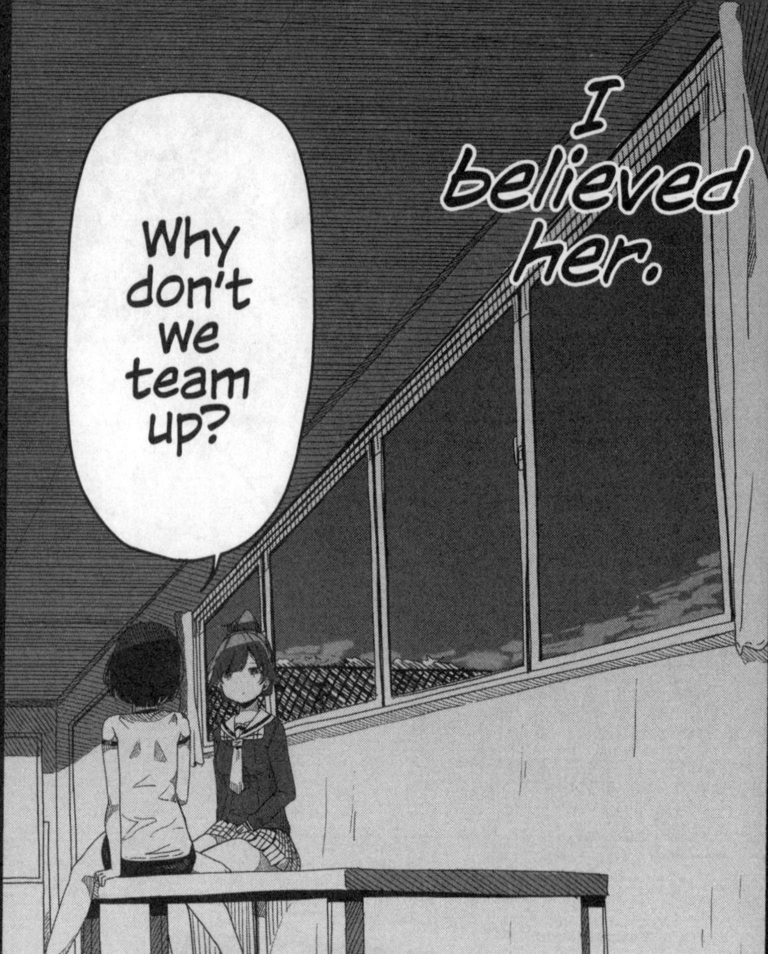
I believed her.
Why don't we team up?

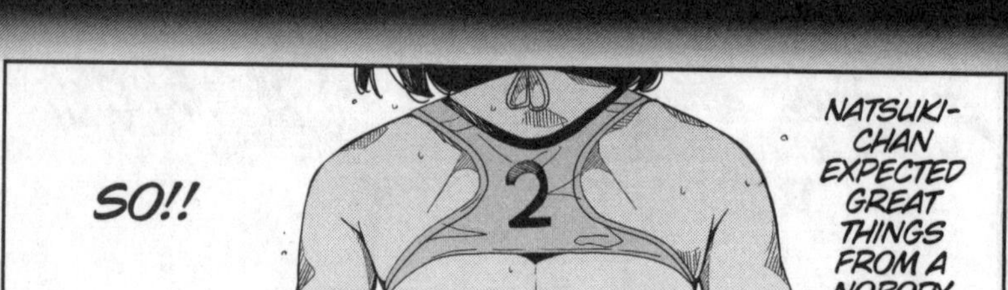
NATSUKI-CHAN EXPECTED GREAT THINGS FROM A NOBODY LIKE ME.
SO!!

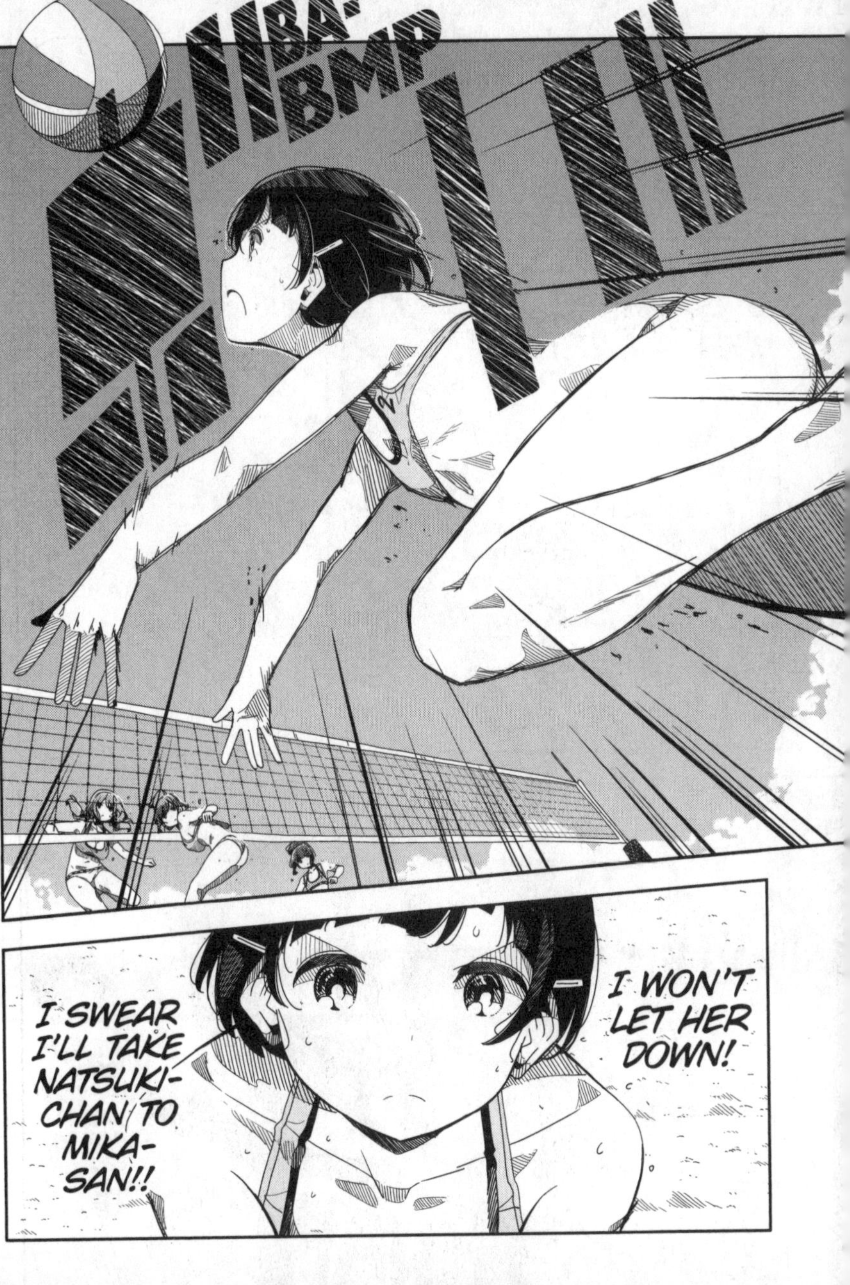
THBA-THBMP
I WON'T LET HER DOWN!
I SWEAR I'LL TAKE NATSUKI-CHAN TO MIKA-SAN!!

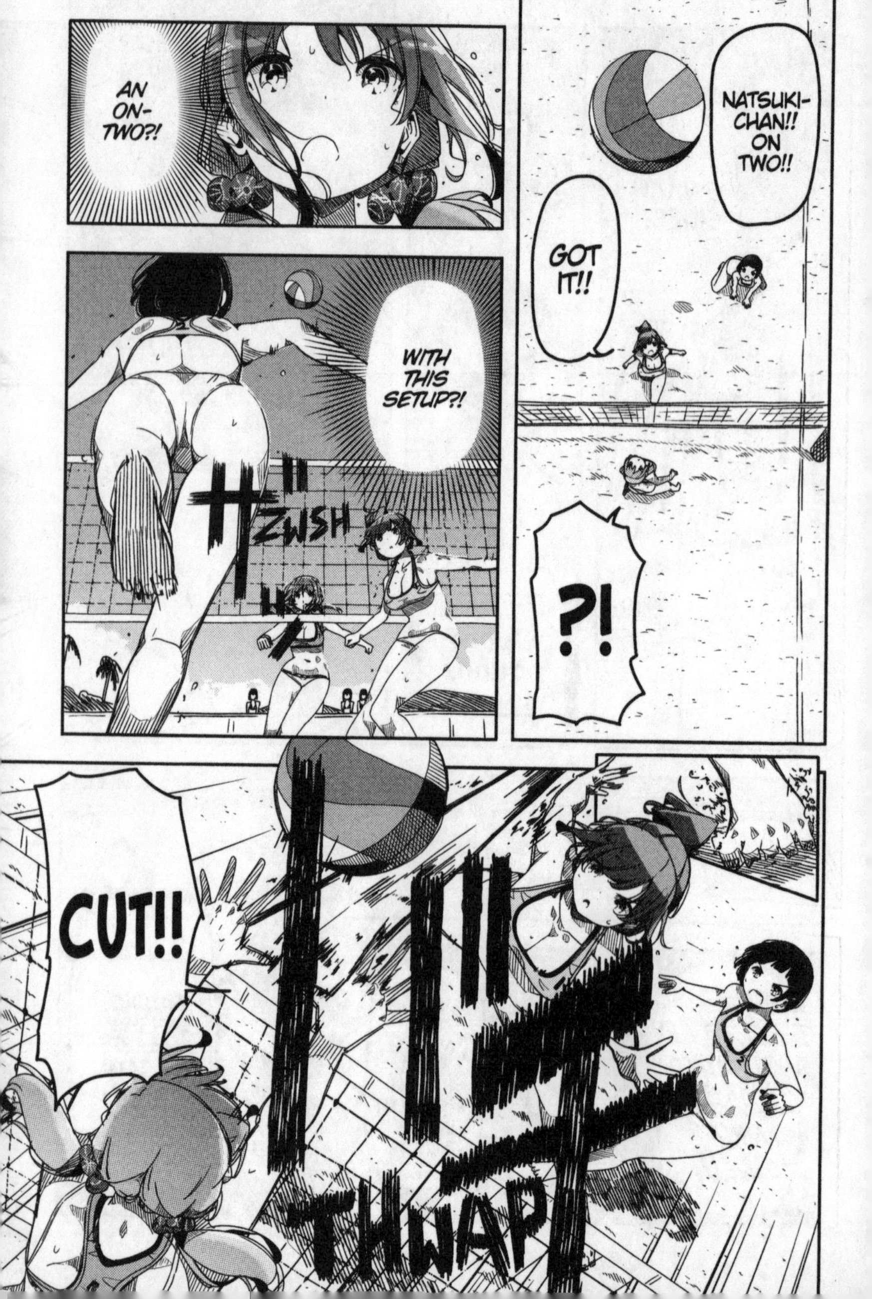
NATSUKI-CHAN!! ON TWO!!
GOT IT!!
?!
AN ON-TWO?!
WITH THIS SETUP?!
ZWSH
CUT!!
THWAP

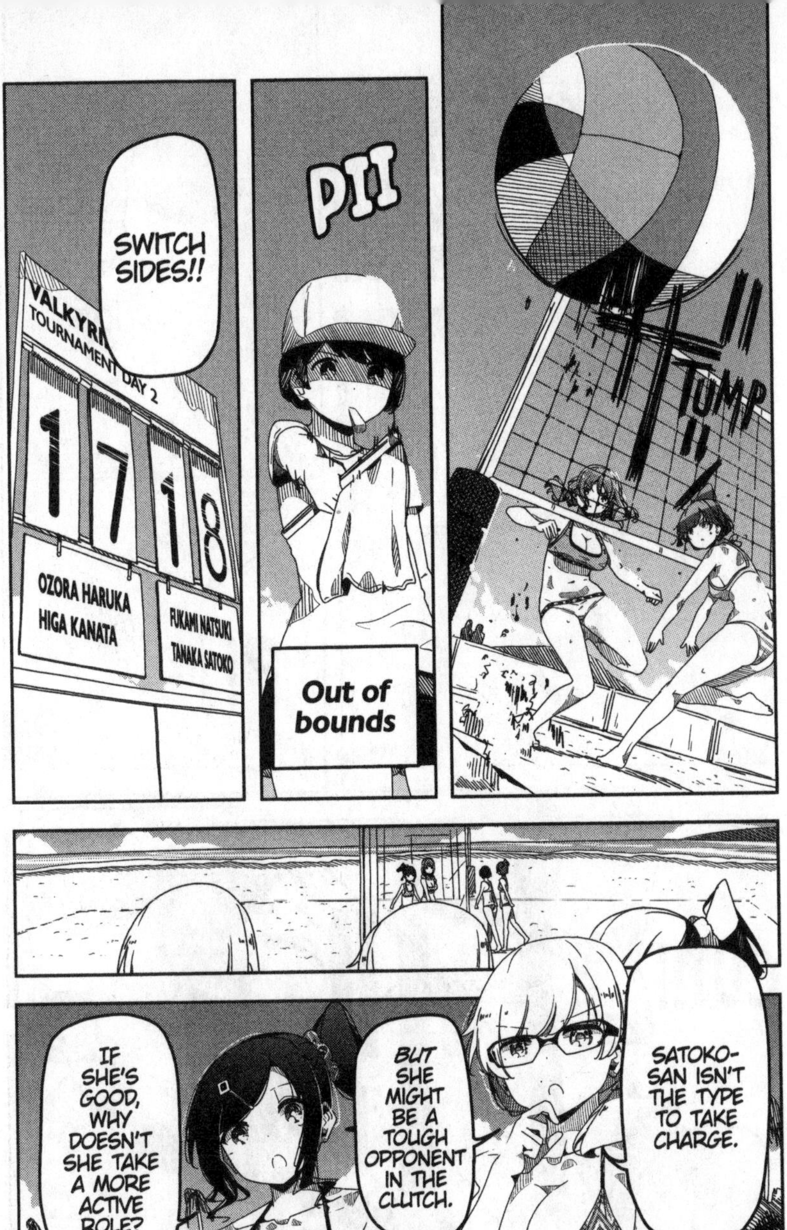
TUMP
PII
Out of bounds
SWITCH SIDES!!
TOURNAMENT DAY 2
17
18
OZORA HARUKA
HIGA KANATA
FUKAMI NATSUKI
TANAKA SATOKO
SATOKO-SAN ISN'T THE TYPE TO TAKE CHARGE.
*BUT* SHE MIGHT BE A TOUGH OPPONENT IN THE CLUTCH.
IF SHE'S GOOD, WHY DOESN'T SHE TAKE A MORE ACTIVE ROLE?

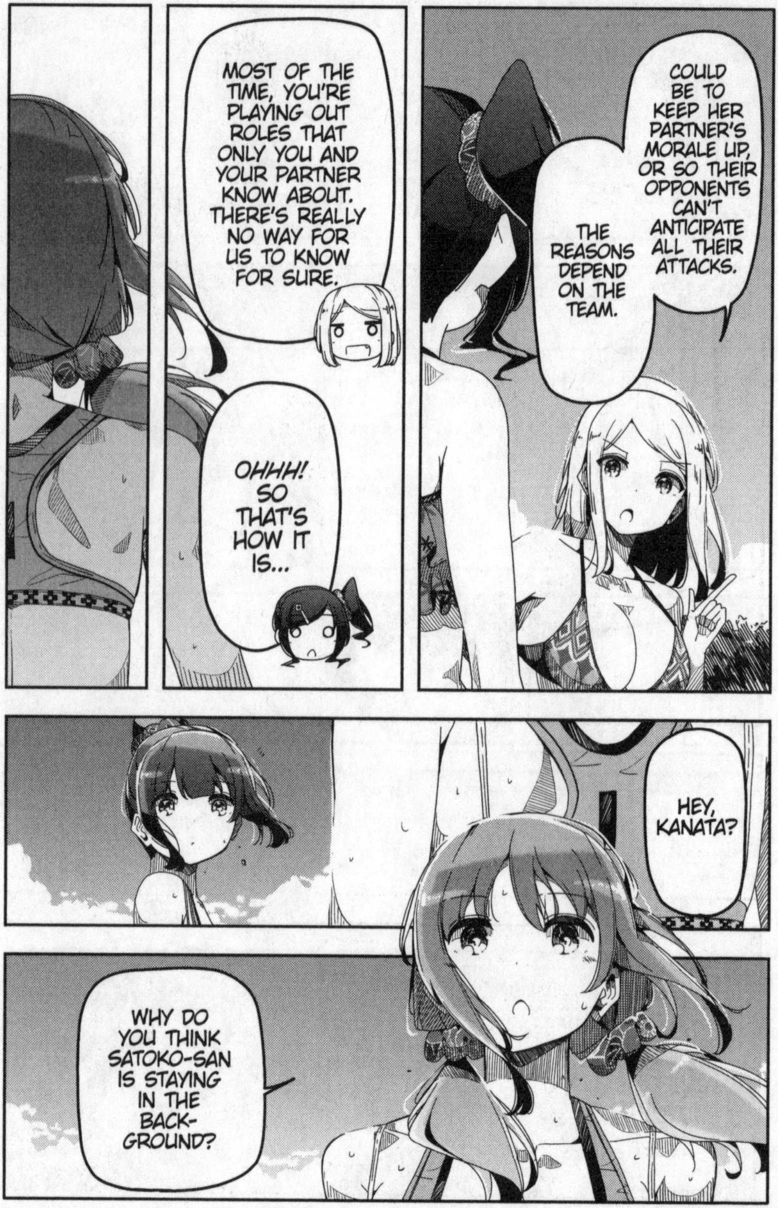
THE REASONS DEPEND ON THE TEAM.
COULD BE TO KEEP HER PARTNER'S MORALE UP, OR SO THEIR OPPONENTS CAN'T ANTICIPATE ALL THEIR ATTACKS.
MOST OF THE TIME, YOU'RE PLAYING OUT ROLES THAT ONLY YOU AND YOUR PARTNER KNOW ABOUT. THERE'S REALLY NO WAY FOR US TO KNOW FOR SURE.
OHHH! SO THAT'S HOW IT IS...
HEY, KANATA?
WHY DO YOU THINK SATOKO-SAN IS STAYING IN THE BACK-GROUND?

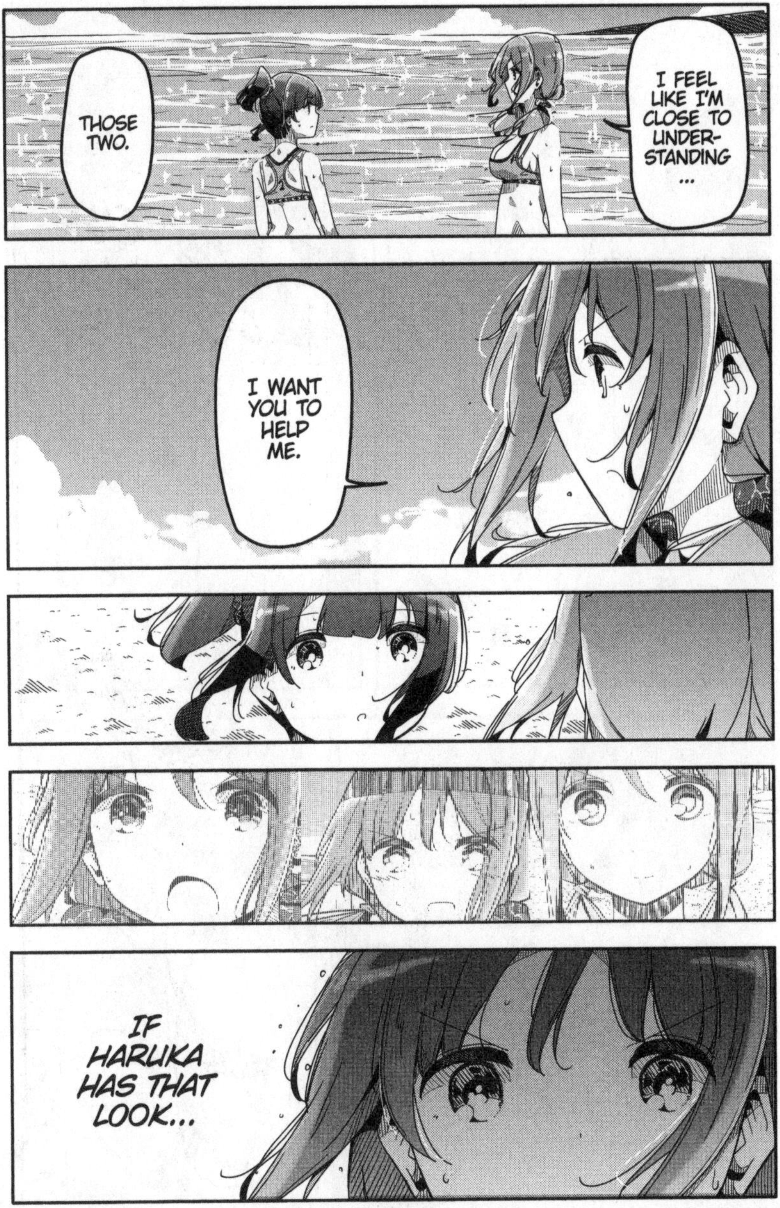
I FEEL LIKE I'M CLOSE TO UNDER-STANDING...
THOSE TWO.
I WANT YOU TO HELP ME.
IF HARUKA HAS THAT LOOK...

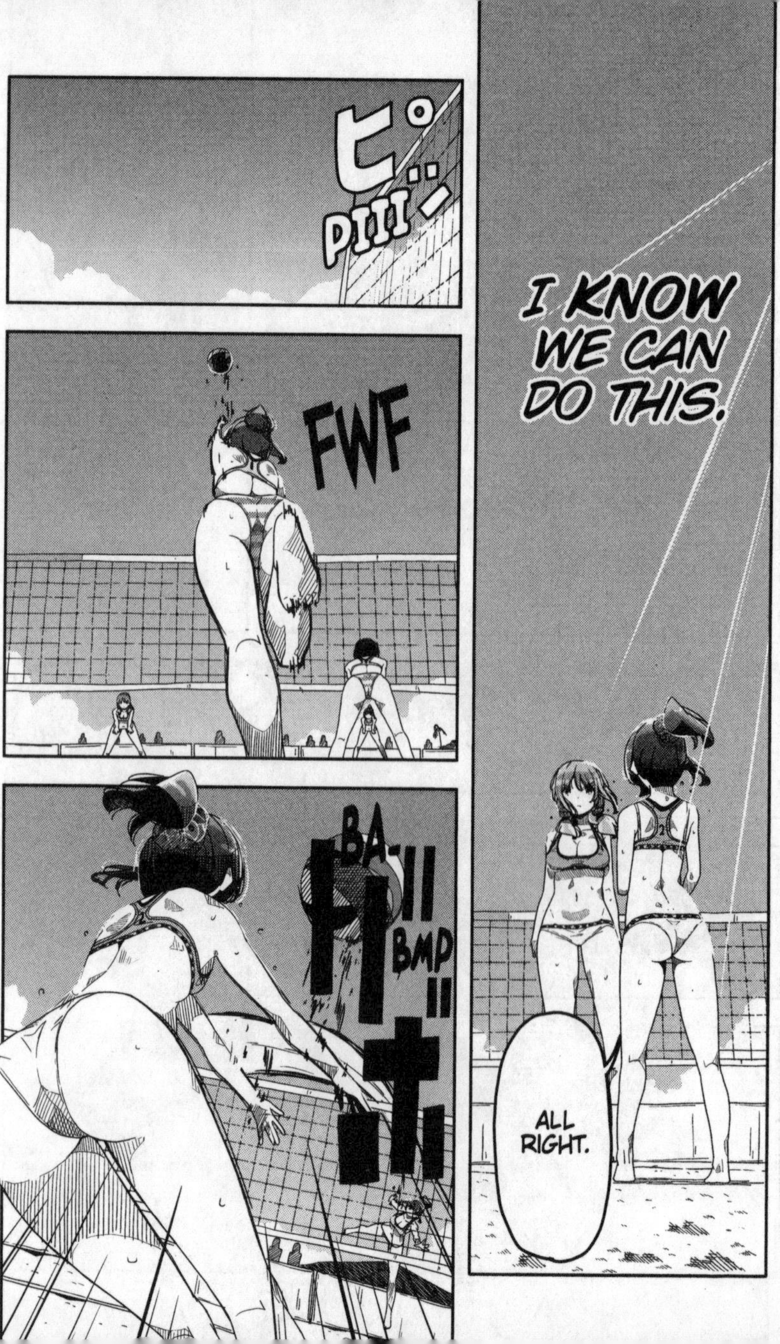
I KNOW WE CAN DO THIS.
ALL RIGHT.
PIII
FWF
BA-!!
BMP!!

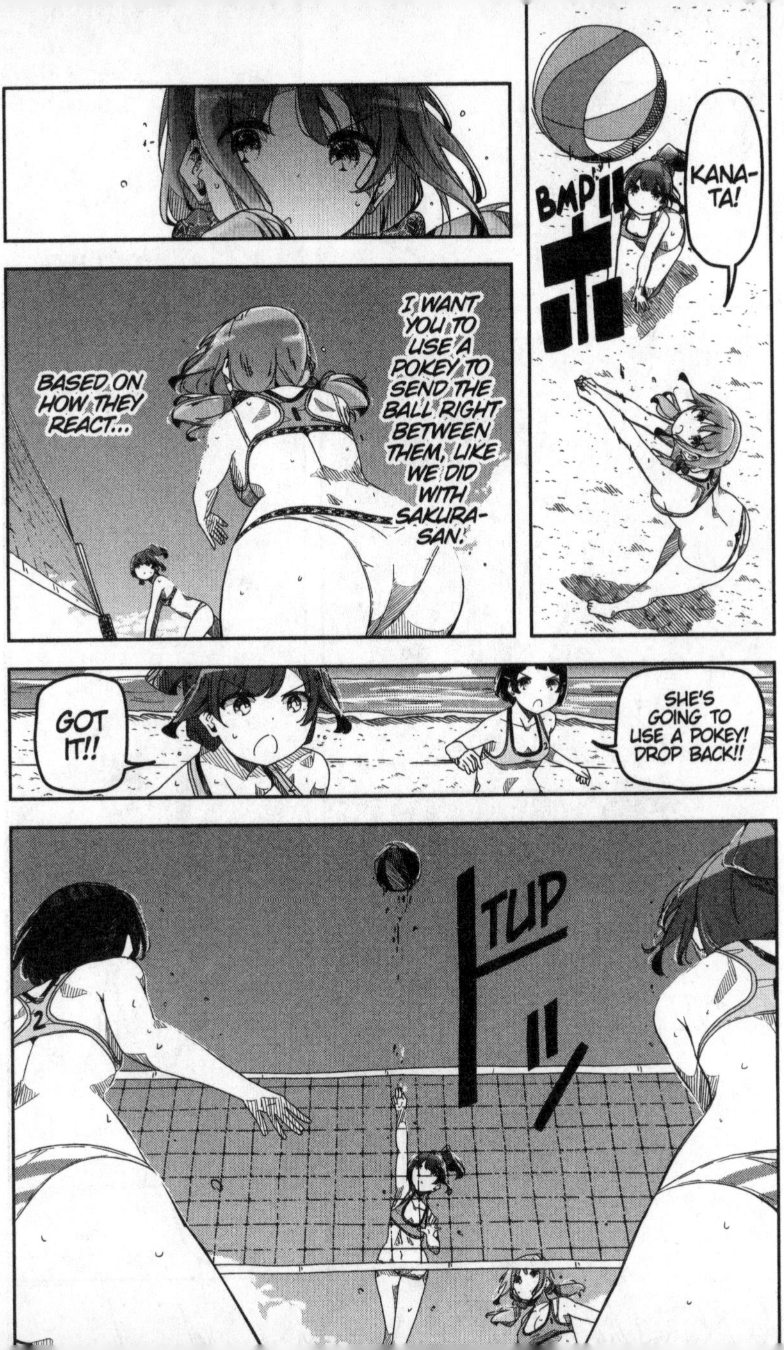
KANA-TA!
BMP
I WANT YOU TO USE A POKEY TO SEND THE BALL RIGHT BETWEEN THEM, LIKE WE DID WITH SAKURA-SAN!
BASED ON HOW THEY REACT...
SHE'S GOING TO USE A POKEY! DROP BACK!!
GOT IT!!
TUP

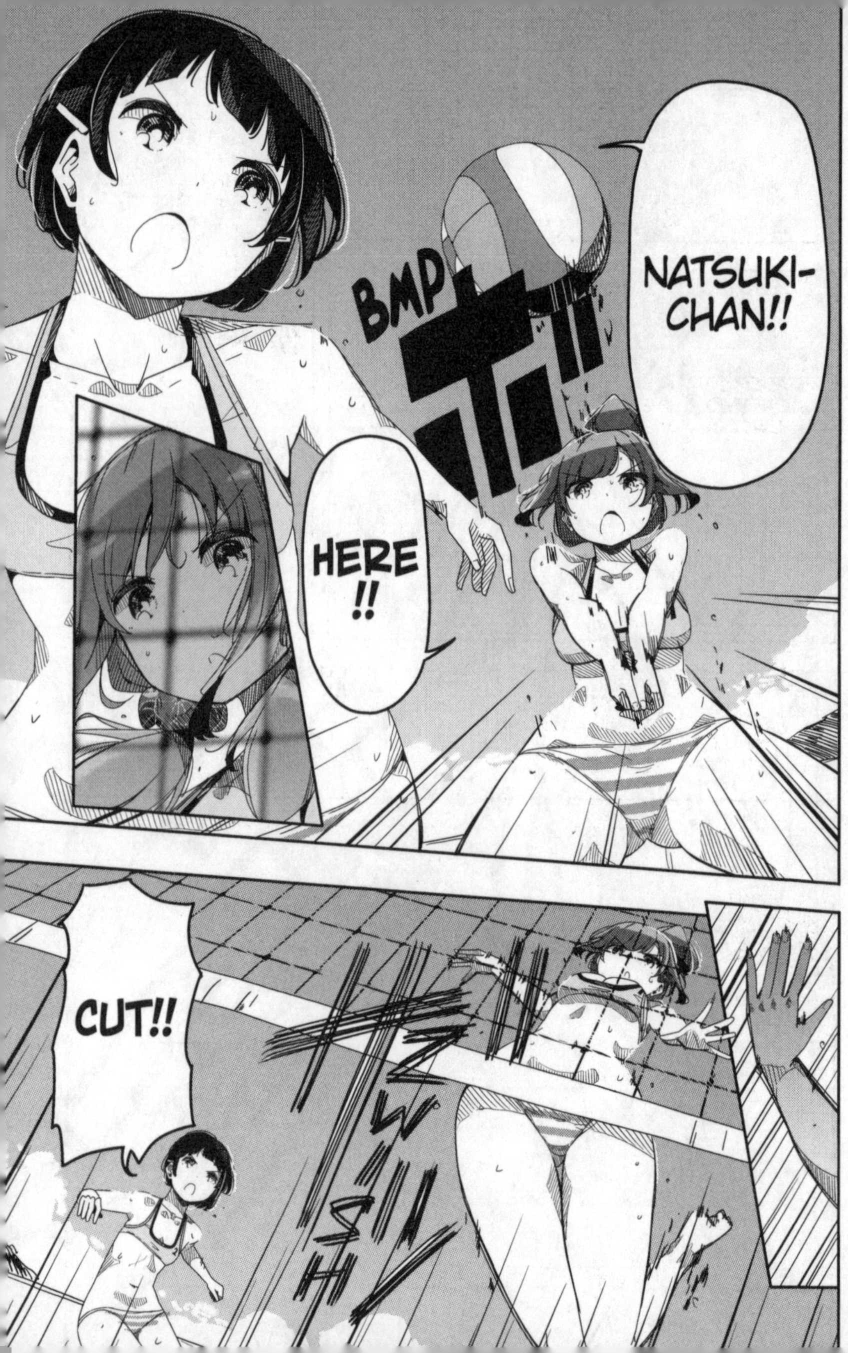
NATSUKI-CHAN!!
BMP
HERE!!
CUT!!

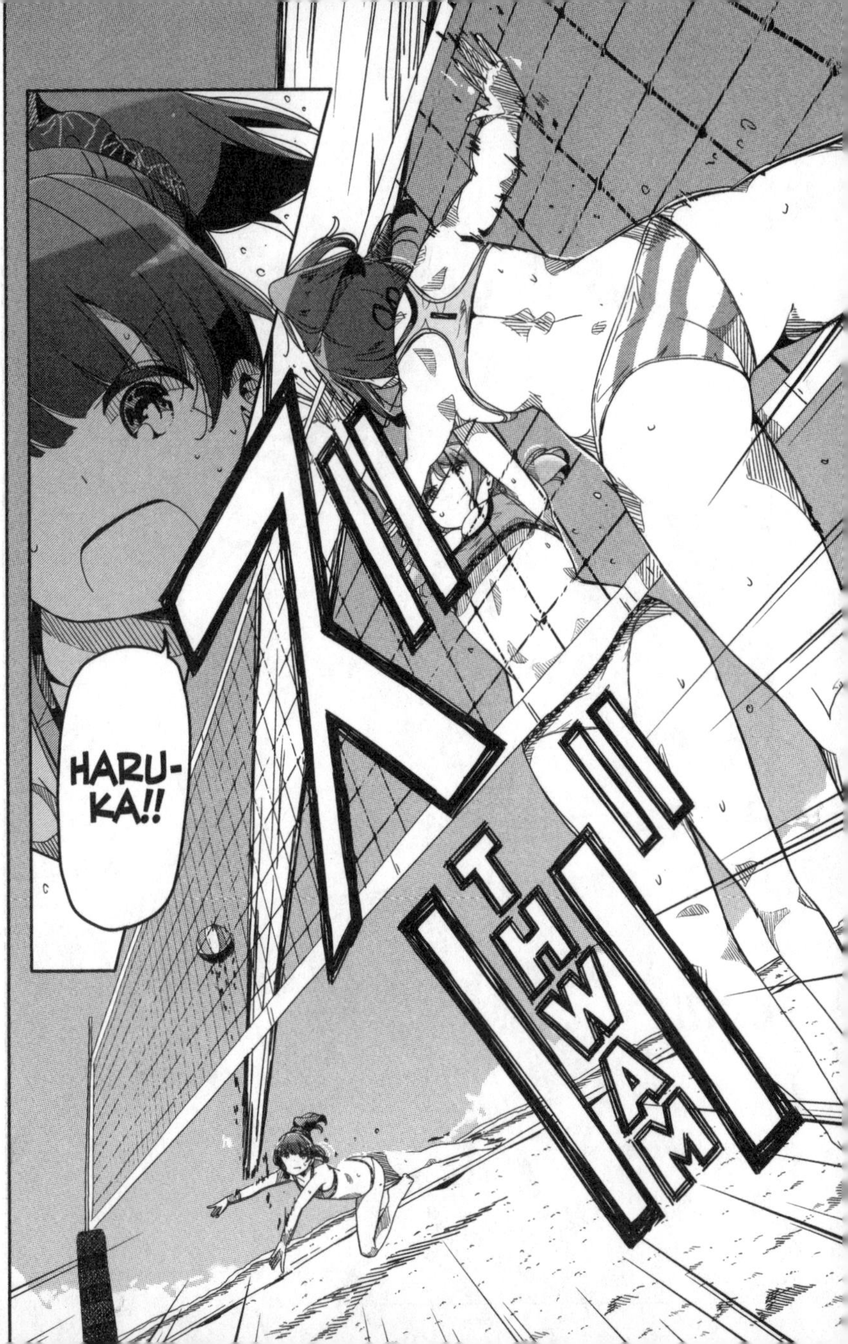
HARU-
KA!!
THWAM

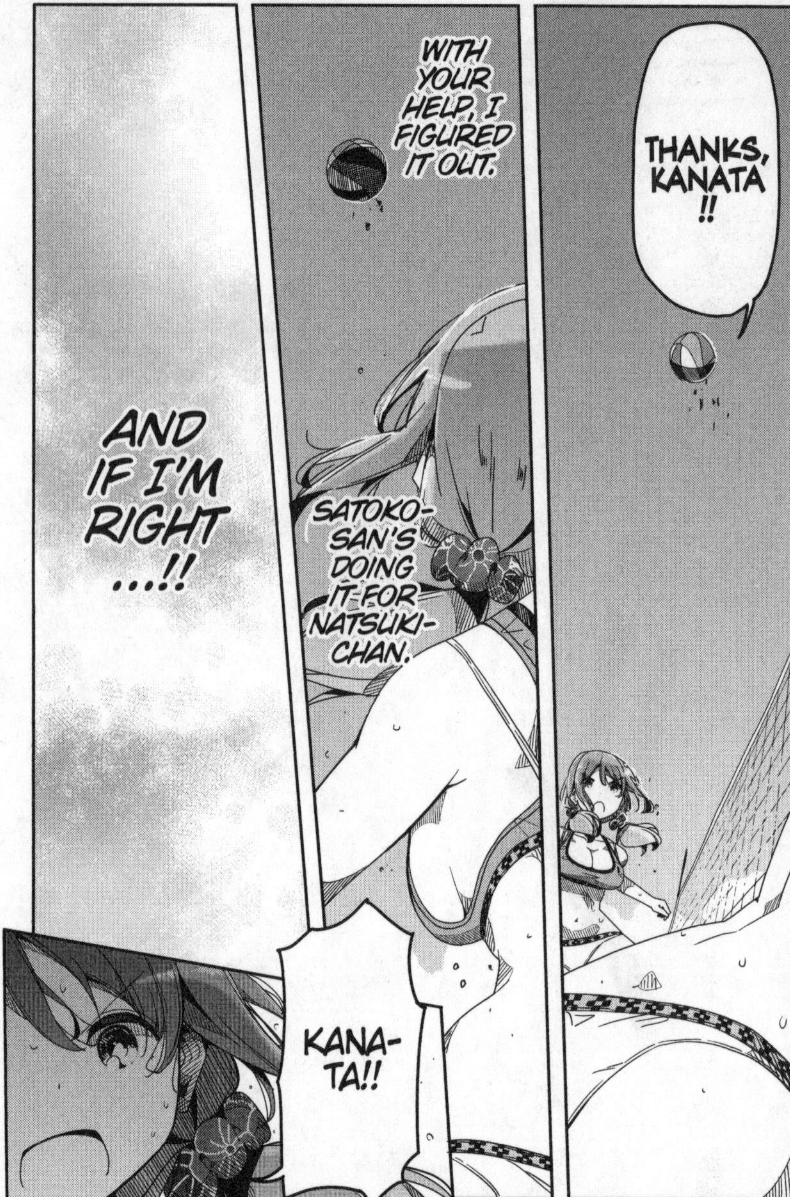
THANKS, KANATA!!
WITH YOUR HELP, I FIGURED IT OUT.
SATOKO-SAN'S DOING IT FOR NATSUKI-CHAN.
AND IF I'M RIGHT...!!
KANA-TA!!

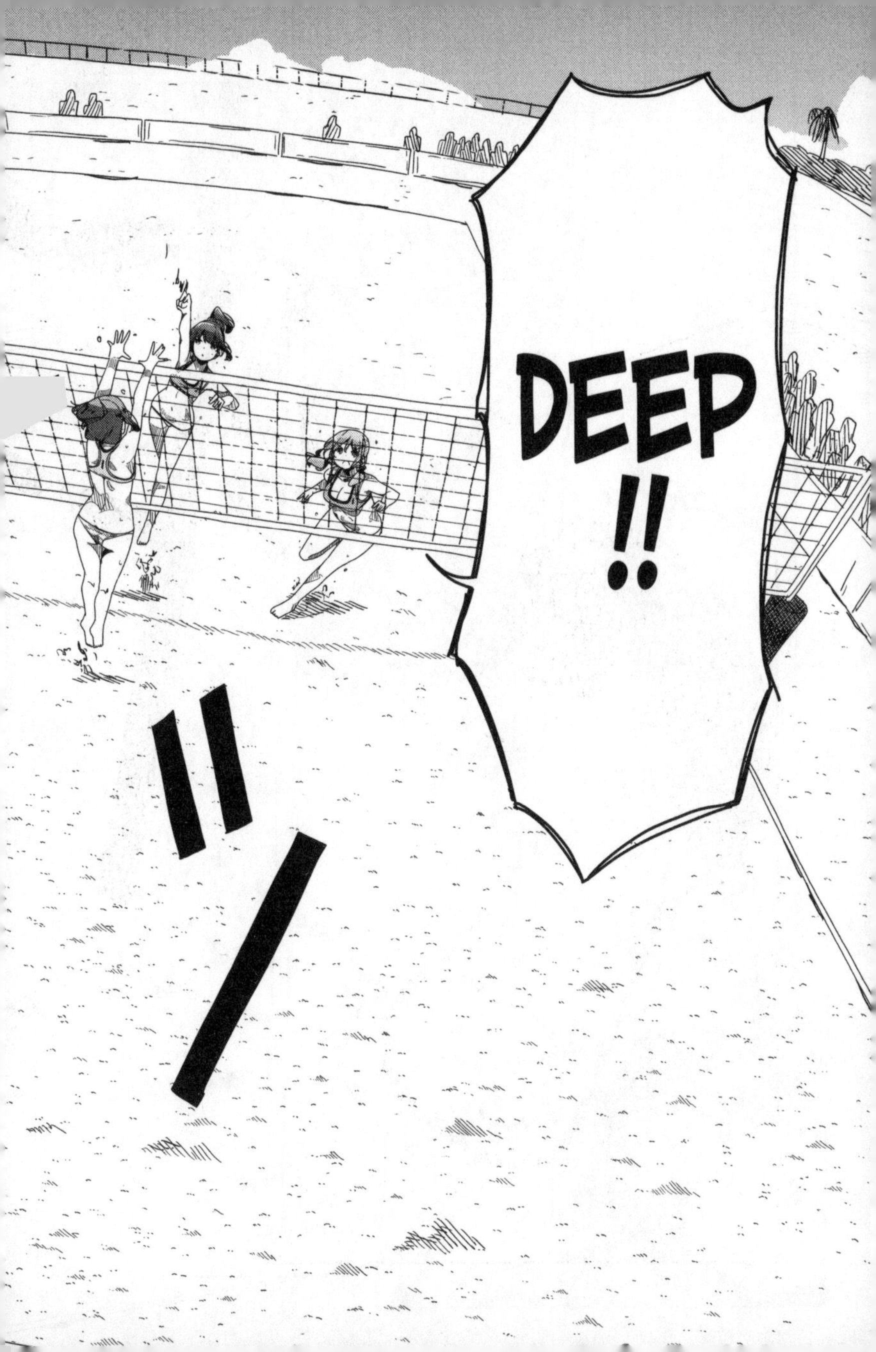
DEEP !!

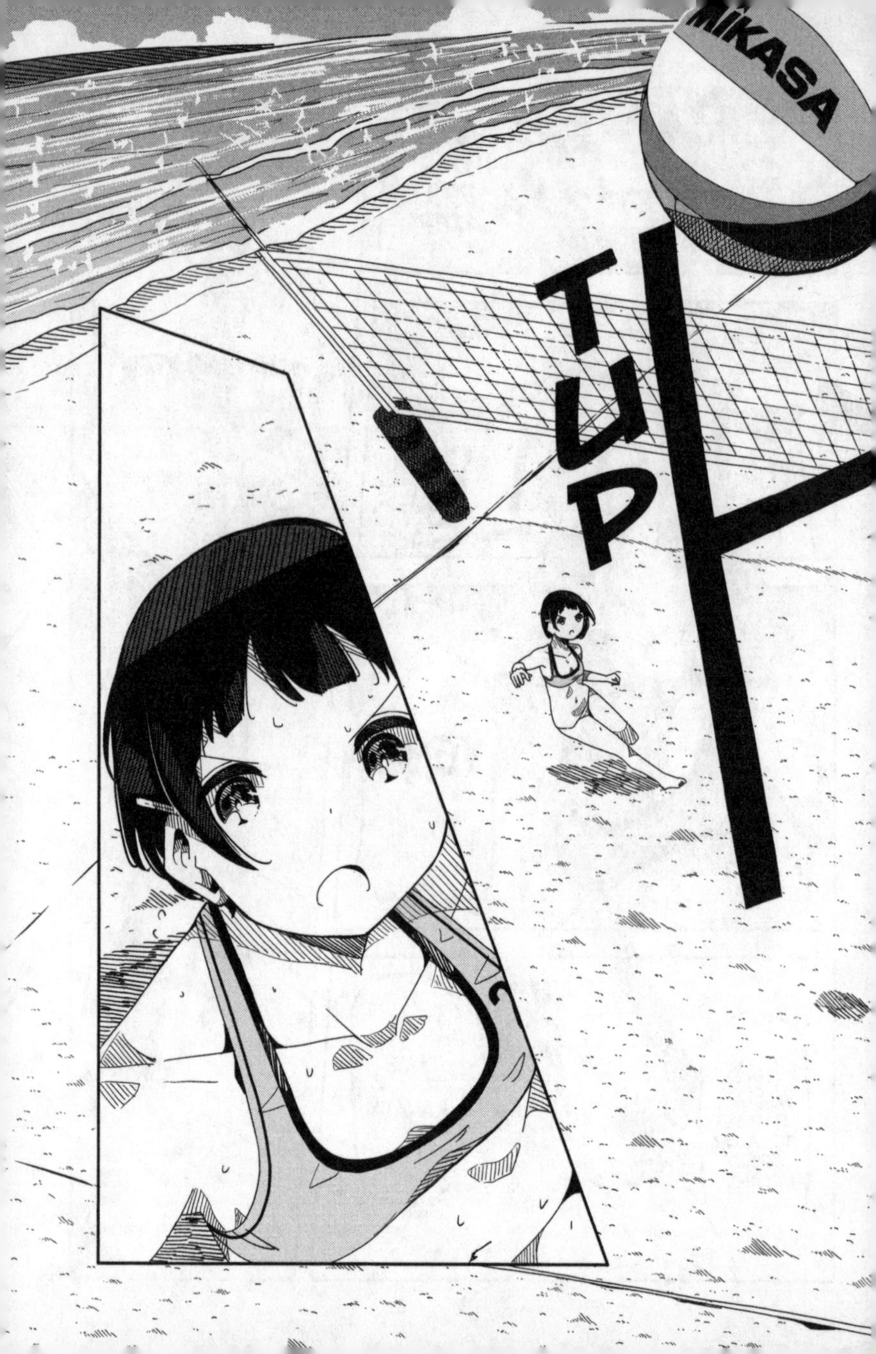
MIKASA
TUP

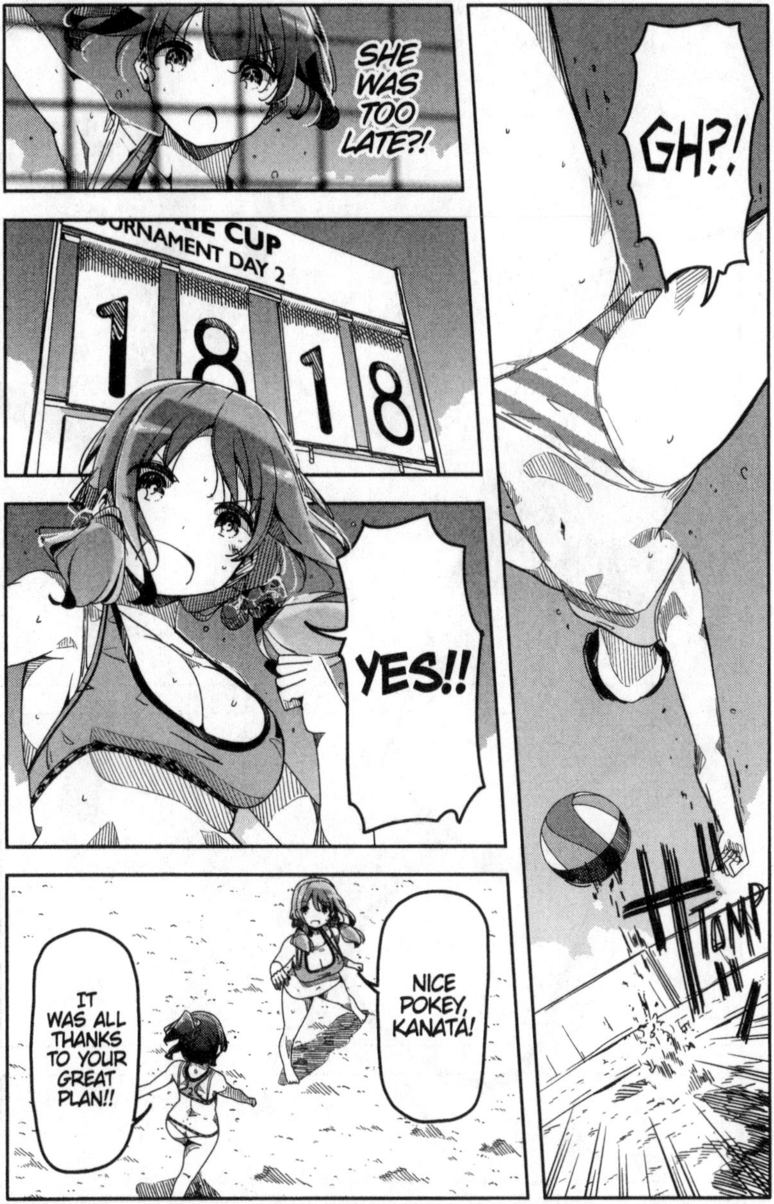
GH?!
TOMP
SHE WAS TOO LATE?!
RIE CUP
URNAMENT DAY 2
18 18
YES!!
NICE POKEY, KANATA!
IT WAS ALL THANKS TO YOUR GREAT PLAN!!

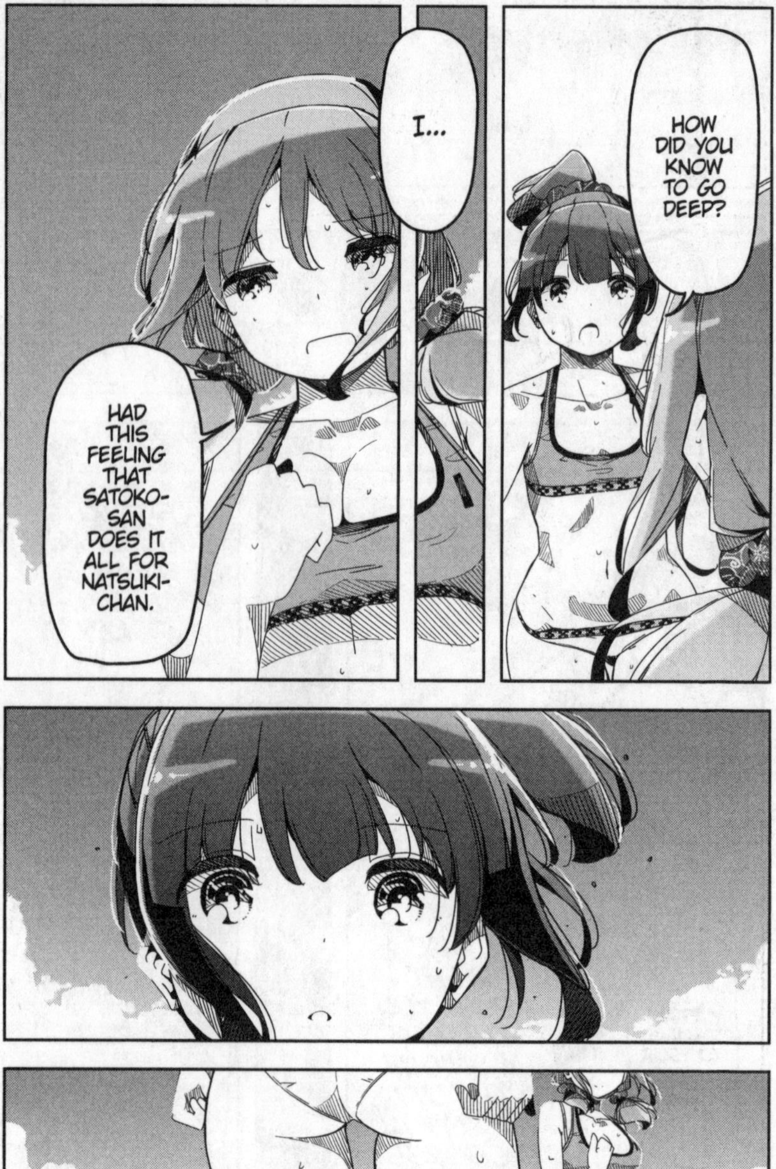
HOW DID YOU KNOW TO GO DEEP?
I...
HAD THIS FEELING THAT SATOKO-SAN DOES IT ALL FOR NATSUKI-CHAN.

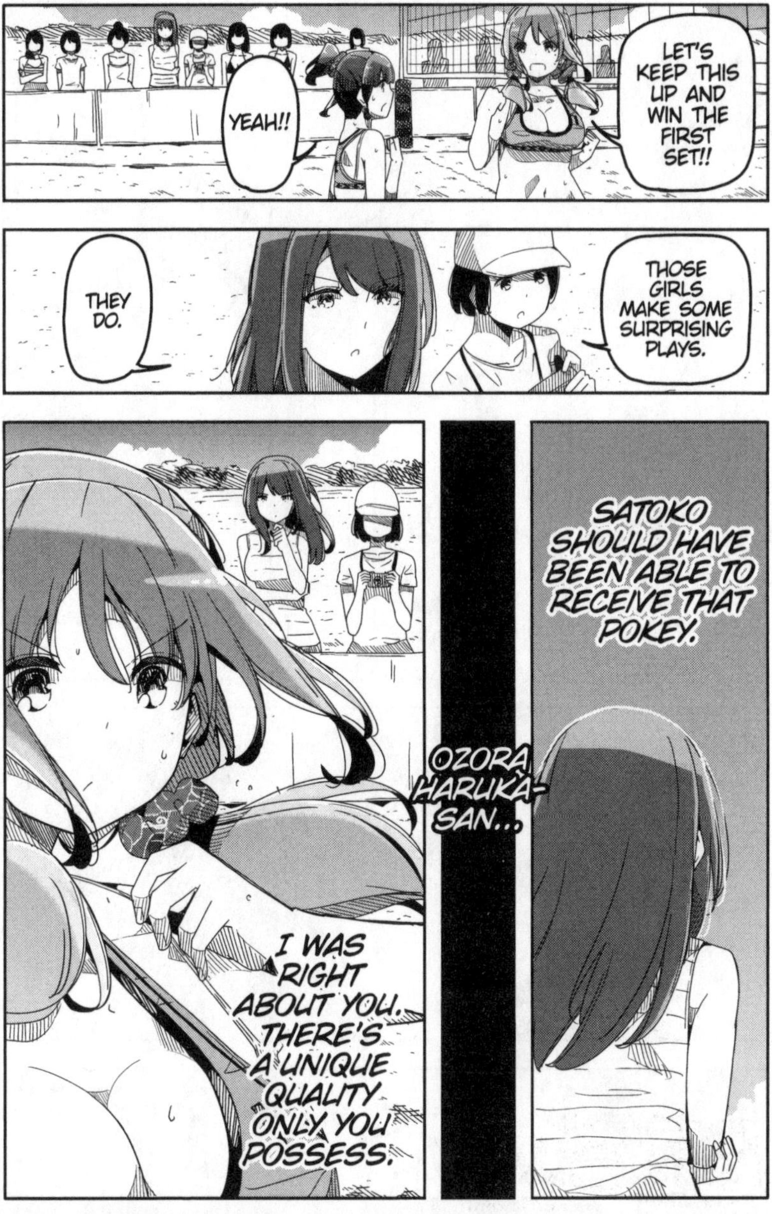
LET'S KEEP THIS UP AND WIN THE FIRST SET!!
YEAH!!
THOSE GIRLS MAKE SOME SURPRISING PLAYS.
THEY DO.
SATOKO SHOULD HAVE BEEN ABLE TO RECEIVE THAT POKEY.
OZORA HARUKA-SAN...
I WAS RIGHT ABOUT YOU. THERE'S A UNIQUE QUALITY ONLY YOU POSSESS.

Harukana Receive

Presented by Nyoijizai

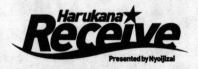

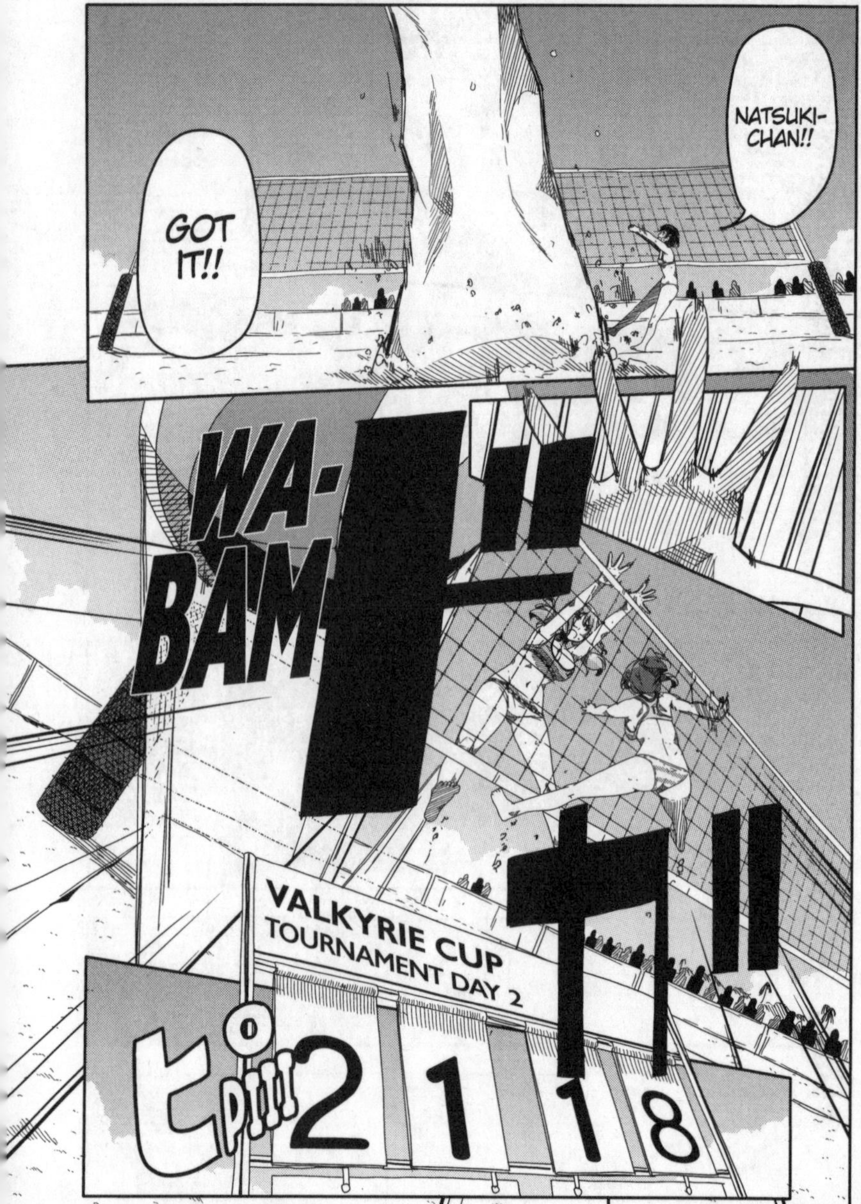
NATSUKI-CHAN!!
GOT IT!!
WA-BAM
VALKYRIE CUP
TOURNAMENT DAY 2
PTIII
21 18

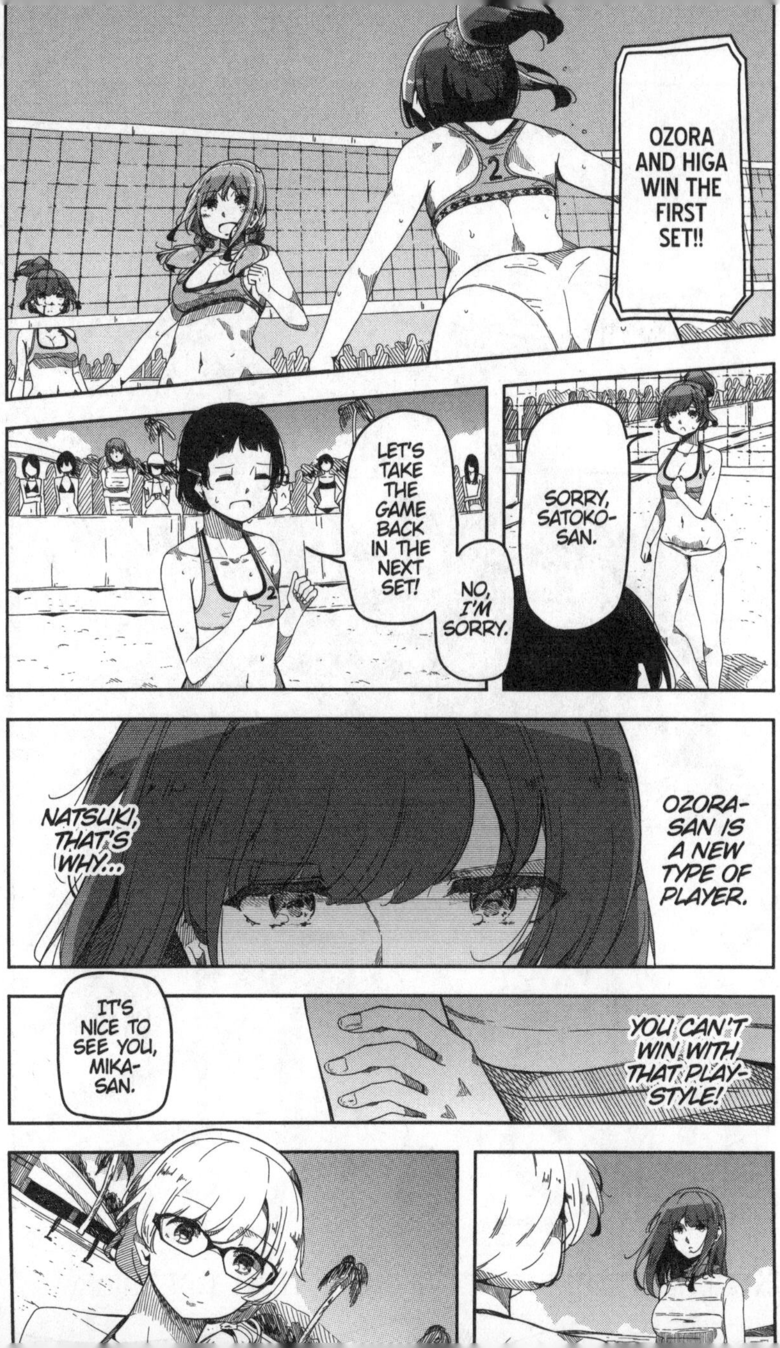
OZORA AND HIGA WIN THE FIRST SET!!
SORRY, SATOKO-SAN.
NO, I'M SORRY.
LET'S TAKE THE GAME BACK IN THE NEXT SET!
OZORA-SAN IS A NEW TYPE OF PLAYER.
NATSUKI, THAT'S WHY...
YOU CAN'T WIN WITH THAT PLAY-STYLE!
IT'S NICE TO SEE YOU, MIKA-SAN.

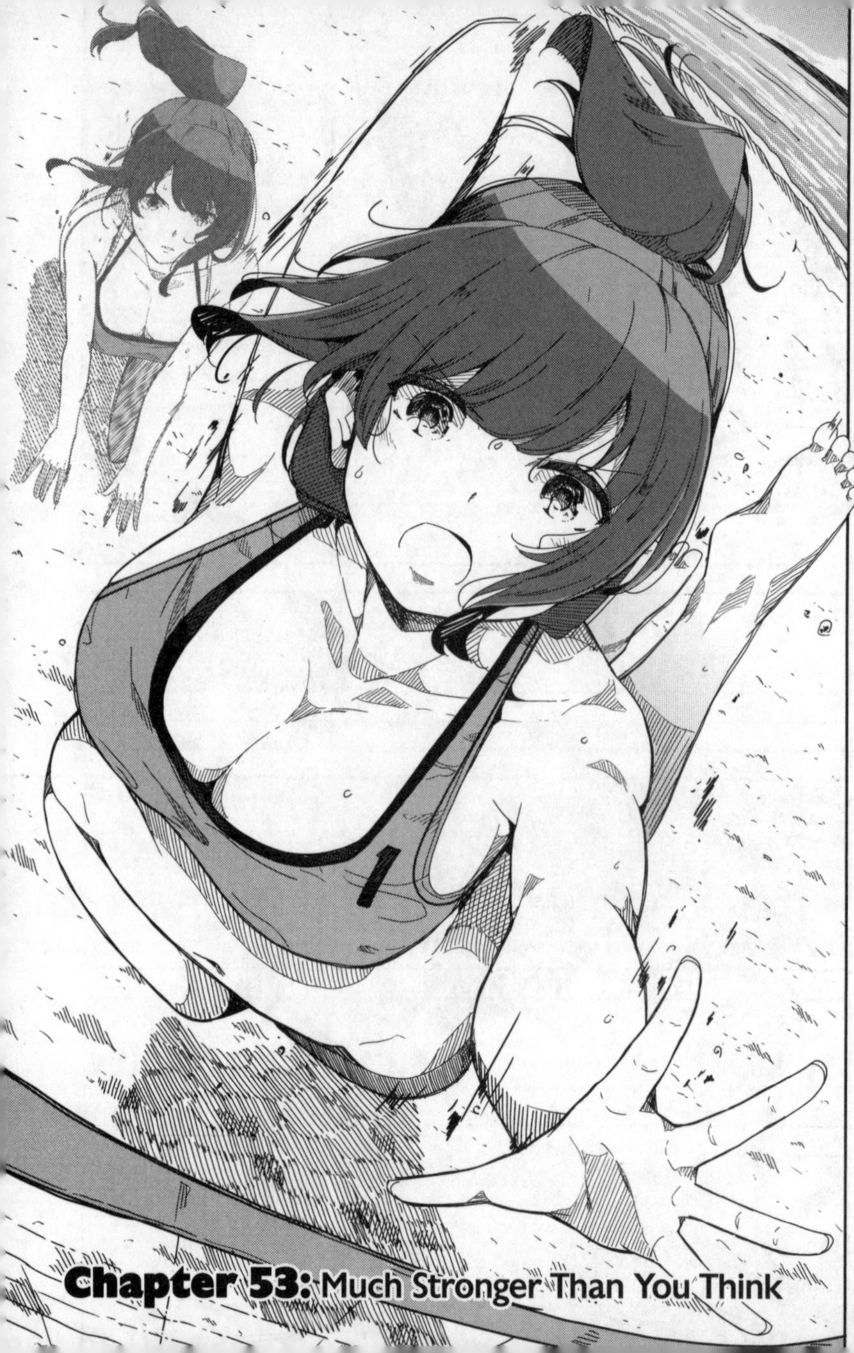

# Chapter 53: Much Stronger Than You Think

VALKYRIE CUP
TOURNAMENT DAY 2

# 12  07

OZORA HARUKA
HIGA KANATA

FUKAMI NATSUKI
TANAKA SATOKO

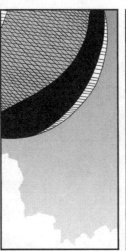

BMP!!

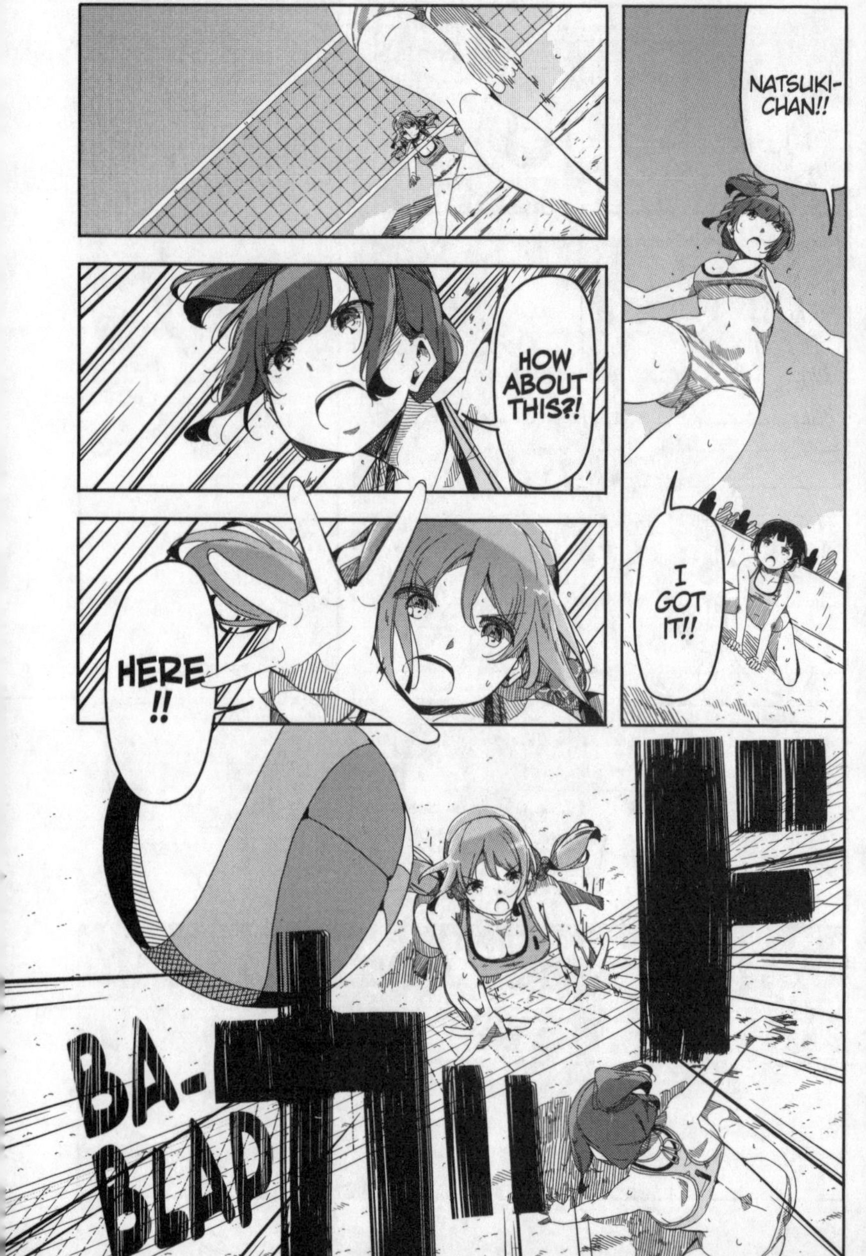
NATSUKI-CHAN!!
HOW ABOUT THIS?!
I GOT IT!!
HERE!!
BA-BLAP

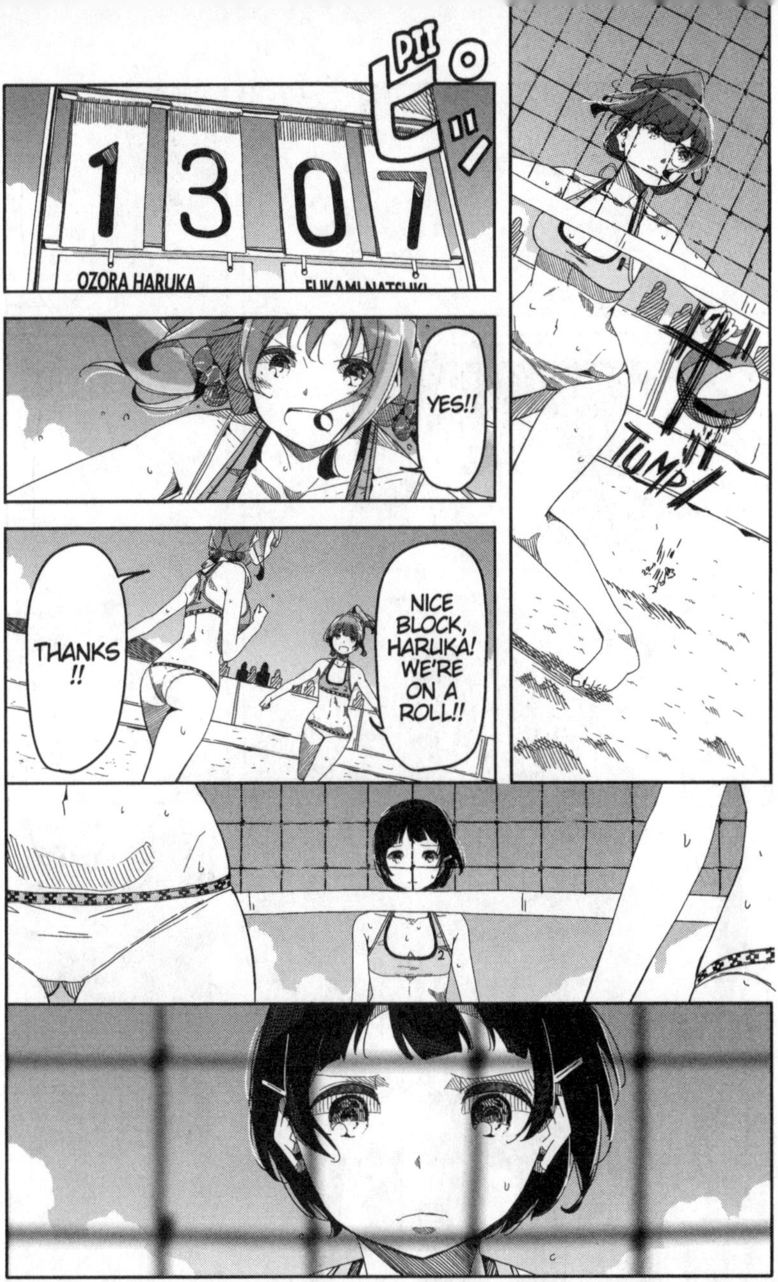

TUMP!
PII
13
07
OZORA HARUKA
FUKAMI NATSUKI
YES!!
NICE BLOCK, HARUKA! WE'RE ON A ROLL!!
THANKS!!

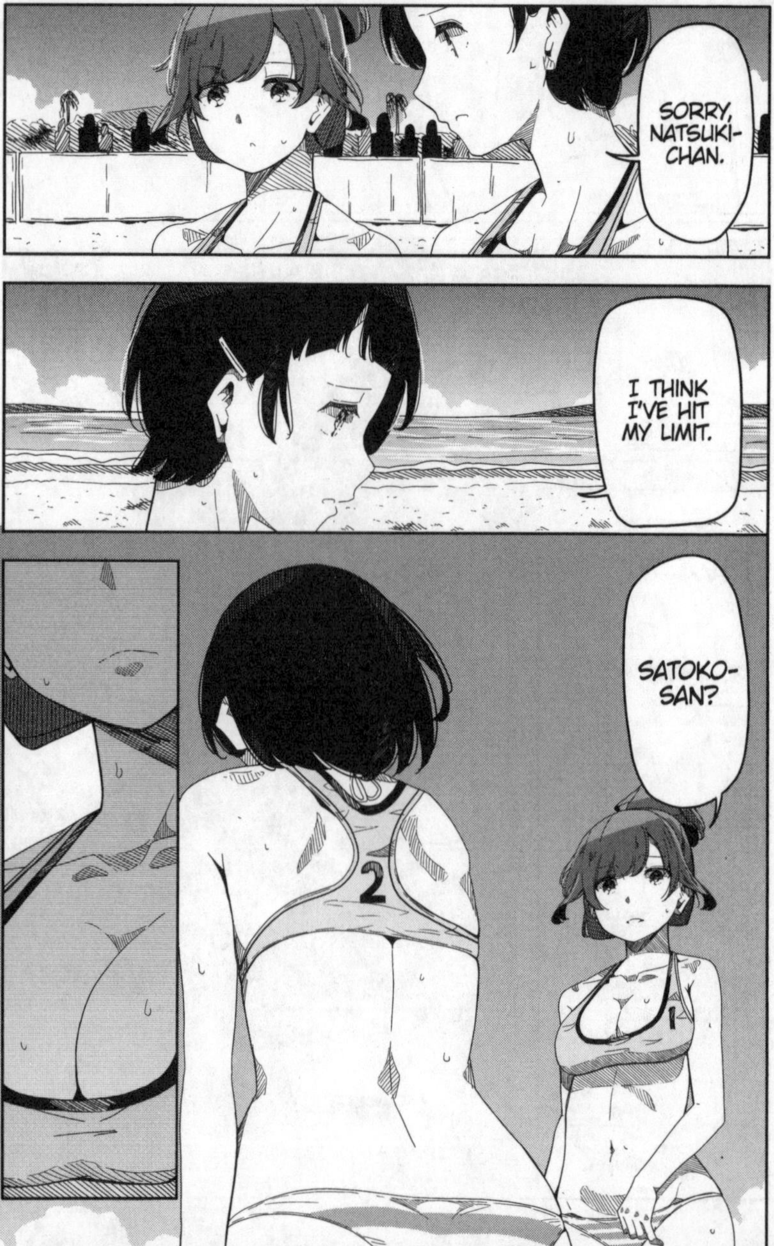
SORRY, NATSUKI-CHAN.
I THINK I'VE HIT MY LIMIT.
SATOKO-SAN?

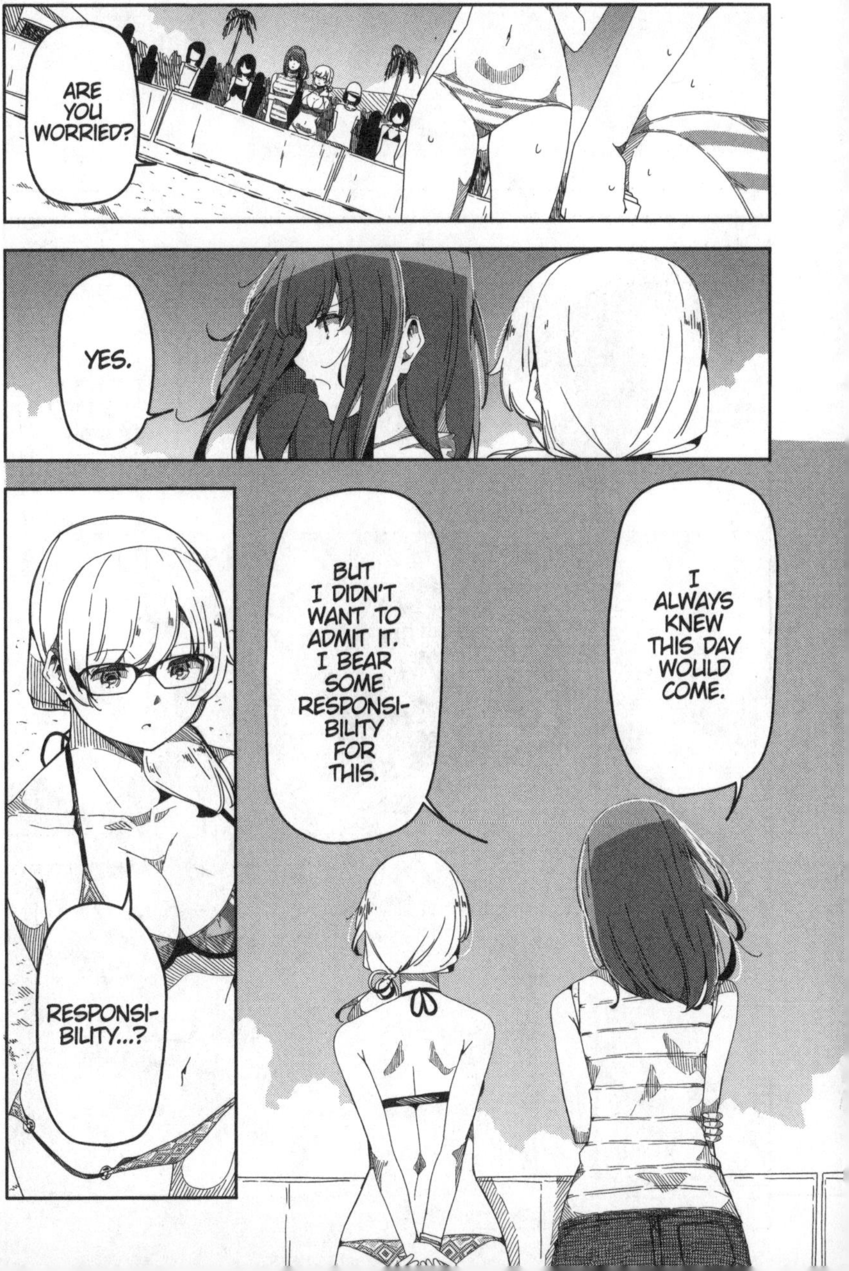
ARE YOU WORRIED?
YES.
I ALWAYS KNEW THIS DAY WOULD COME.
BUT I DIDN'T WANT TO ADMIT IT. I BEAR SOME RESPONSIBILITY FOR THIS.
RESPONSIBILITY...?

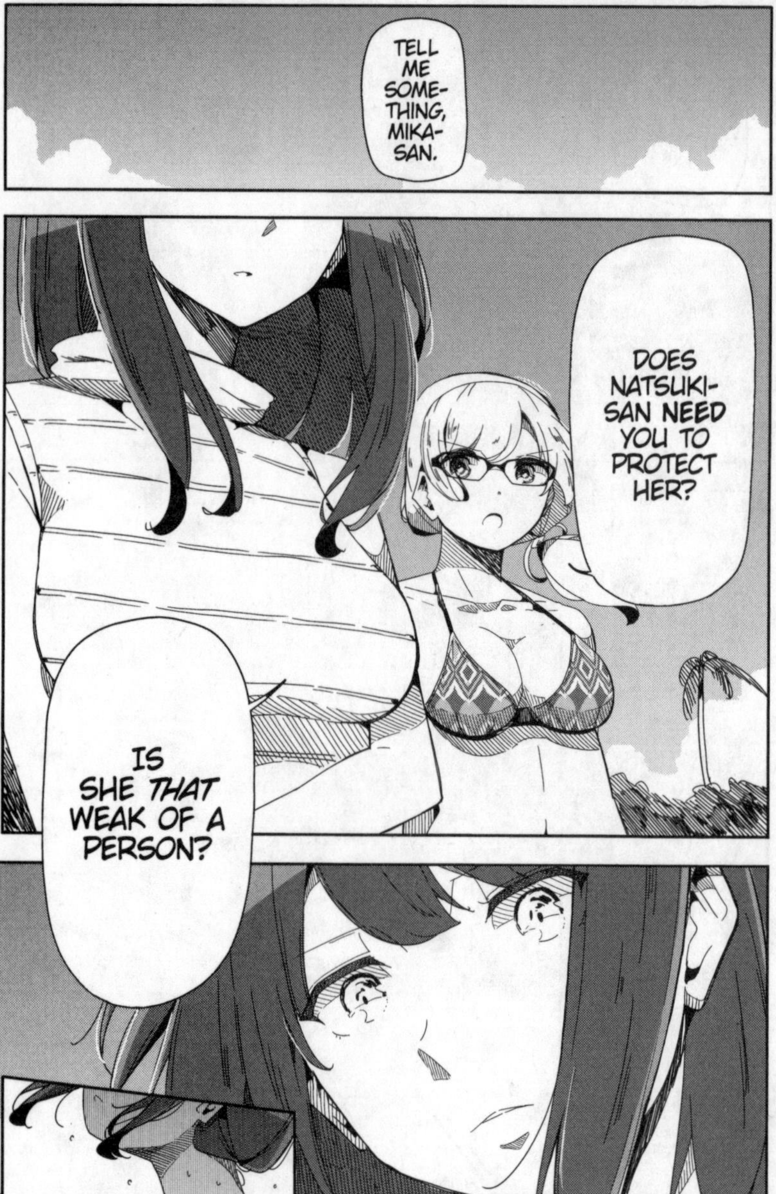
TELL ME SOMETHING, MIKA-SAN.
DOES NATSUKI-SAN NEED YOU TO PROTECT HER?
IS SHE *THAT* WEAK OF A PERSON?

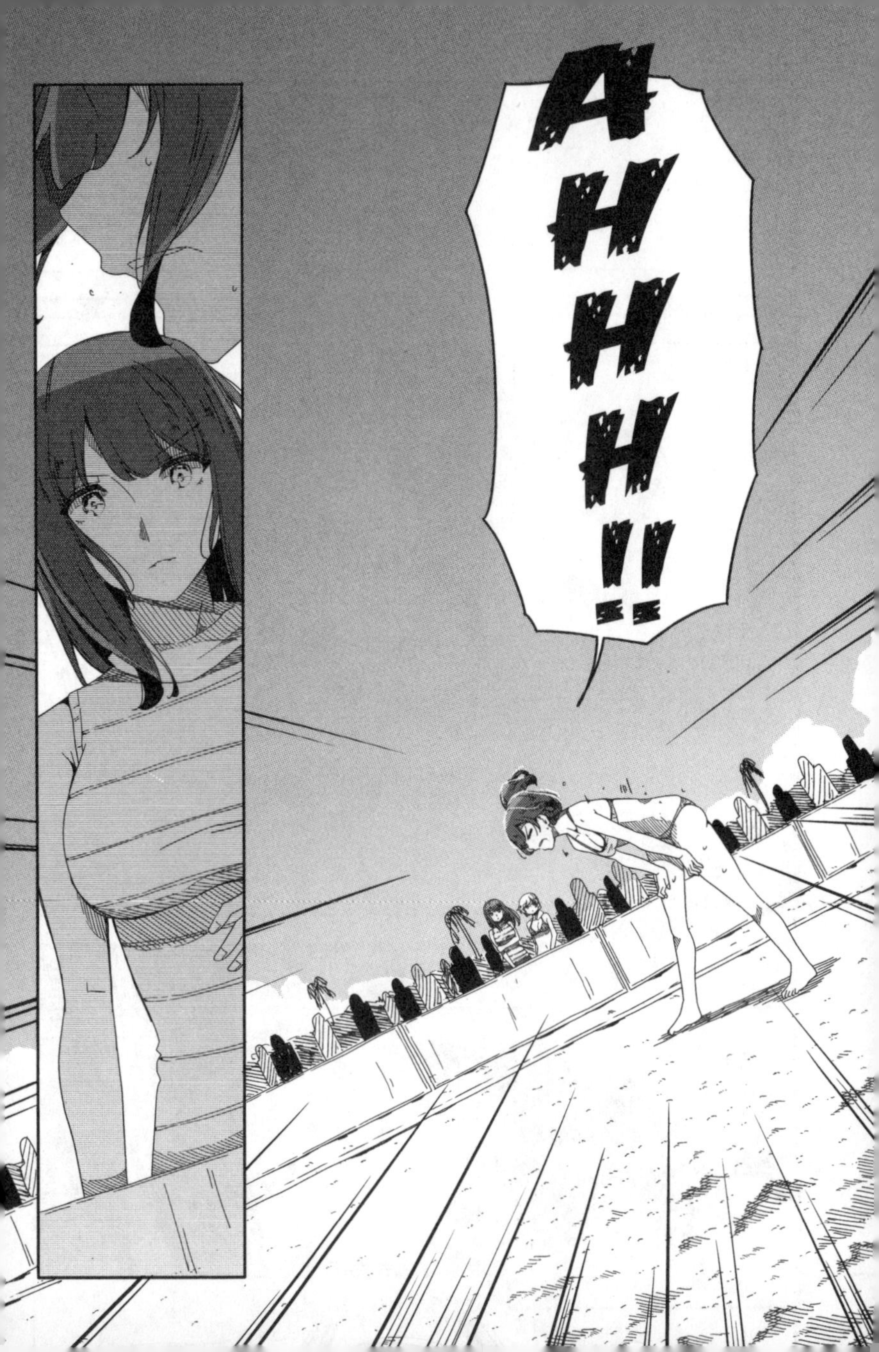
AHHHH!!

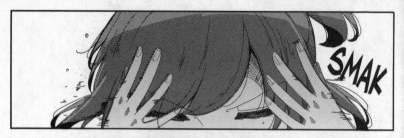

SMAK

WE'RE GONNA ...

WIN THIS!!

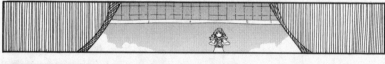

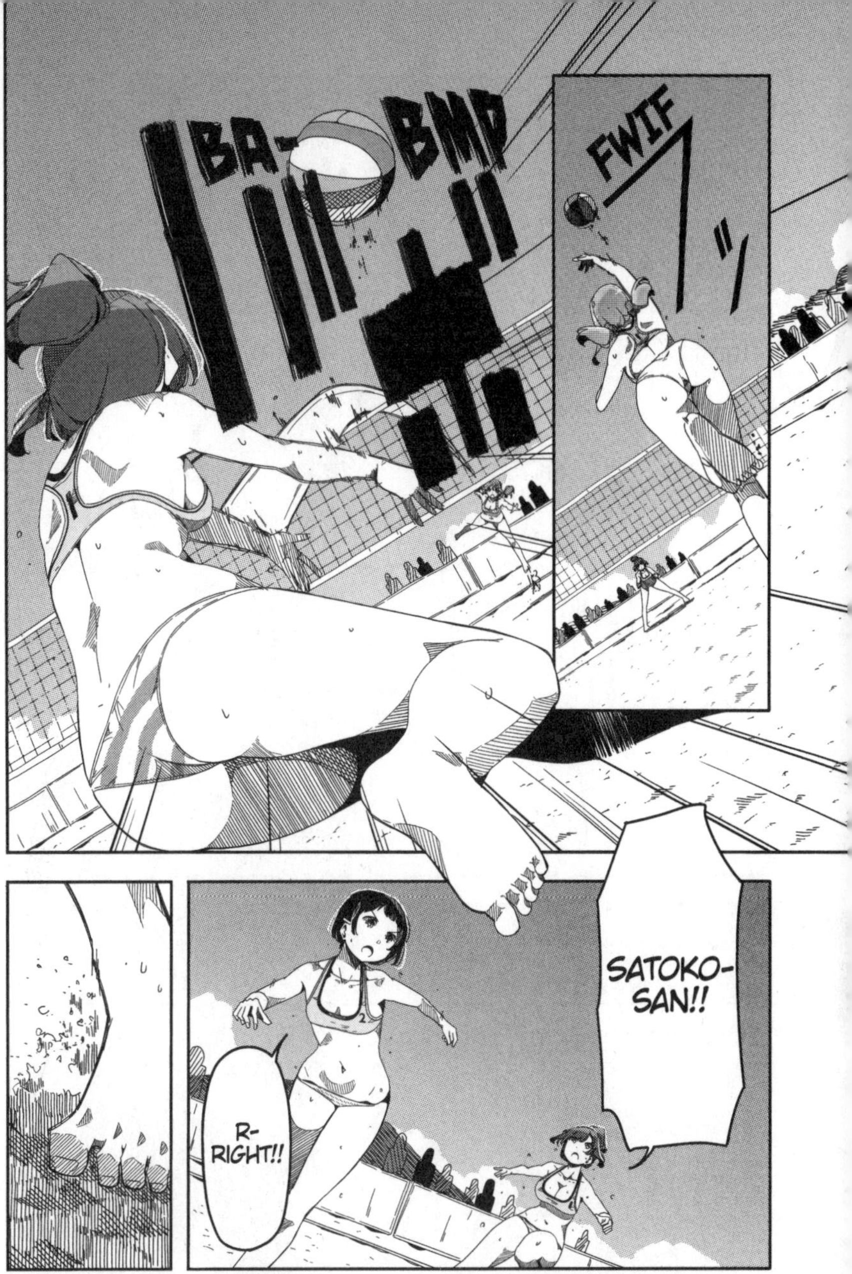
FWIF
BA-BMP
SATOKO-SAN!!
R-RIGHT!!

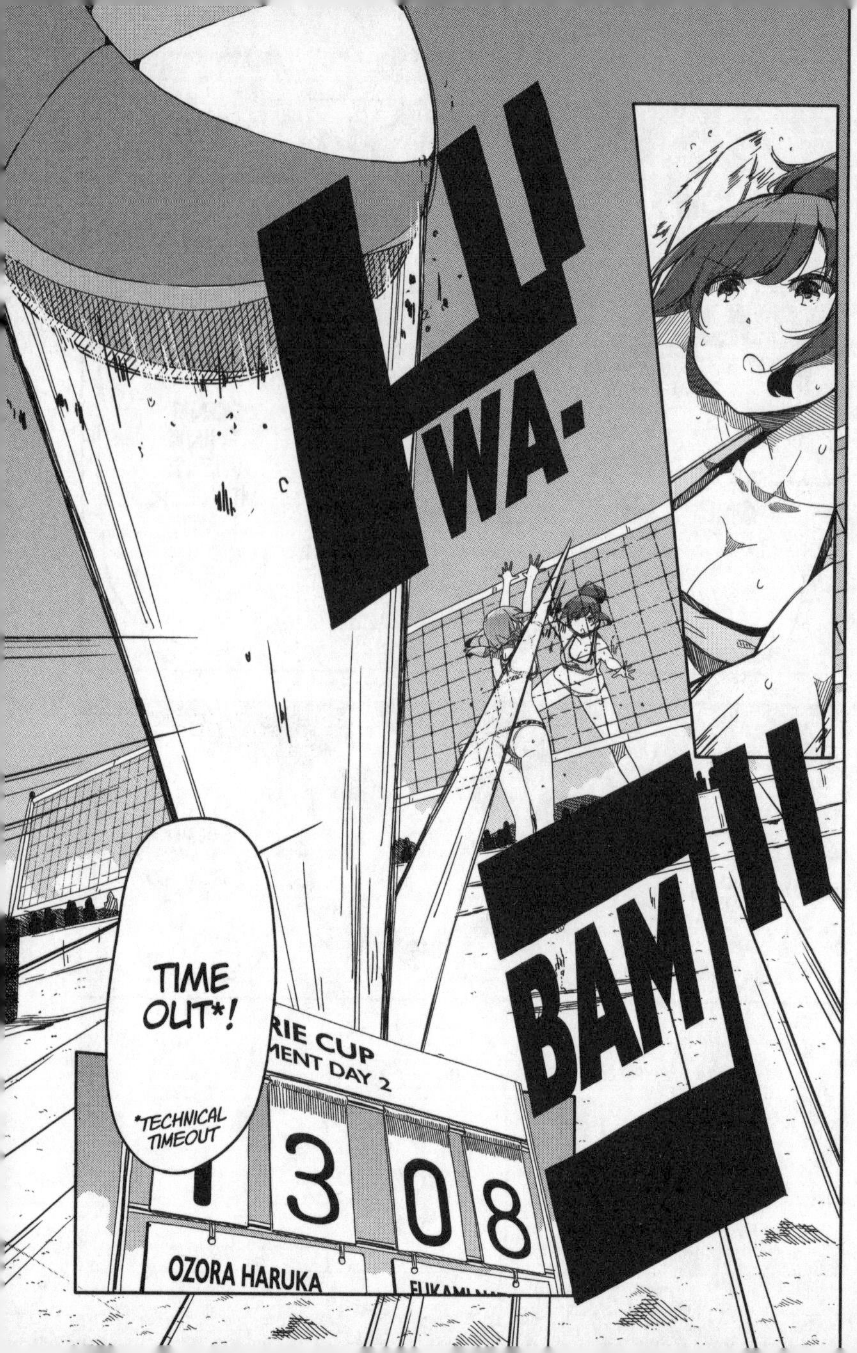
WA-
BAM!!
TIME OUT*!
*TECHNICAL TIMEOUT
RIE CUP
MENT DAY 2
1 3 0 8
OZORA HARUKA

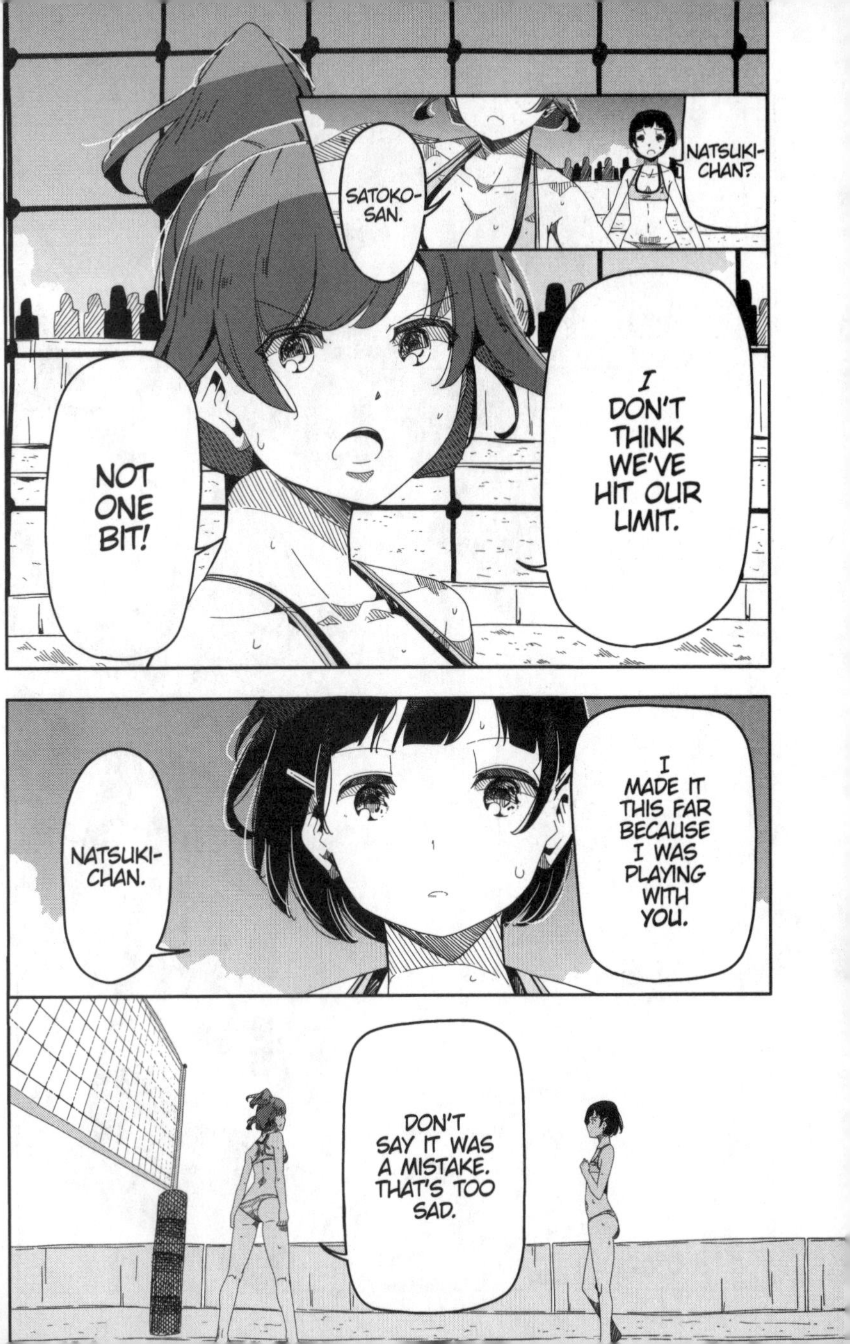
NATSUKI-CHAN?
SATOKO-SAN.
I DON'T THINK WE'VE HIT OUR LIMIT.
NOT ONE BIT!
I MADE IT THIS FAR BECAUSE I WAS PLAYING WITH YOU.
NATSUKI-CHAN.
DON'T SAY IT WAS A MISTAKE. THAT'S TOO SAD.

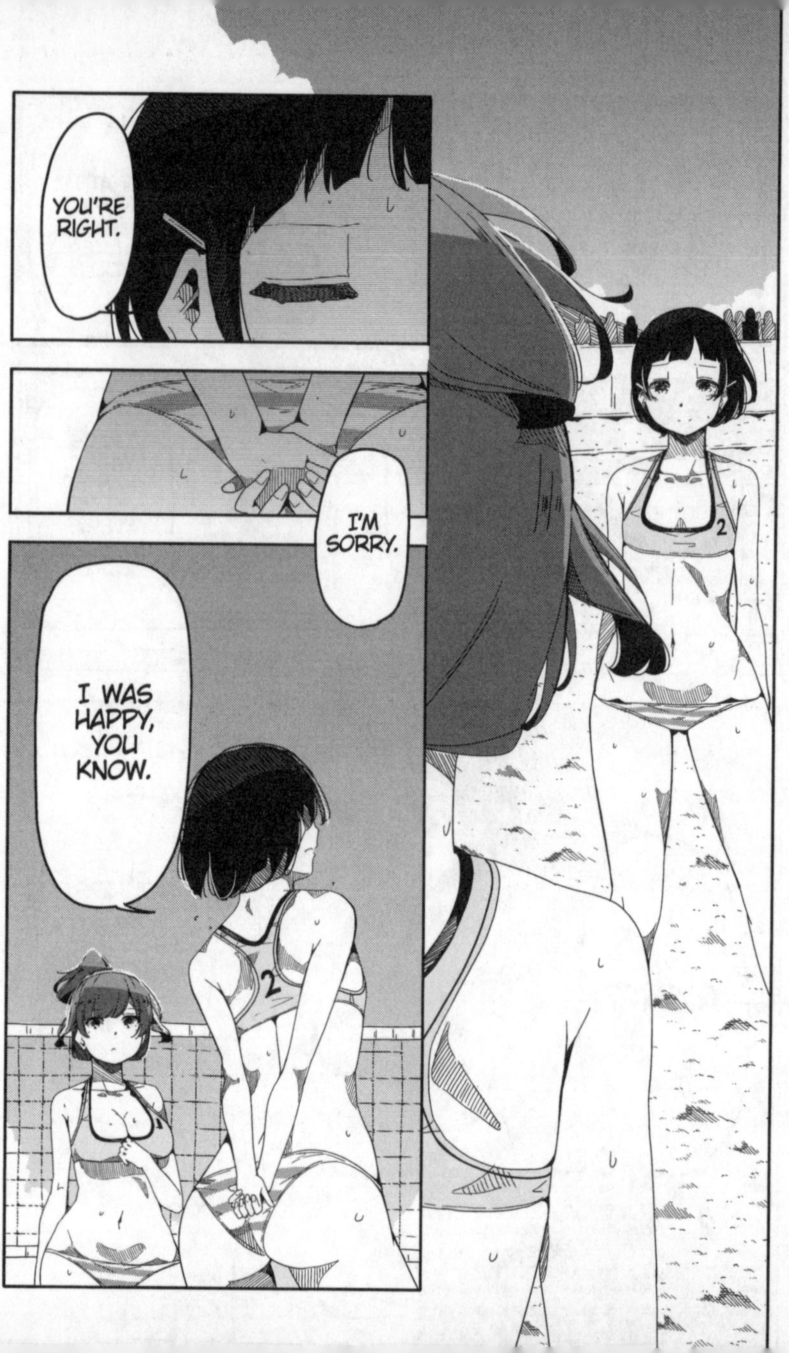
YOU'RE RIGHT.
I'M SORRY.
I WAS HAPPY, YOU KNOW.

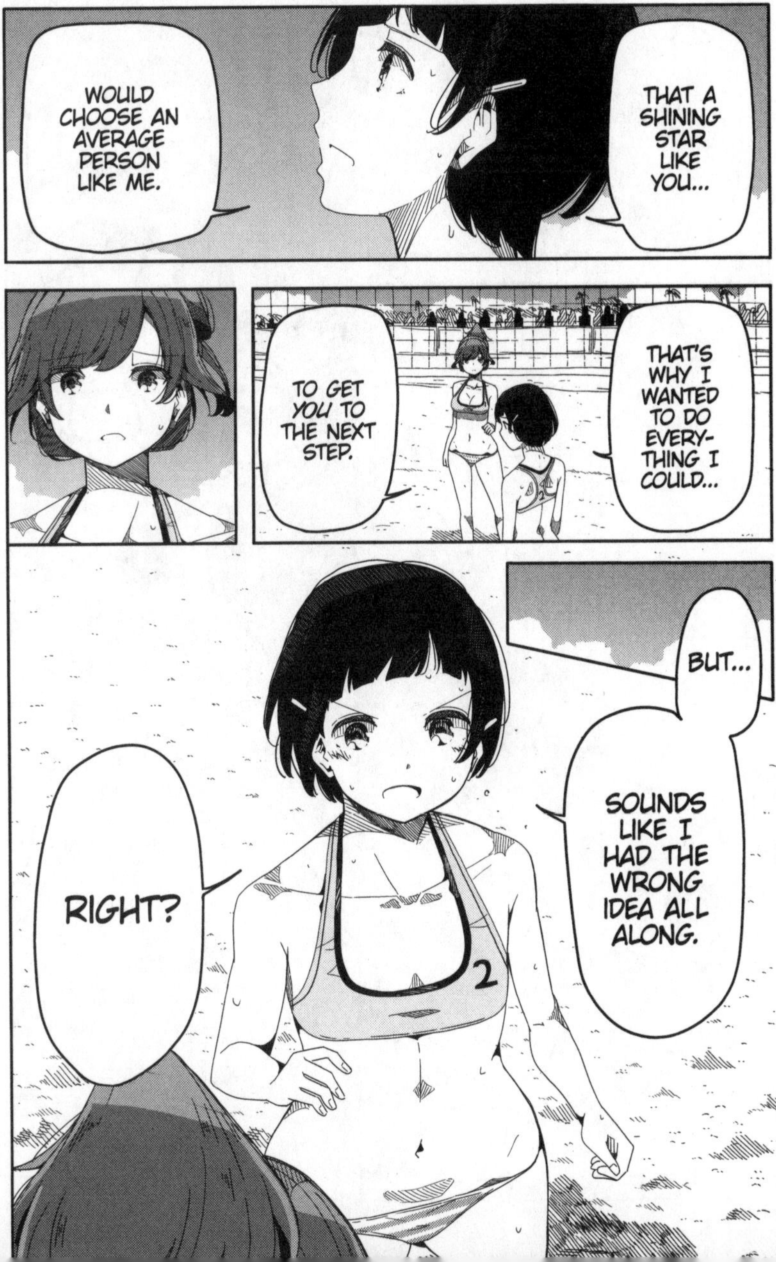
THAT A SHINING STAR LIKE YOU...
WOULD CHOOSE AN AVERAGE PERSON LIKE ME.
THAT'S WHY I WANTED TO DO EVERYTHING I COULD...
TO GET *YOU* TO THE NEXT STEP.
BUT...
SOUNDS LIKE I HAD THE WRONG IDEA ALL ALONG.
RIGHT?

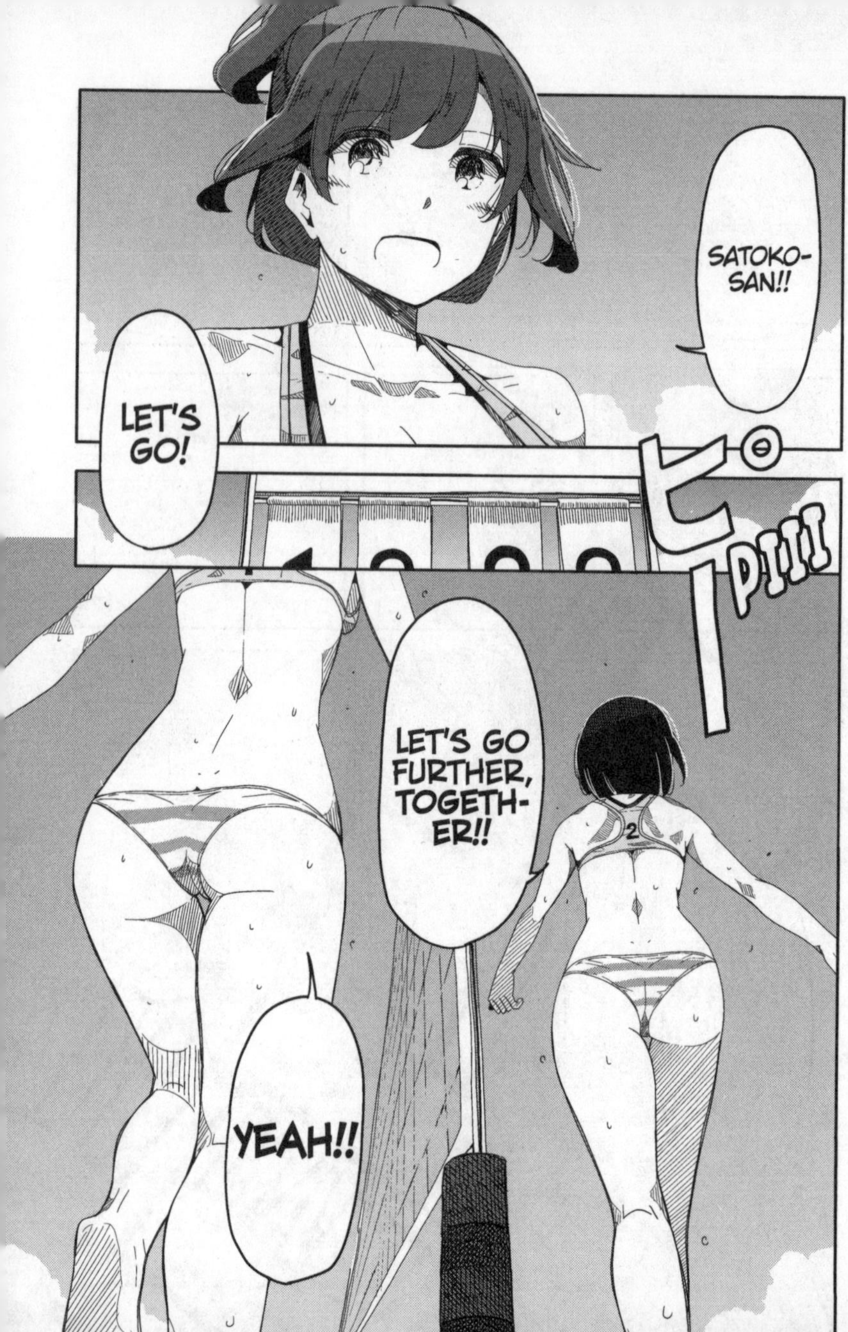
SATOKO-SAN!!
LET'S GO!
ピー
PIII
LET'S GO FURTHER, TOGETHER!!
YEAH!!

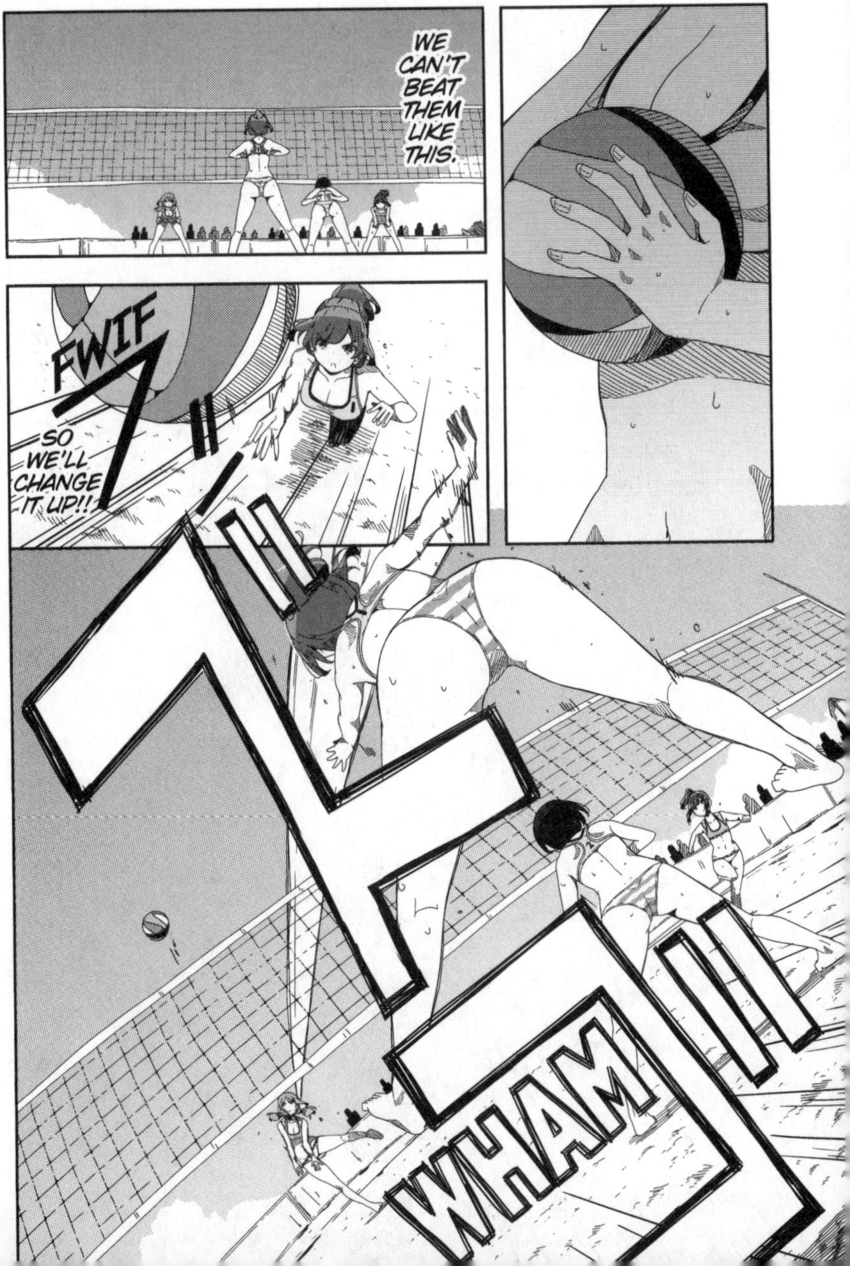
WE CAN'T BEAT THEM LIKE THIS.
FWIF
SO WE'LL CHANGE IT UP!!
WHAM!!

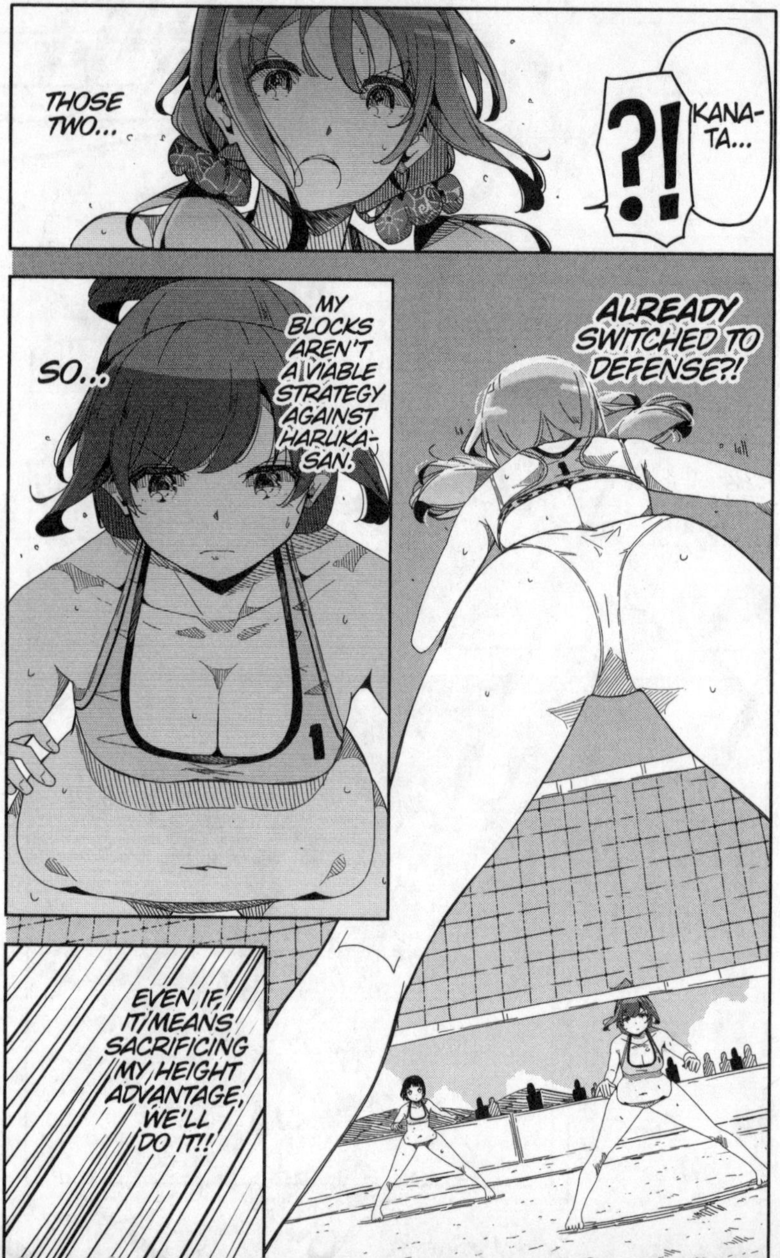
KANATA...
?!
THOSE TWO...
ALREADY SWITCHED TO DEFENSE?!
MY BLOCKS AREN'T A VIABLE STRATEGY AGAINST HARUKA-SAN.
SO...
EVEN IF IT MEANS SACRIFICING MY HEIGHT ADVANTAGE, WE'LL DO IT!!

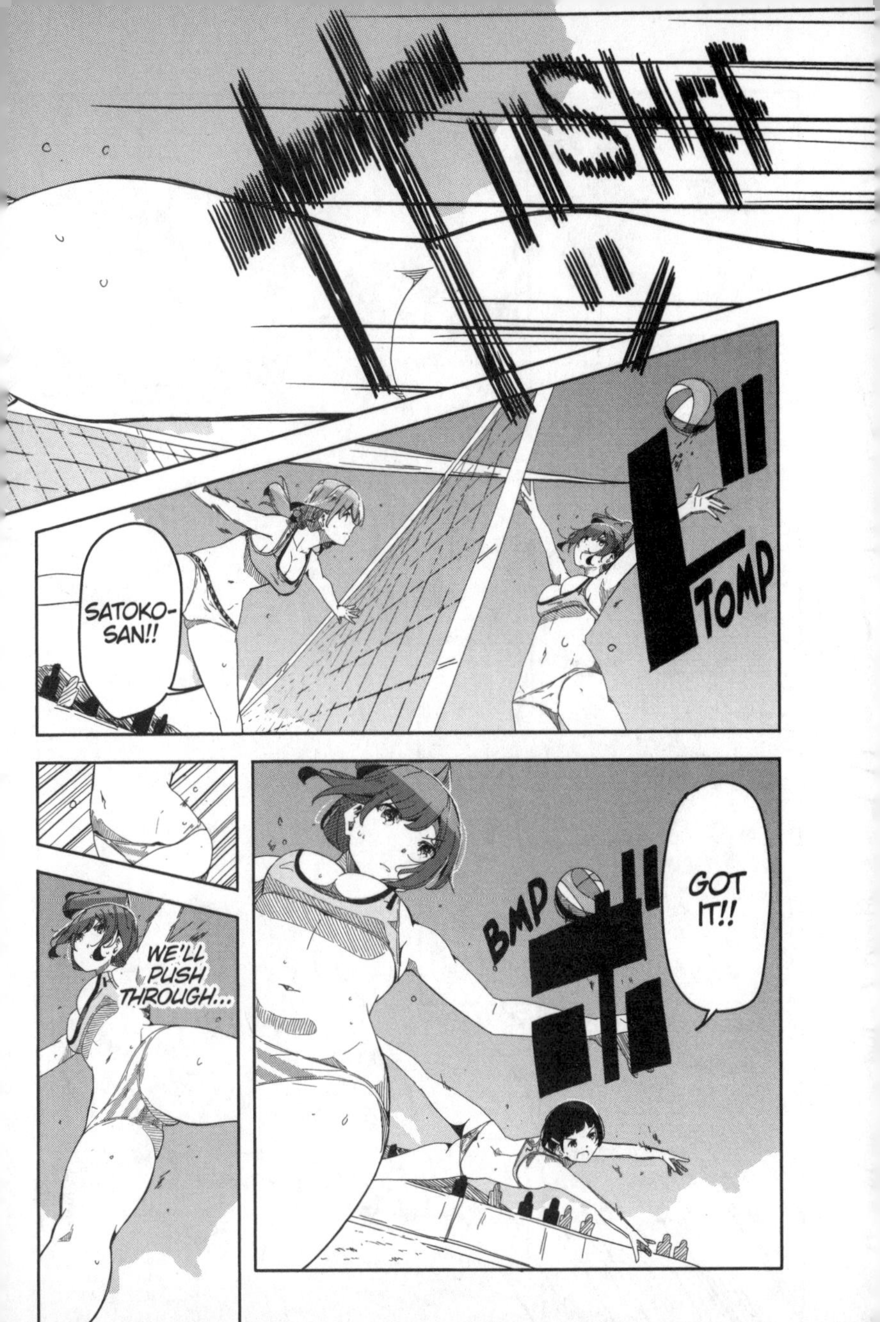
SHFF
TOMP
SATOKO-SAN!!
GOT IT!!
BMP
WE'LL PUSH THROUGH...

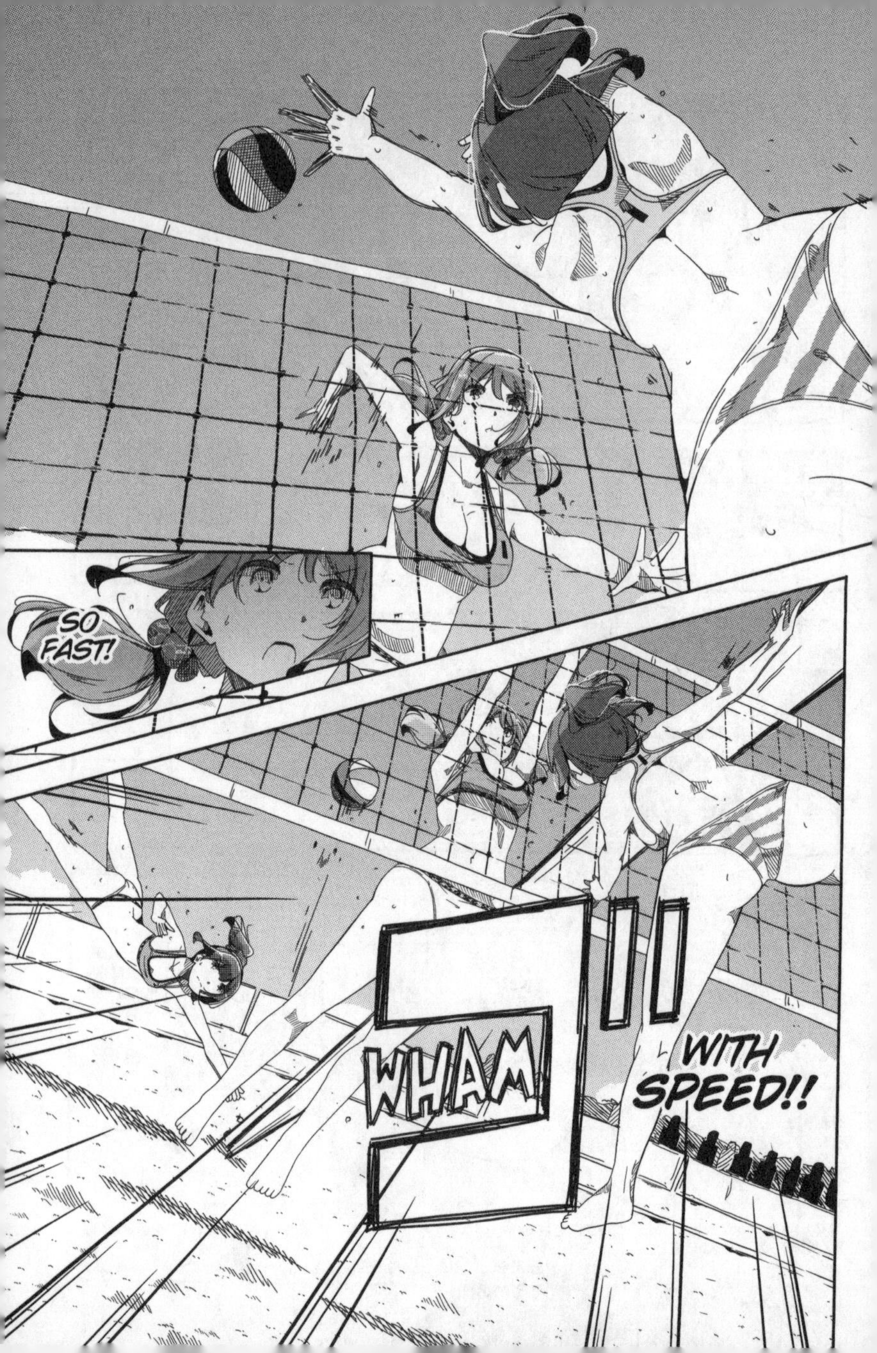
SO FAST!
WHAM
WITH SPEED!!

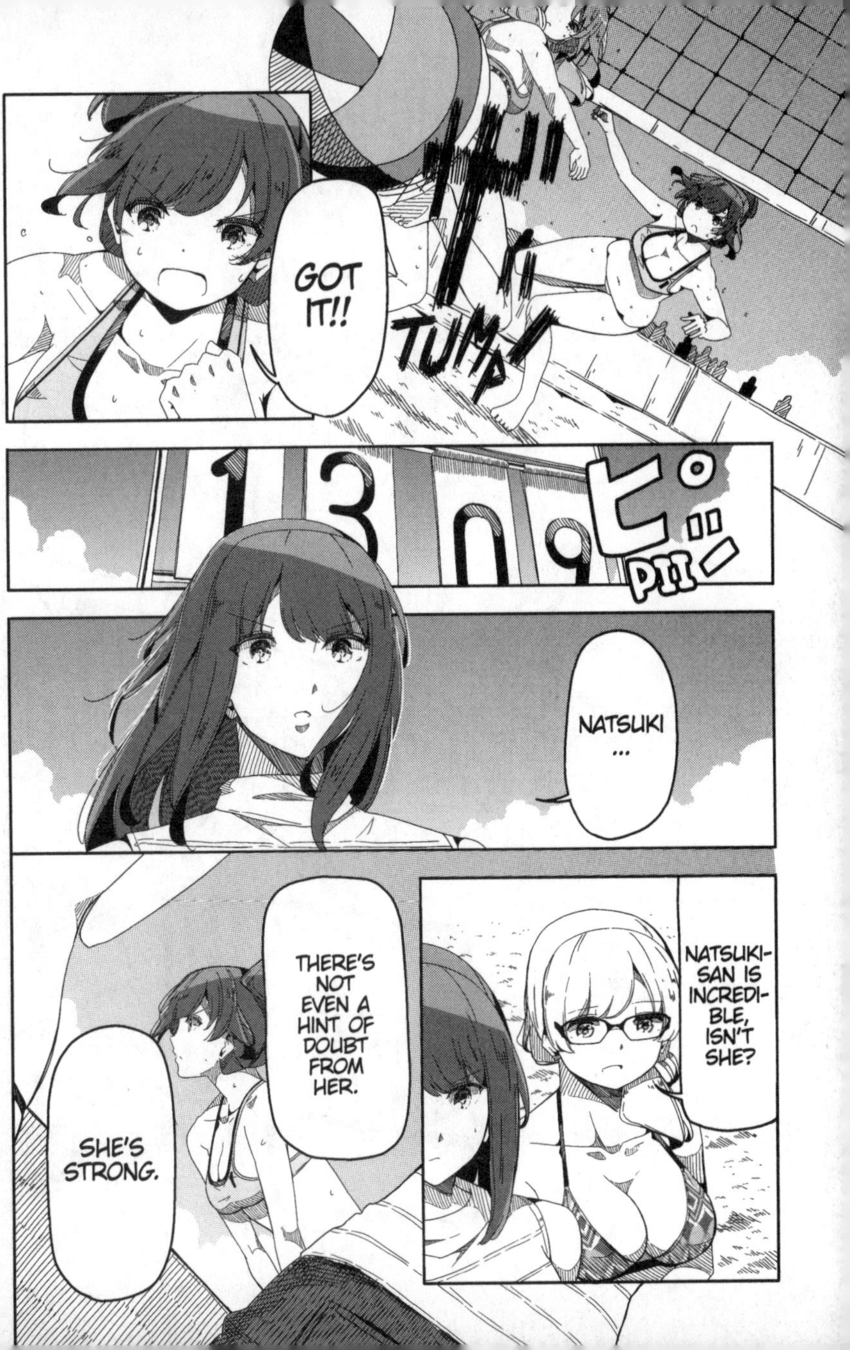
TUMP
GOT IT!!
PII
NATSUKI ...
NATSUKI-SAN IS INCREDIBLE, ISN'T SHE?
THERE'S NOT EVEN A HINT OF DOUBT FROM HER.
SHE'S STRONG.

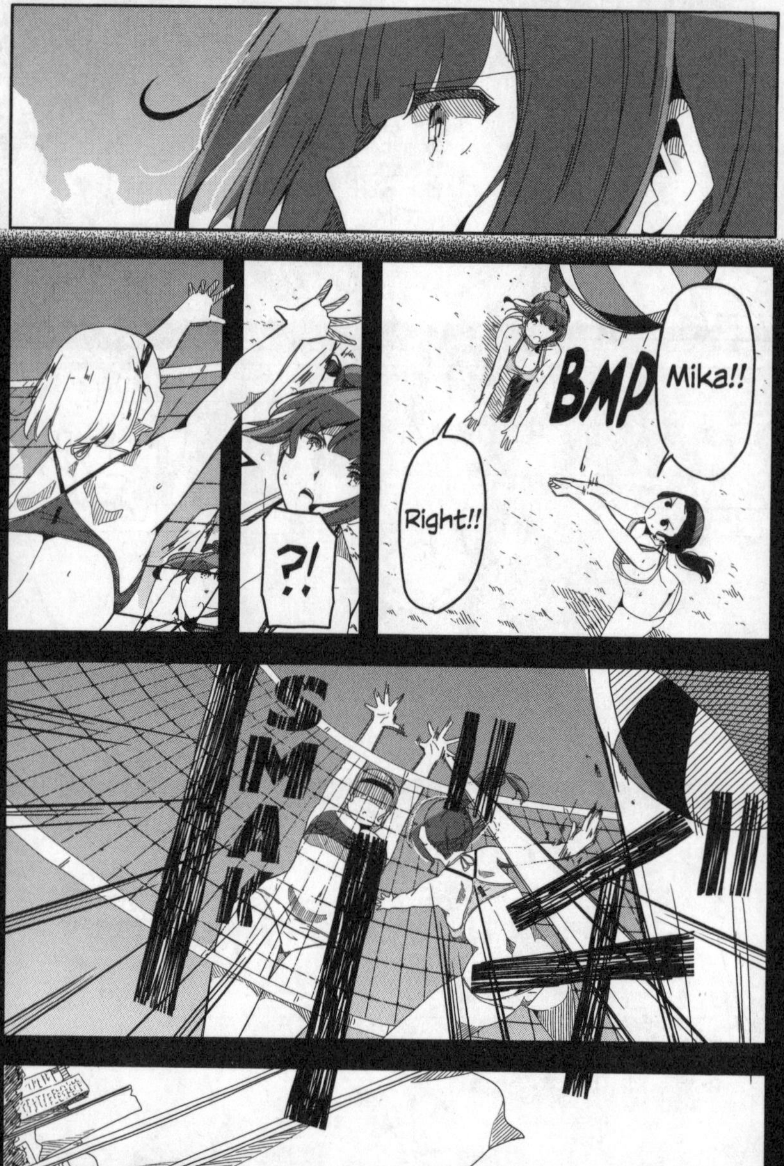
Mika!!
BMP
Right!!
?!
SMAK

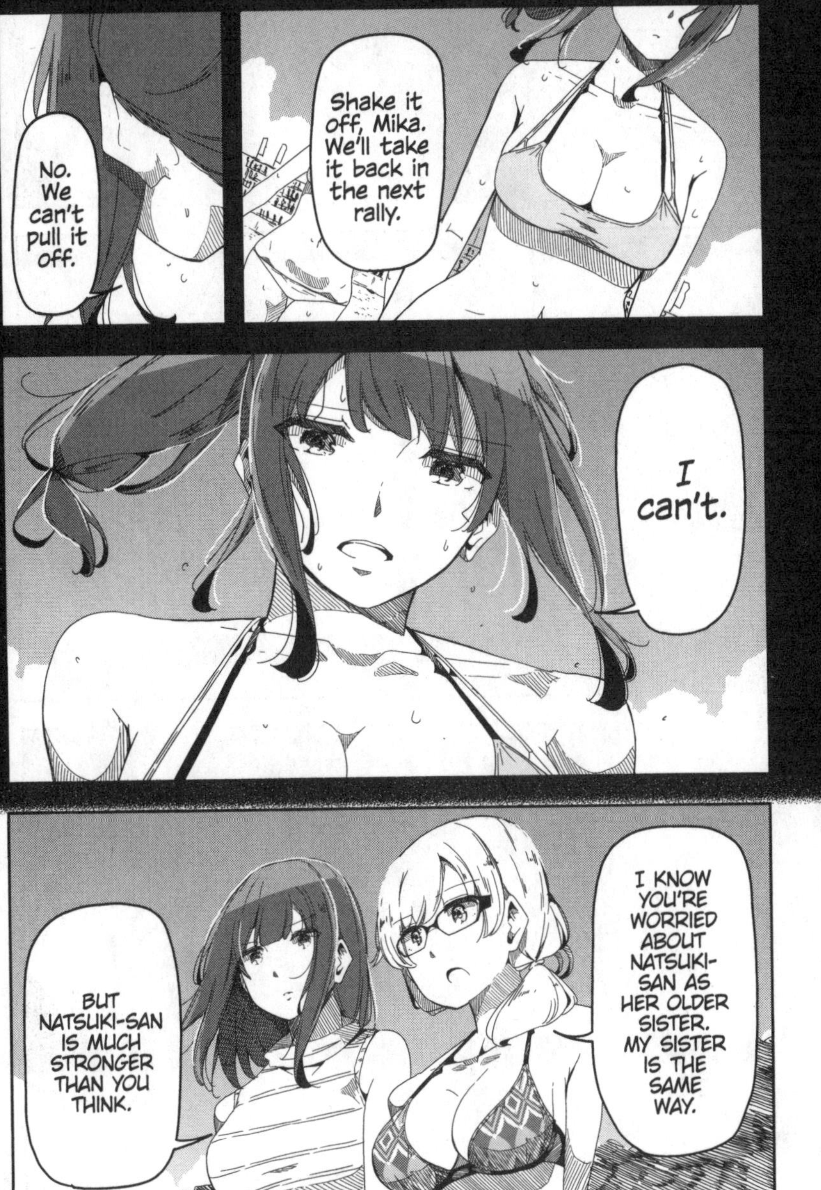
Shake it off, Mika. We'll take it back in the next rally.
No. We can't pull it off.
I can't.
I KNOW YOU'RE WORRIED ABOUT NATSUKI-SAN AS HER OLDER SISTER. MY SISTER IS THE SAME WAY.
BUT NATSUKI-SAN IS MUCH STRONGER THAN YOU THINK.

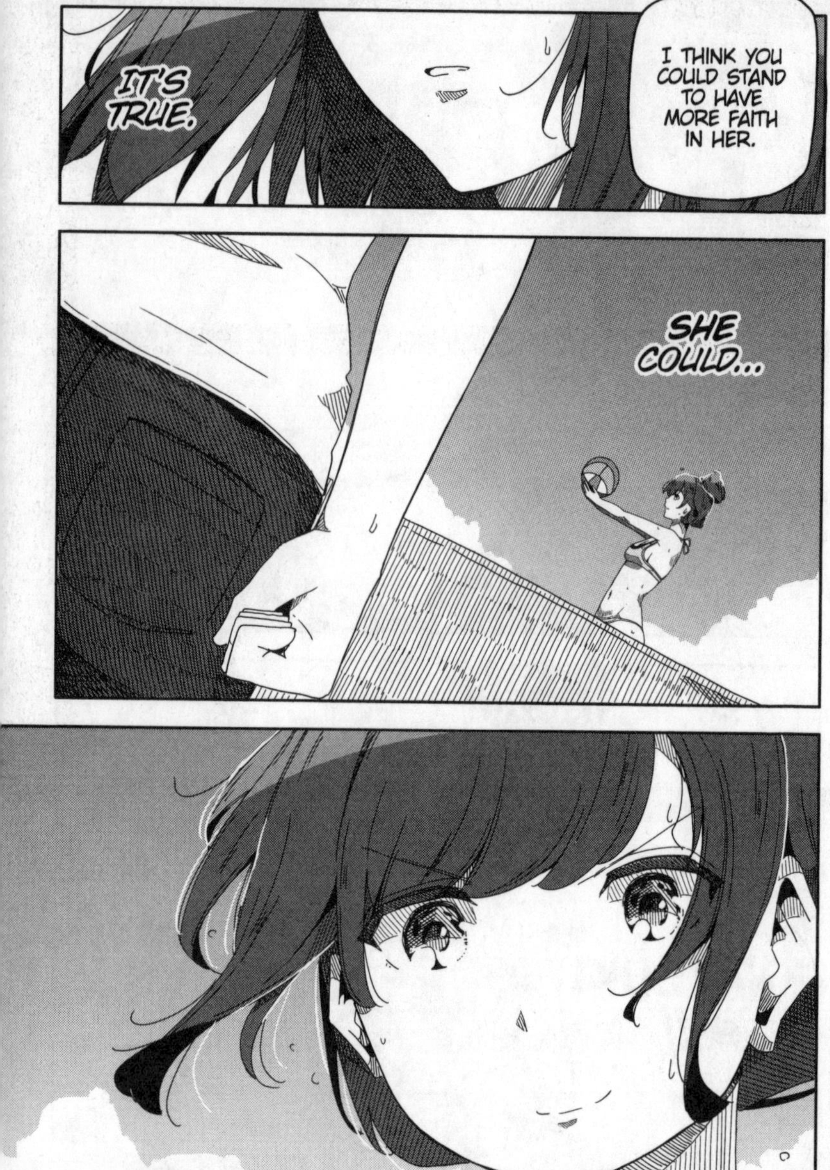
I THINK YOU COULD STAND TO HAVE MORE FAITH IN HER.
IT'S TRUE.
SHE COULD...

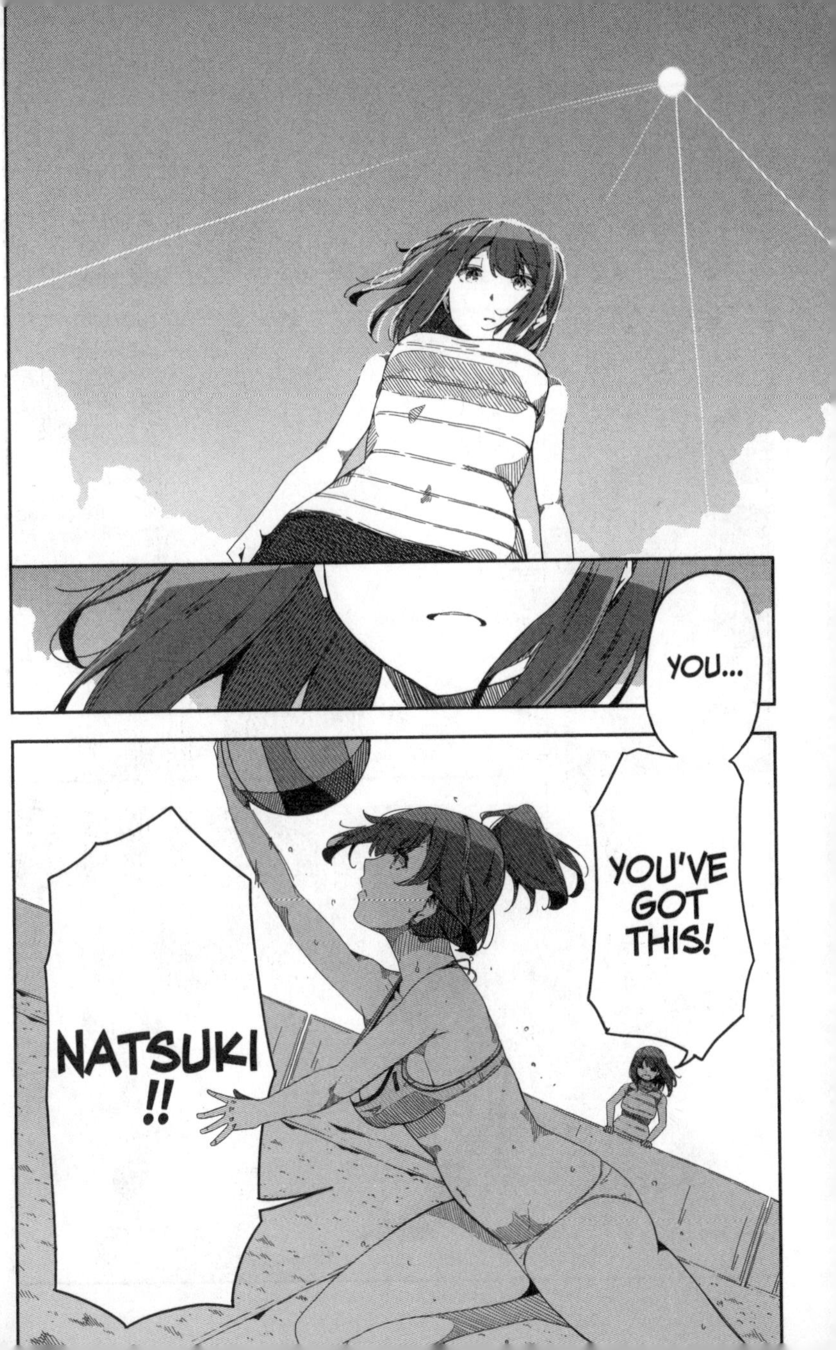
YOU...
YOU'VE GOT THIS!
NATSUKI !!

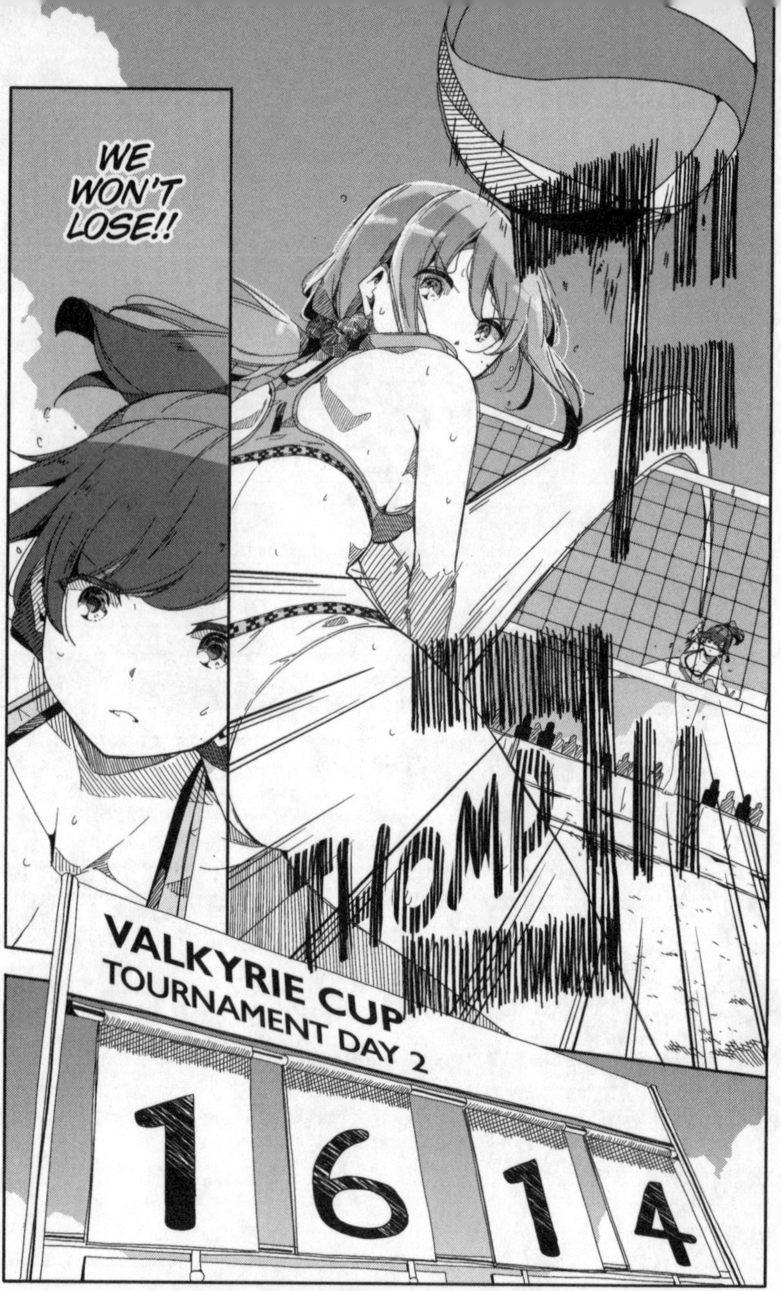
THOMP
WE WON'T LOSE!!
VALKYRIE CUP
TOURNAMENT DAY 2
16
14

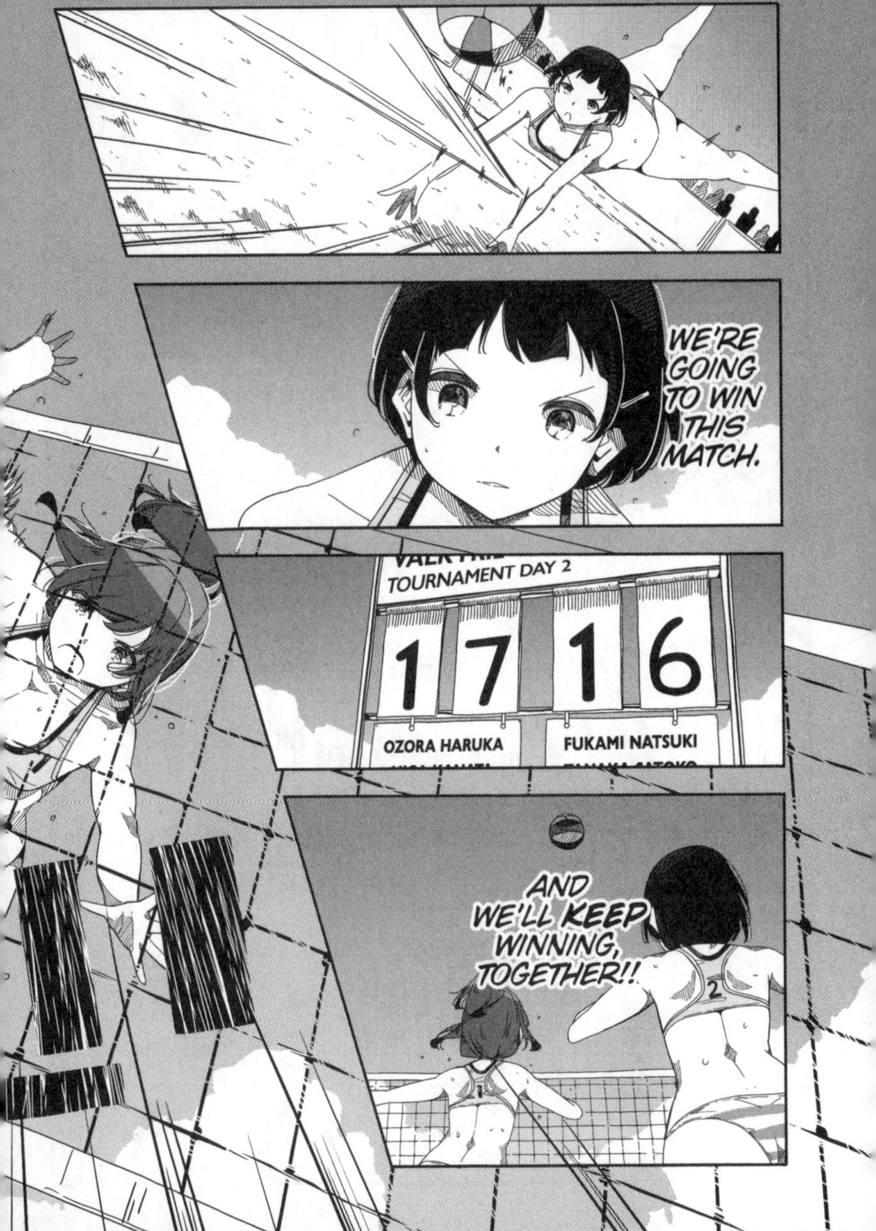
WE'RE GOING TO WIN THIS MATCH.
TOURNAMENT DAY 2
17
16
OZORA HARUKA
FUKAMI NATSUKI
AND WE'LL KEEP WINNING, TOGETHER!!

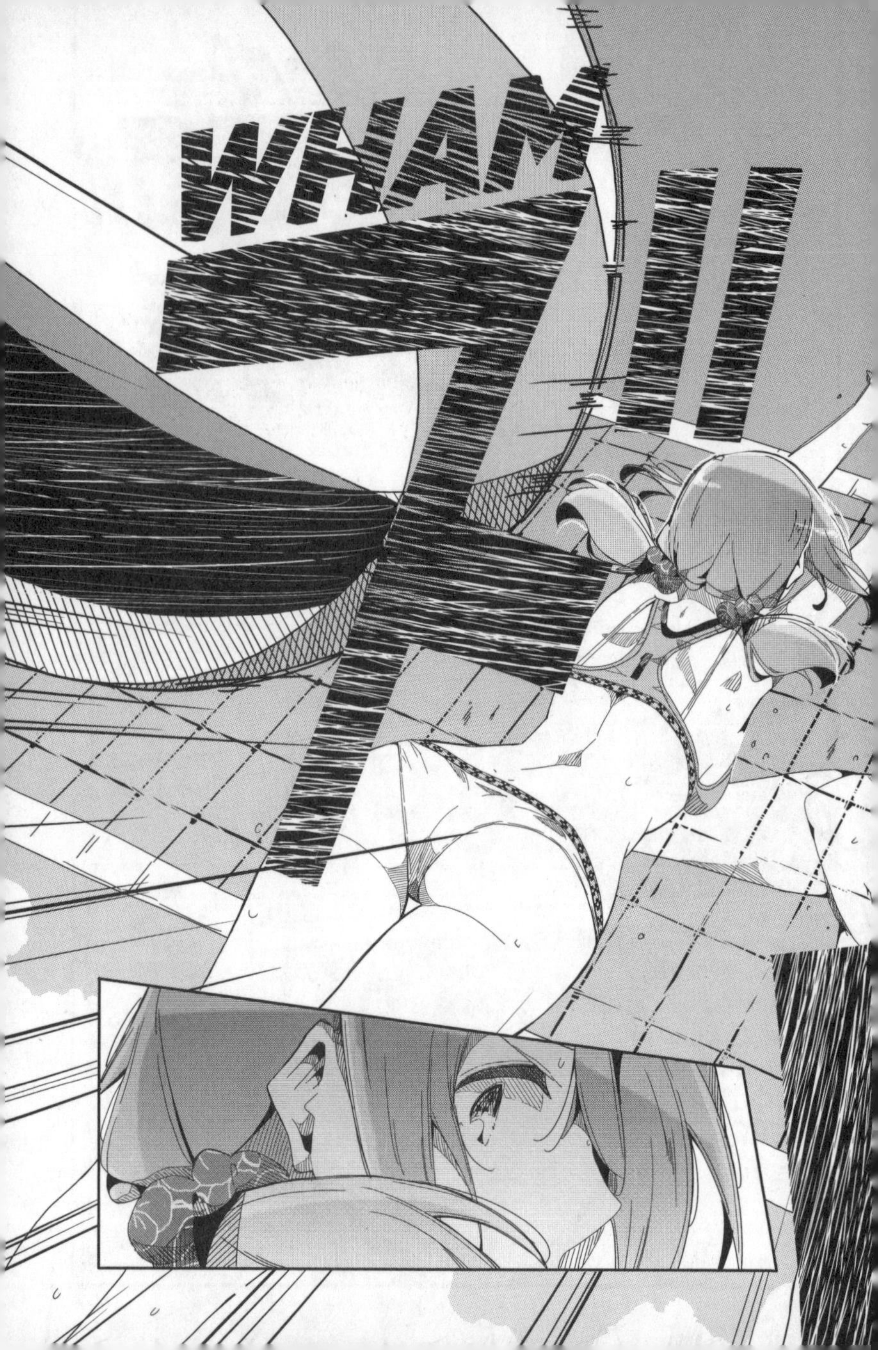
WHAM!!!

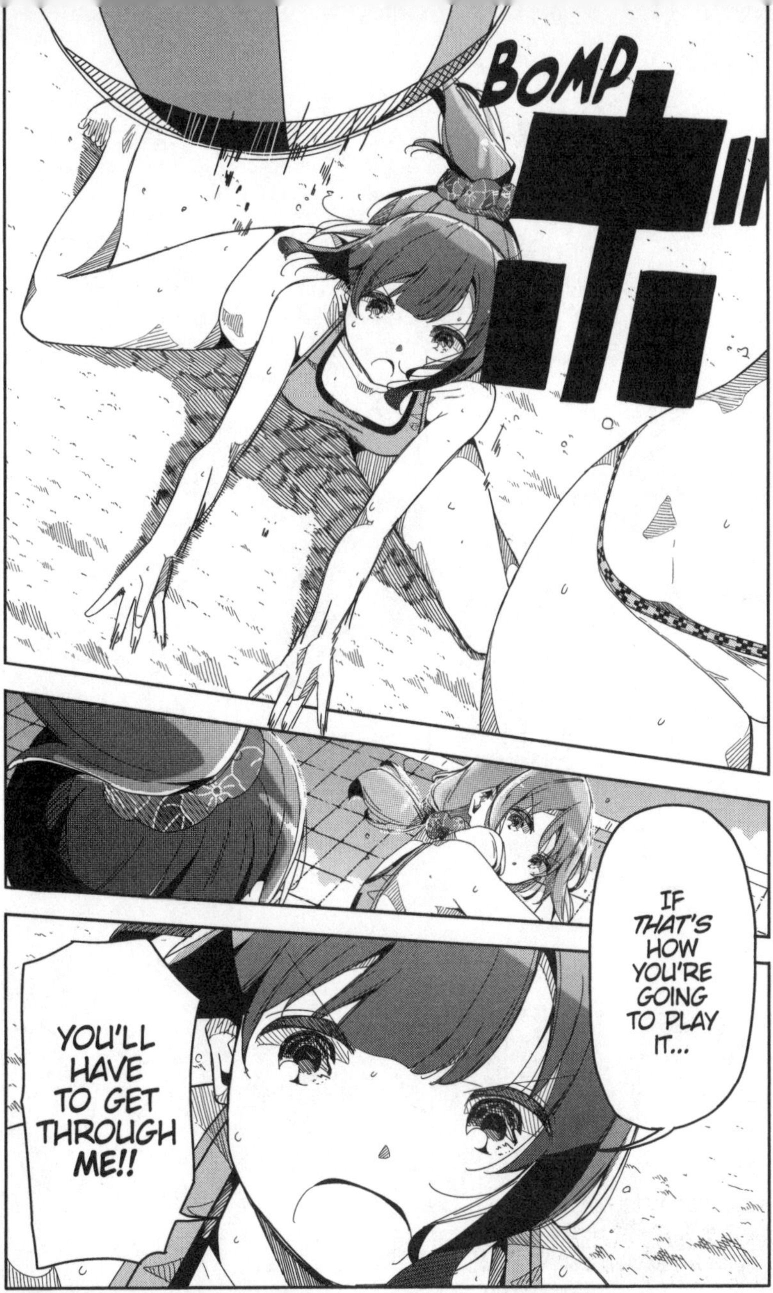
BOMP
IF THAT'S HOW YOU'RE GOING TO PLAY IT...
YOU'LL HAVE TO GET THROUGH ME!!

Harukana★Receive

Presented by Nyoijizai

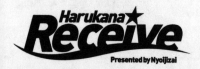

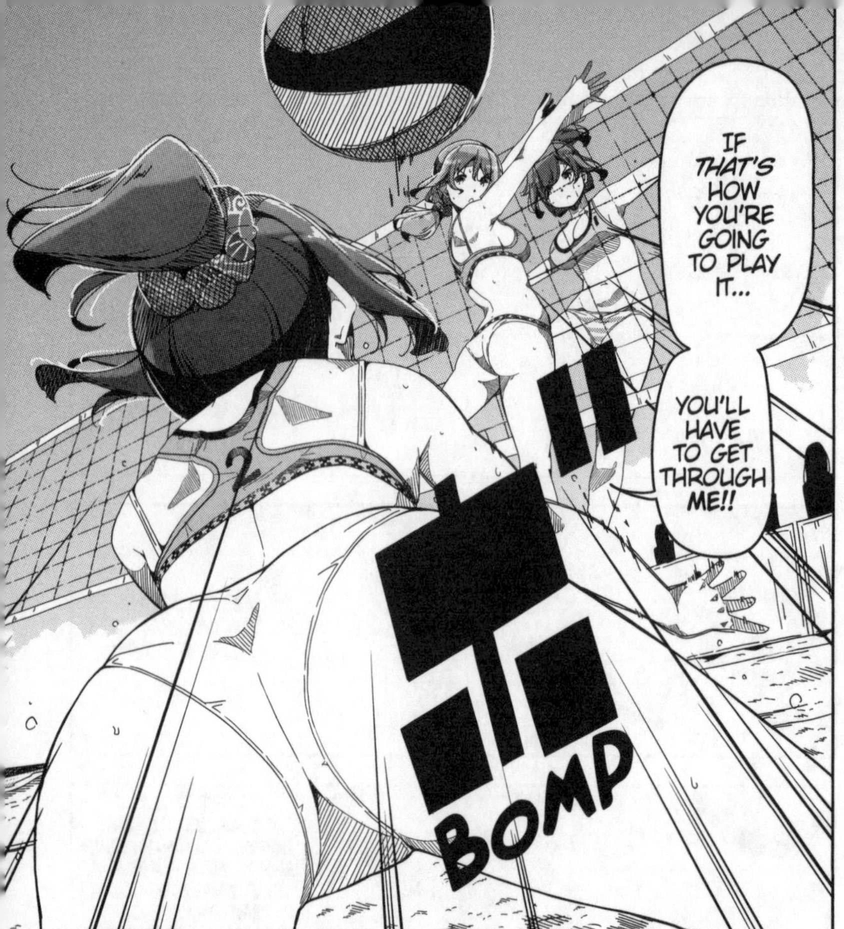
IF THAT'S HOW YOU'RE GOING TO PLAY IT...
YOU'LL HAVE TO GET THROUGH ME!!
BOMP
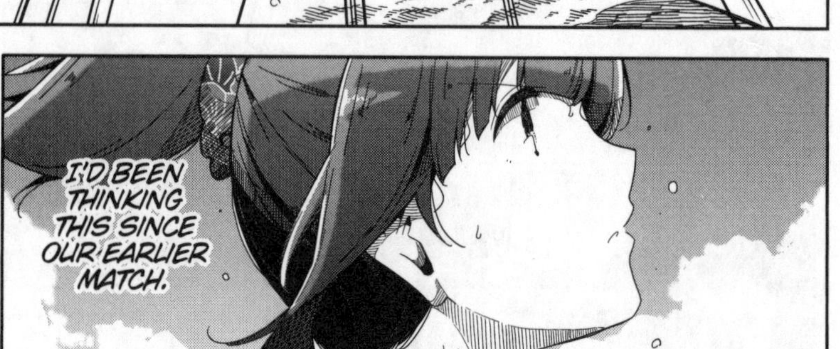
I'D BEEN THINKING THIS SINCE OUR EARLIER MATCH.

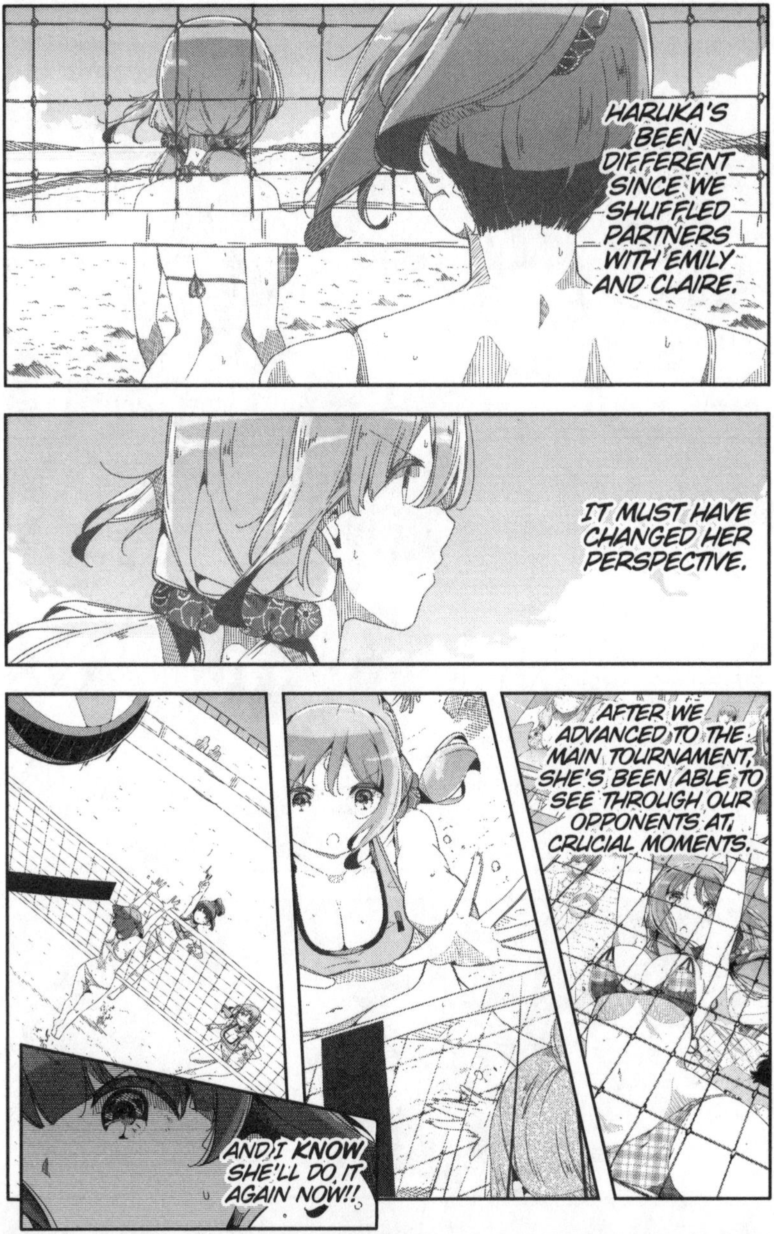
HARUKA'S BEEN DIFFERENT SINCE WE SHUFFLED PARTNERS WITH EMILY AND CLAIRE.
IT MUST HAVE CHANGED HER PERSPECTIVE.
AFTER WE ADVANCED TO THE MAIN TOURNAMENT, SHE'S BEEN ABLE TO SEE THROUGH OUR OPPONENTS AT CRUCIAL MOMENTS.
AND I KNOW SHE'LL DO IT AGAIN NOW!!

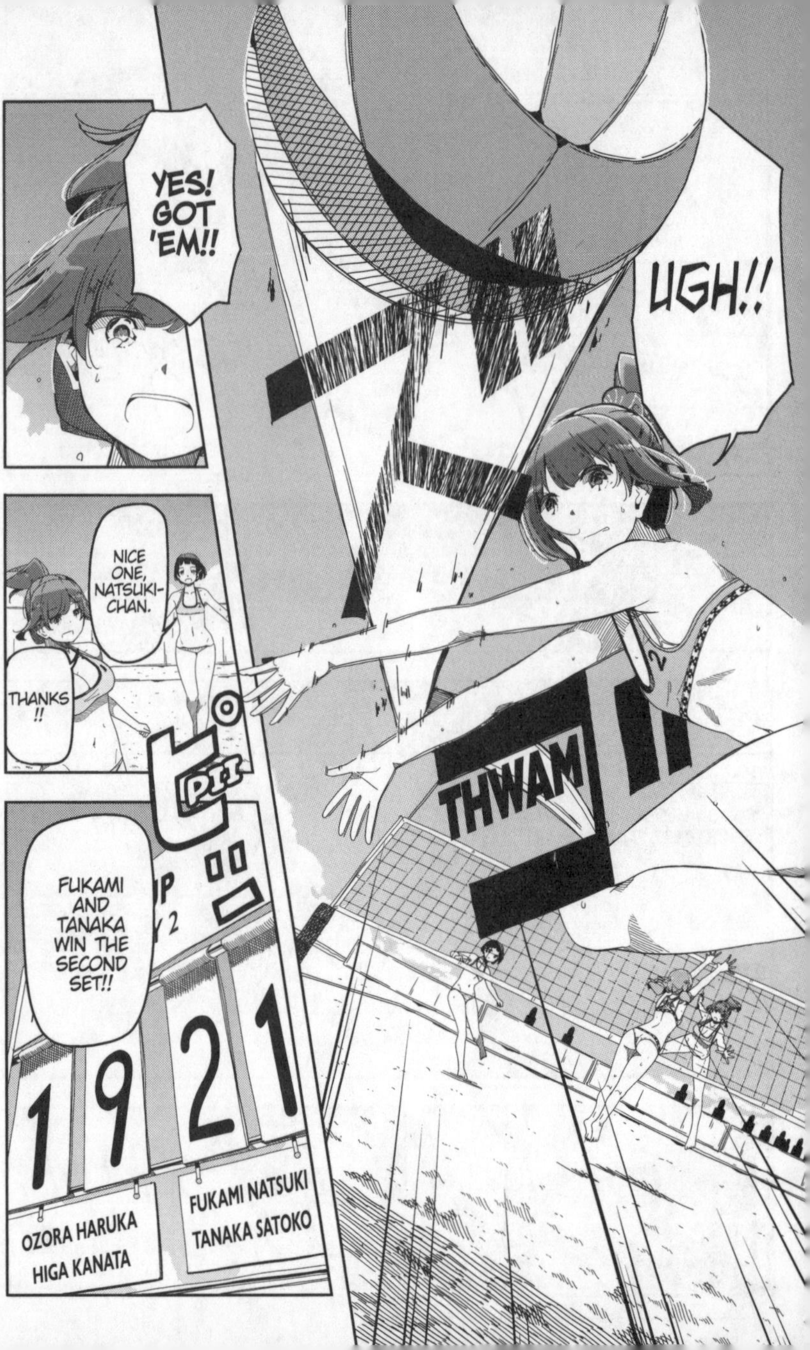
UGH!!
THWAM
YES! GOT 'EM!!
NICE ONE, NATSUKI-CHAN.
THANKS!!
PII
FUKAMI AND TANAKA WIN THE SECOND SET!!
19
21
OZORA HARUKA
HIGA KANATA
FUKAMI NATSUKI
TANAKA SATOKO

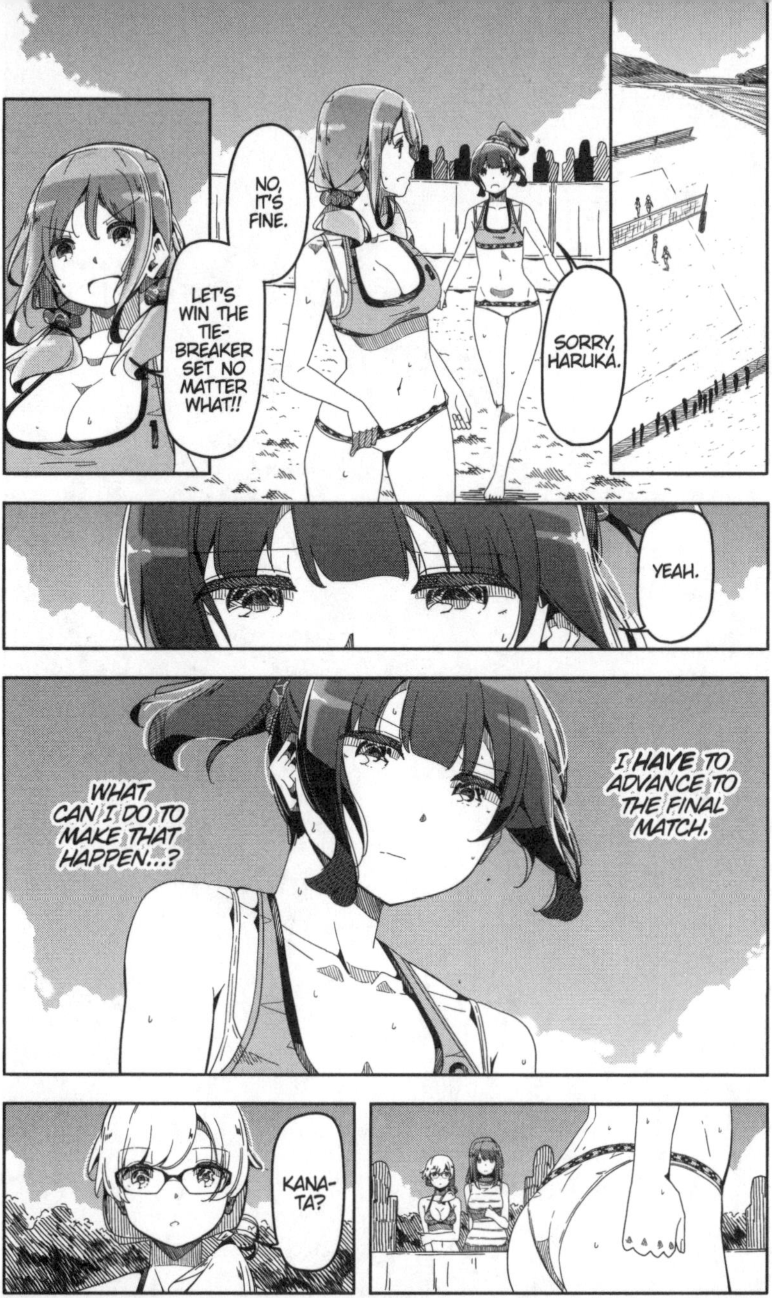
SORRY, HARUKA.
NO, IT'S FINE.
LET'S WIN THE TIE-BREAKER SET NO MATTER WHAT!!
YEAH.
I HAVE TO ADVANCE TO THE FINAL MATCH.
WHAT CAN I DO TO MAKE THAT HAPPEN...?
KANA-TA?

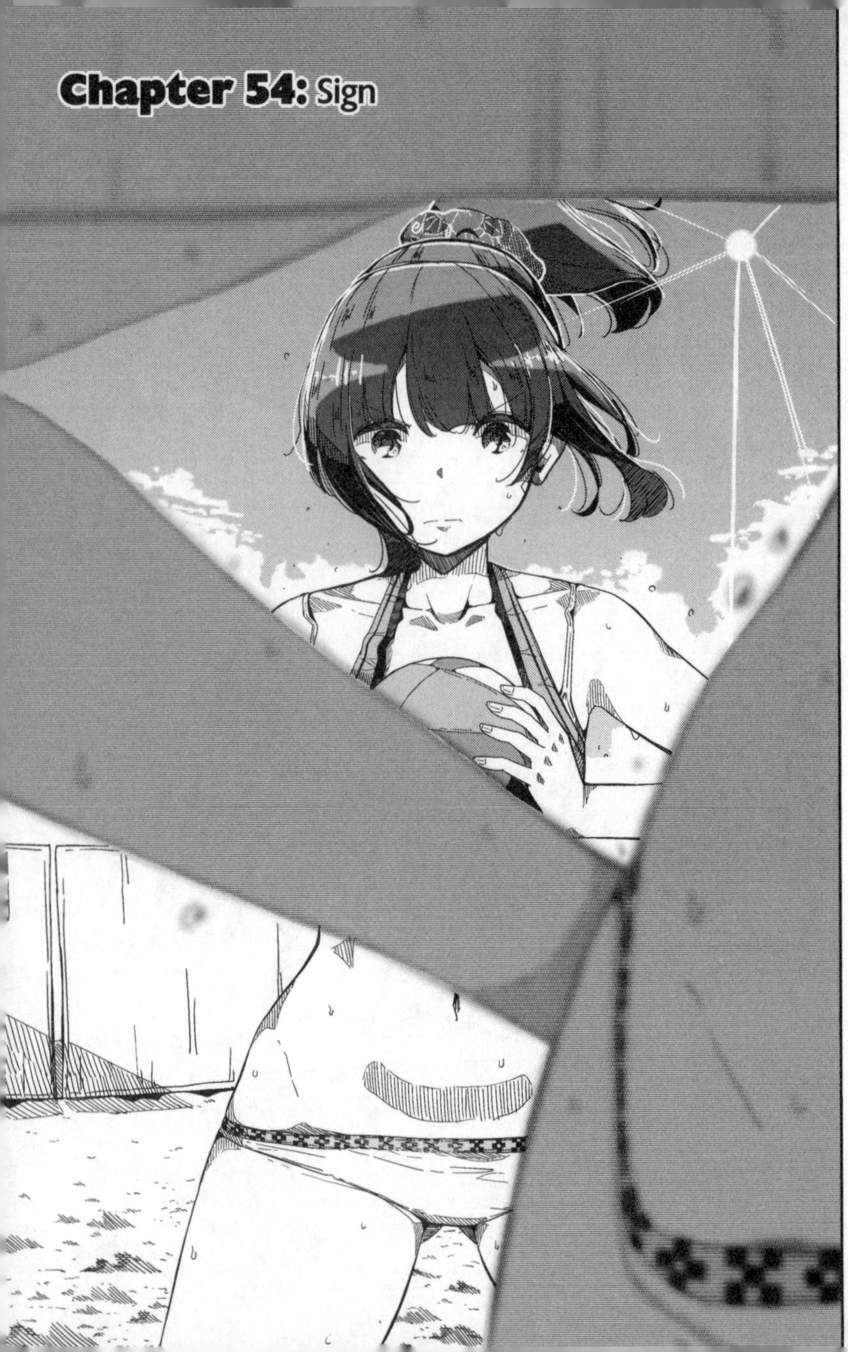
Chapter 54: Sign

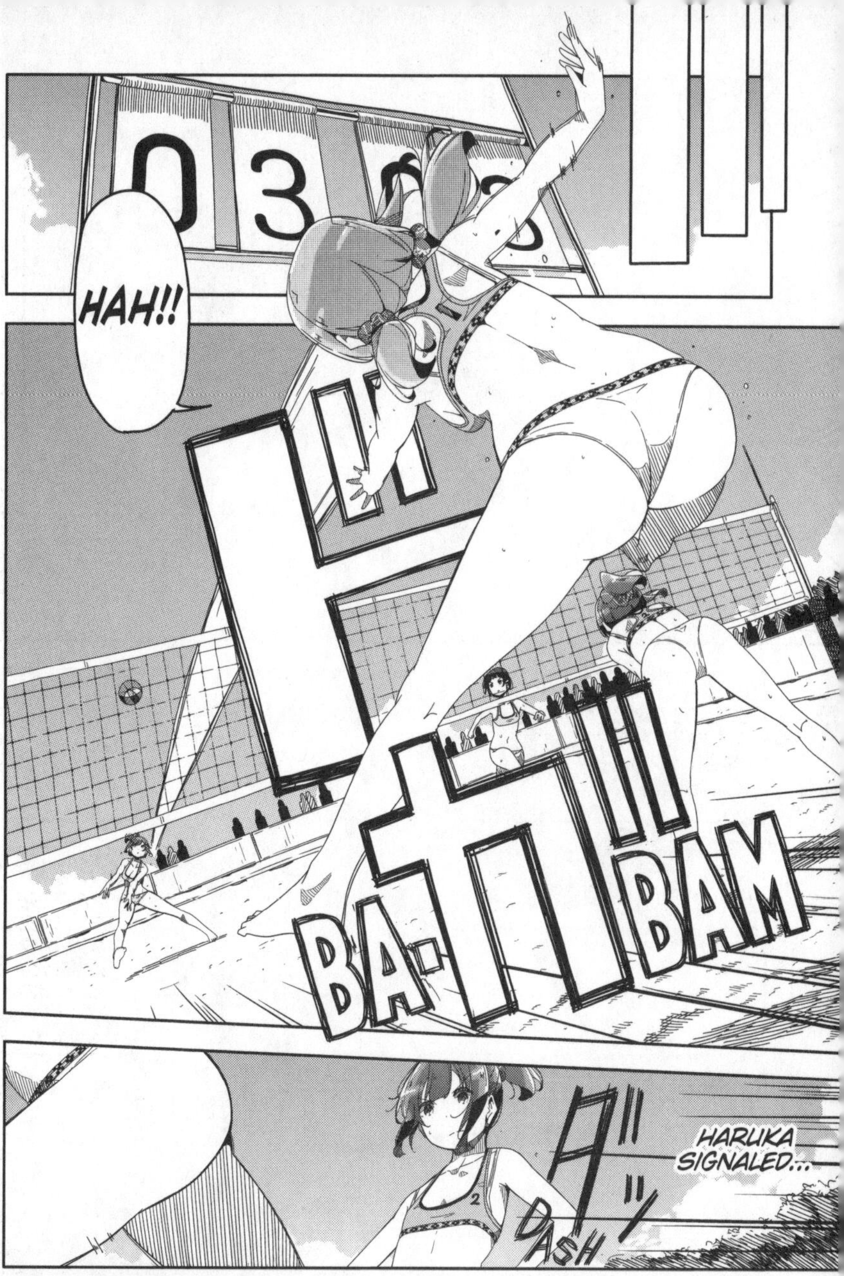
HAH!!
BA-BAM
HARUKA SIGNALED...
DASH

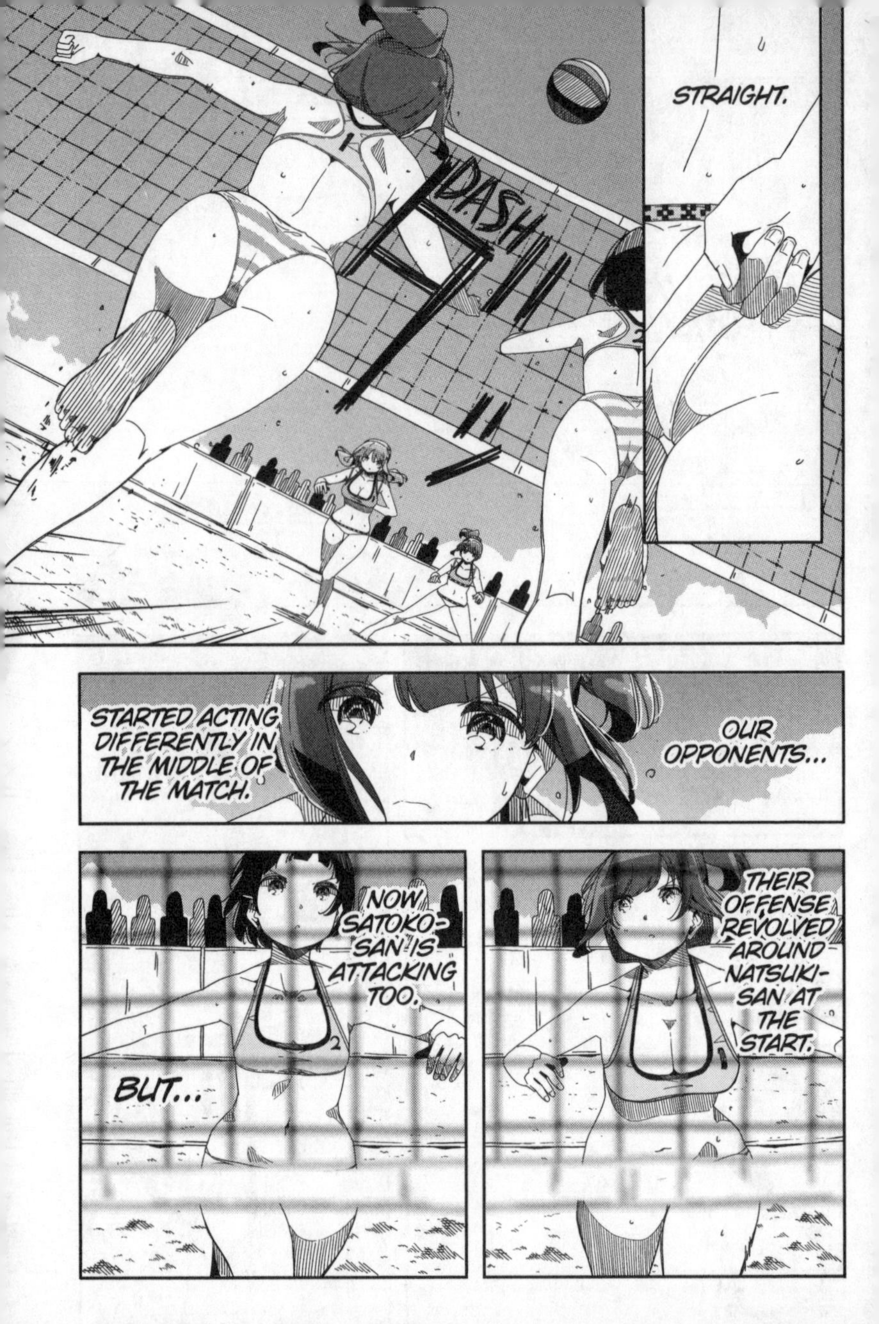
STRAIGHT.
DASH
OUR OPPONENTS...
STARTED ACTING DIFFERENTLY IN THE MIDDLE OF THE MATCH.
THEIR OFFENSE REVOLVED AROUND NATSUKI-SAN AT THE START.
NOW SATOKO-SAN IS ATTACKING TOO.
BUT...

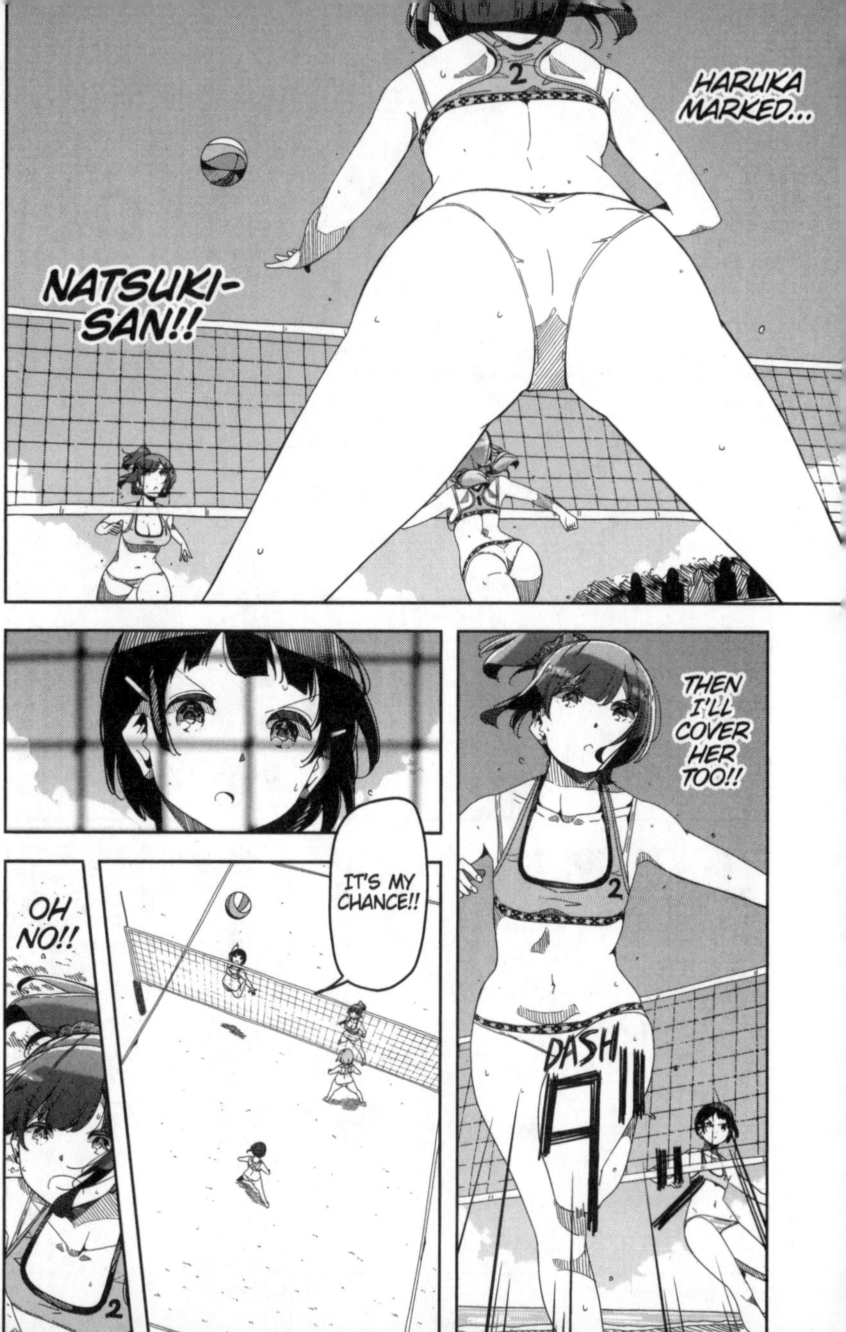
HARUKA MARKED...
NATSUKI-SAN!!
THEN I'LL COVER HER TOO!!
DASH
IT'S MY CHANCE!!
OH NO!!

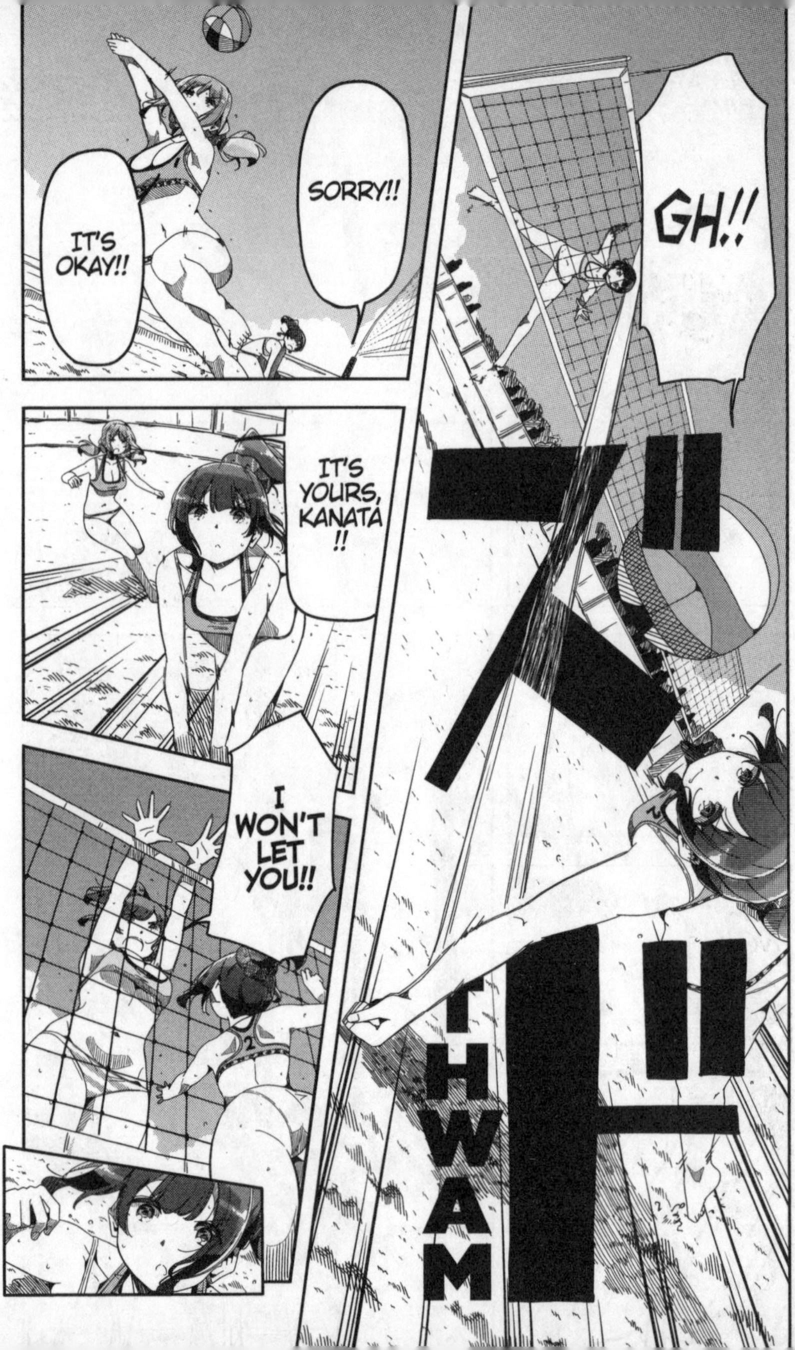
SORRY!!
IT'S OKAY!!
IT'S YOURS, KANATA!!
I WON'T LET YOU!!
GH!!
THWAM

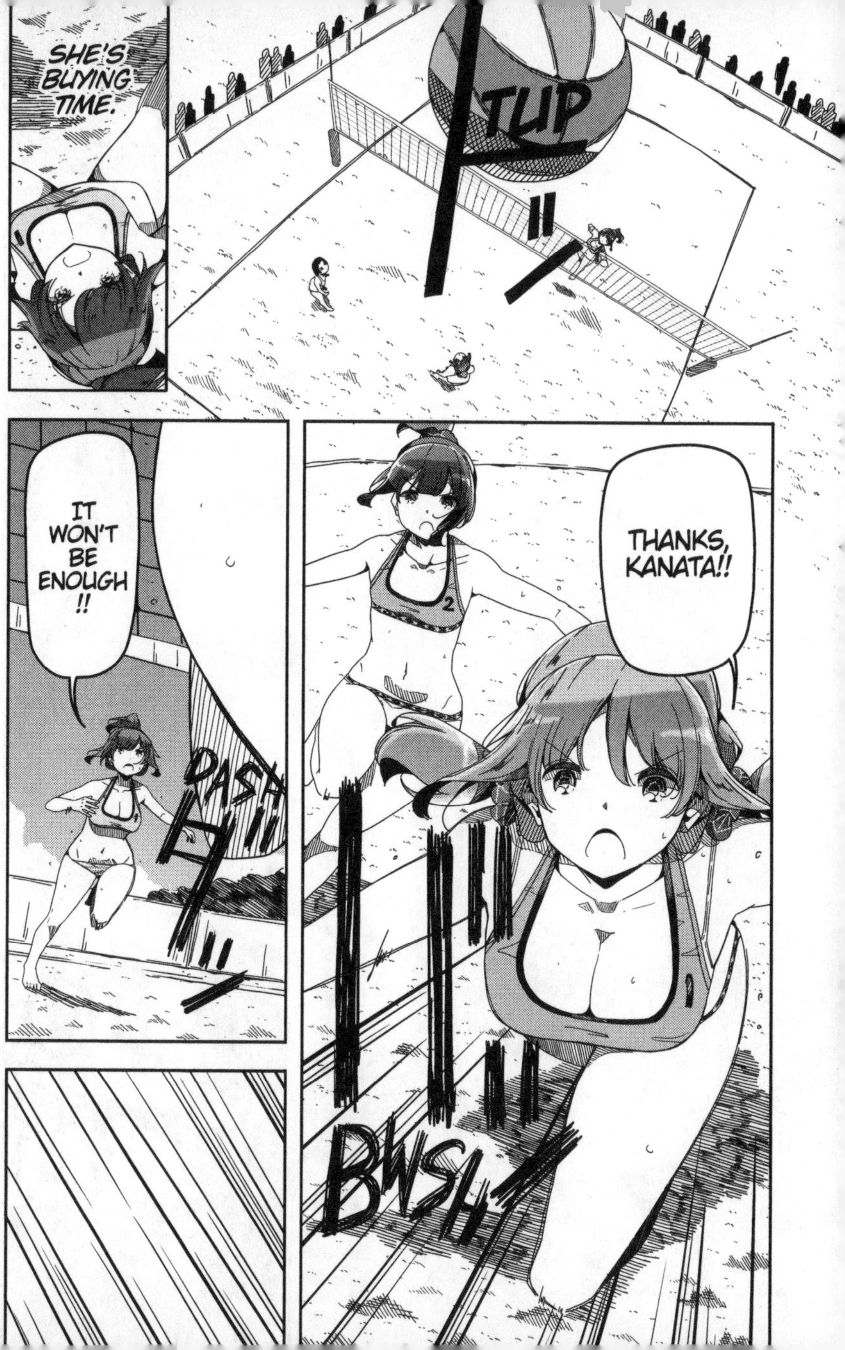
TUP
SHE'S BUYING TIME.
THANKS, KANATA!!
BWSH
IT WON'T BE ENOUGH!!
DASH

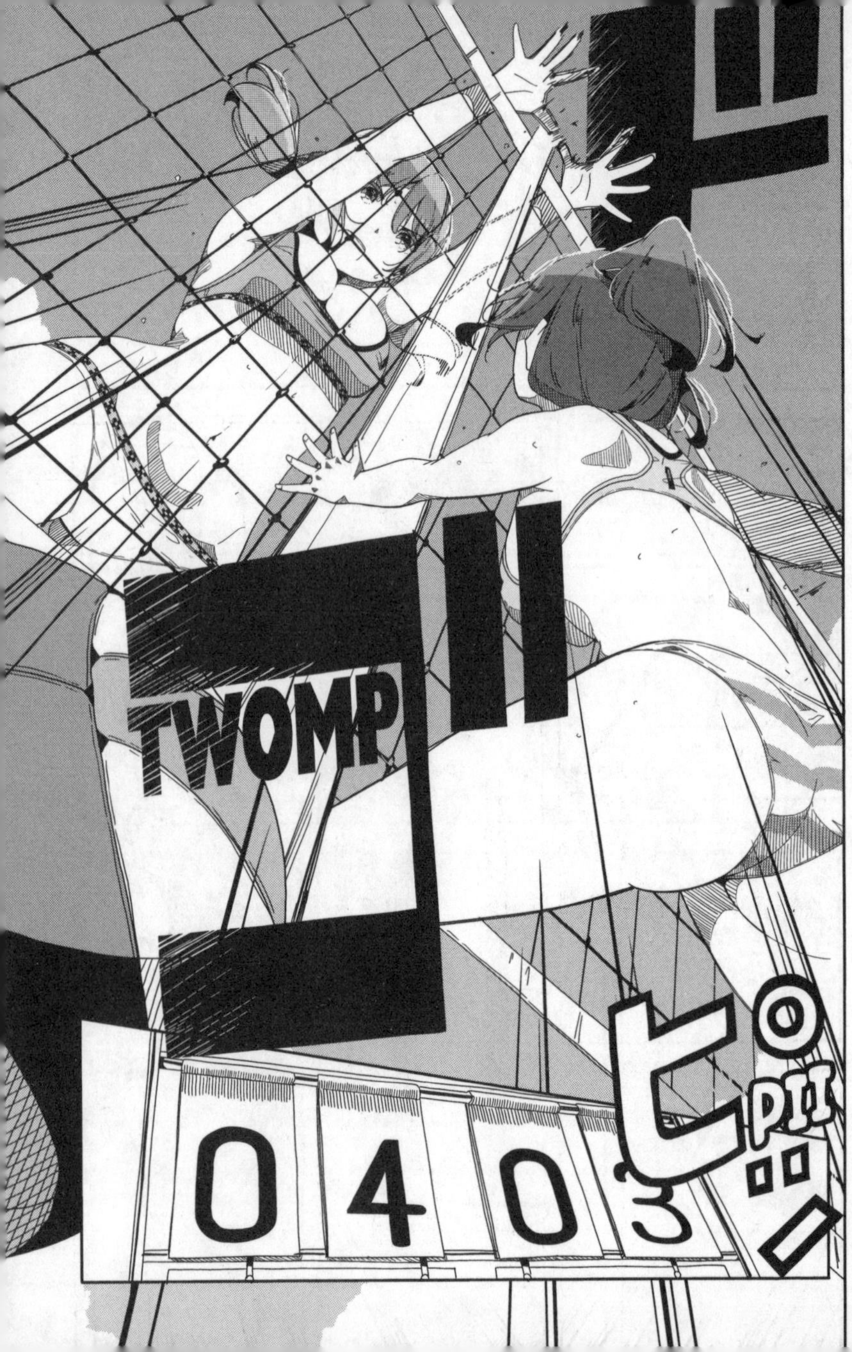
ド!!
TWOMP!!
ピーーッ
PII
0403

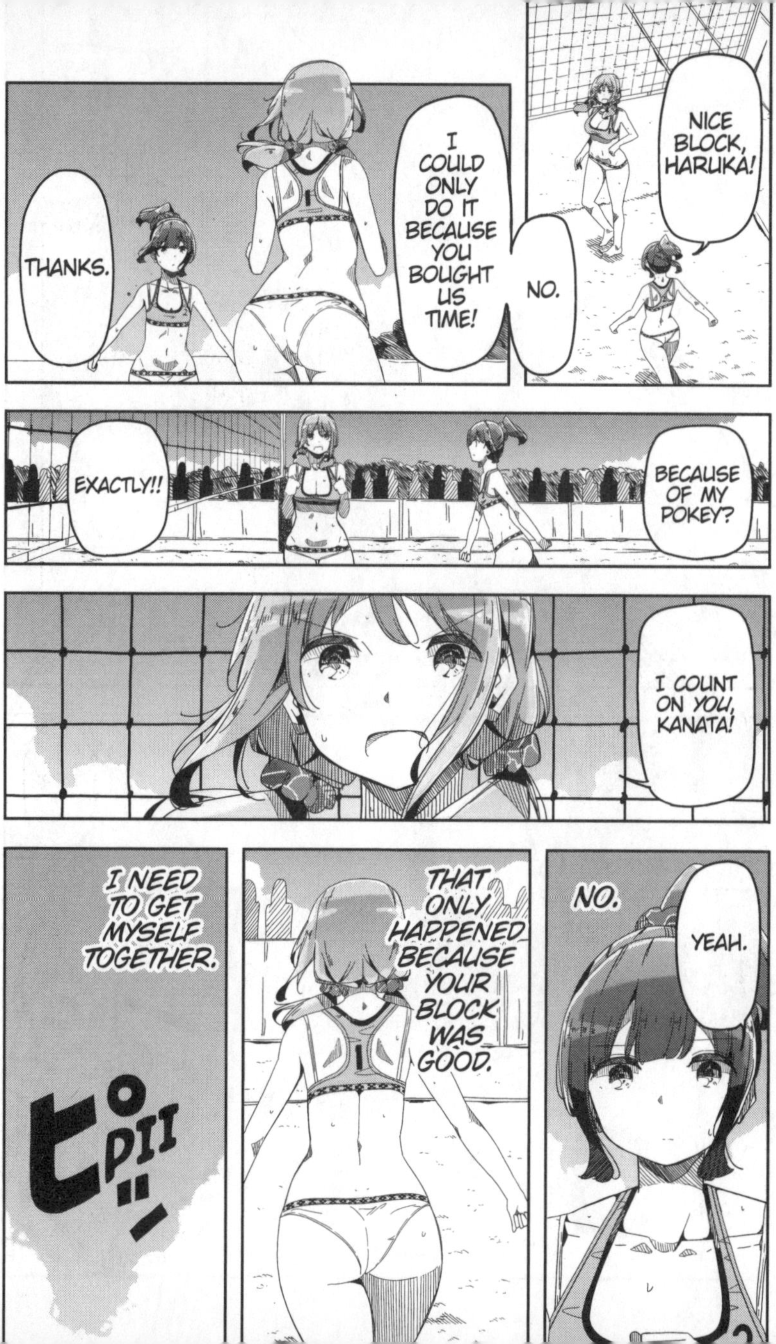
NICE BLOCK, HARUKA!
NO.
I COULD ONLY DO IT BECAUSE YOU BOUGHT US TIME!
THANKS.
BECAUSE OF MY POKEY?
EXACTLY!!
I COUNT ON YOU, KANATA!
YEAH.
NO.
THAT ONLY HAPPENED BECAUSE YOUR BLOCK WAS GOOD.
I NEED TO GET MYSELF TOGETHER.
PII

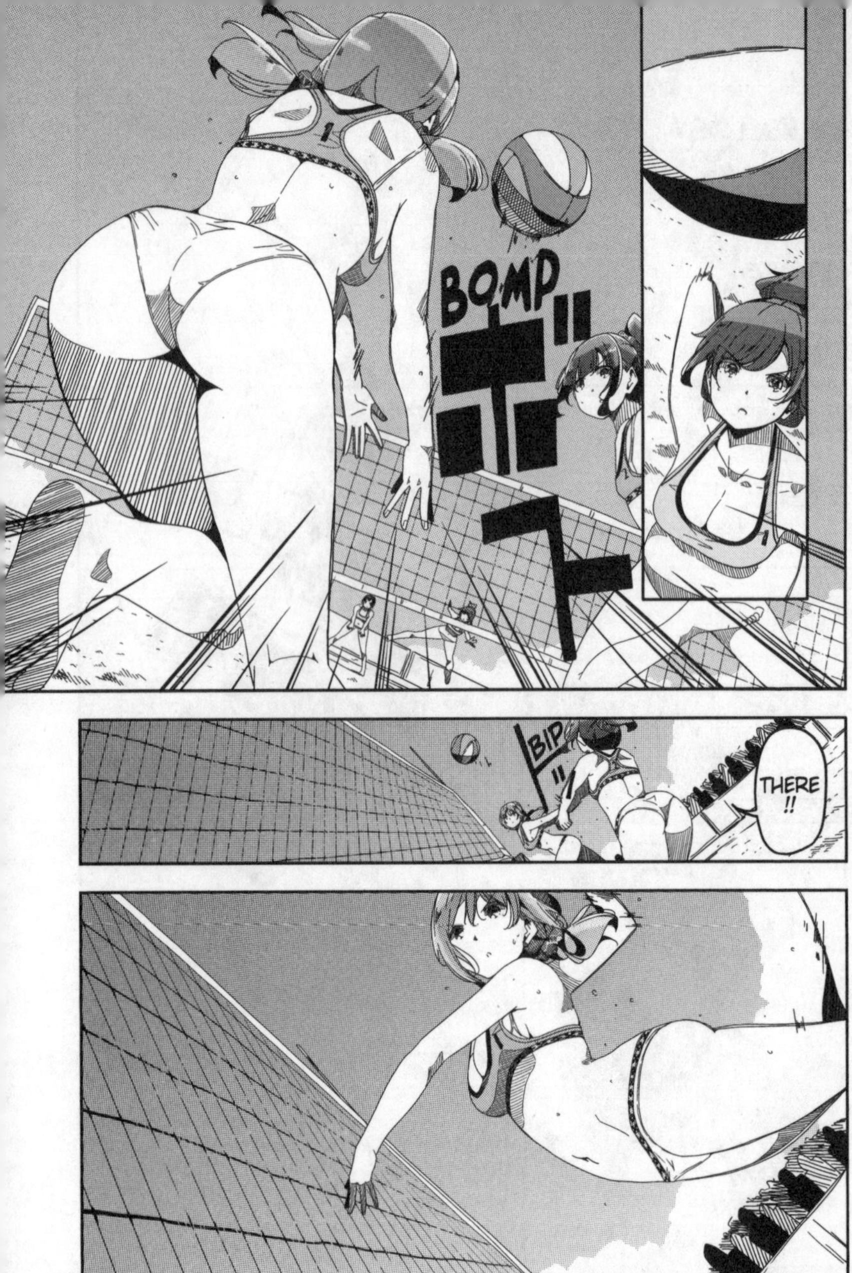
BOMP!!
BIP!!
THERE!!

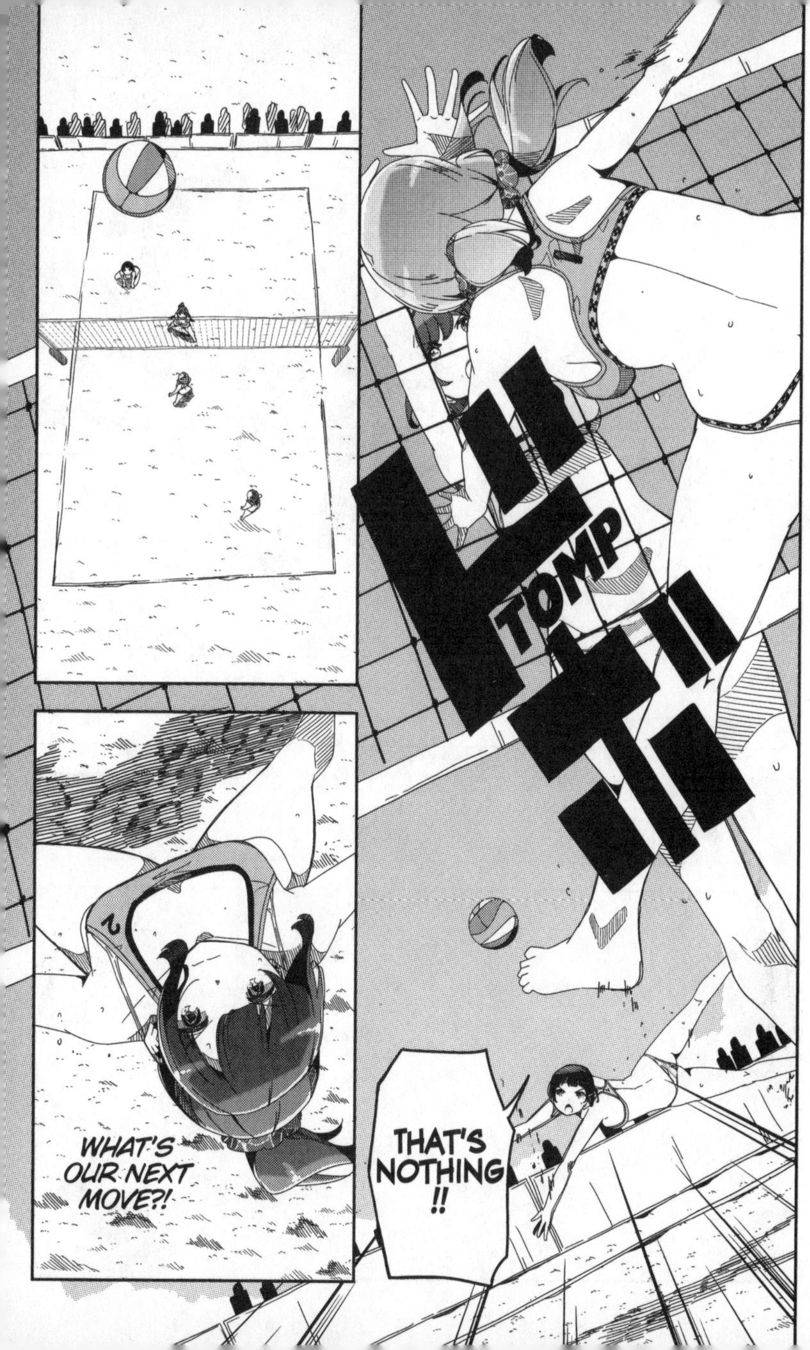
STOMP
THAT'S NOTHING !!
WHAT'S OUR NEXT MOVE?!

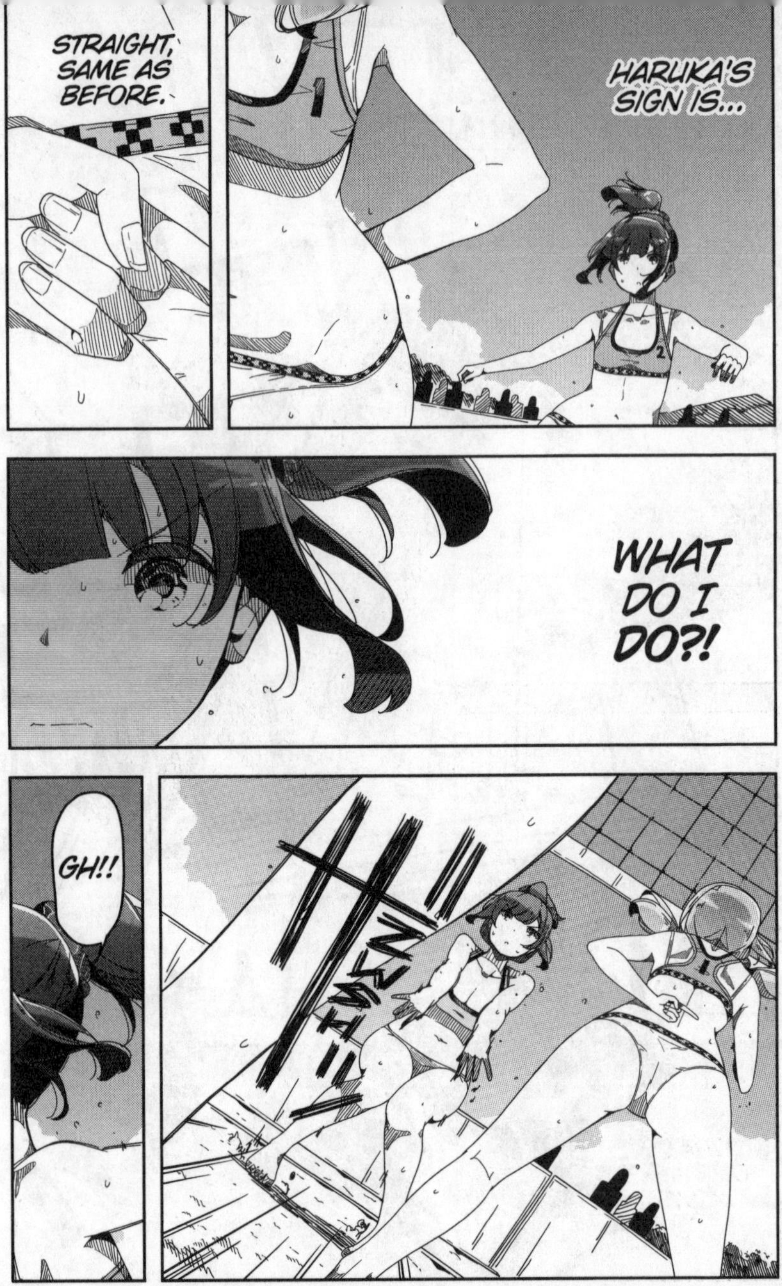
HARUKA'S SIGN IS...
STRAIGHT, SAME AS BEFORE.
WHAT DO I DO?!
GH!!

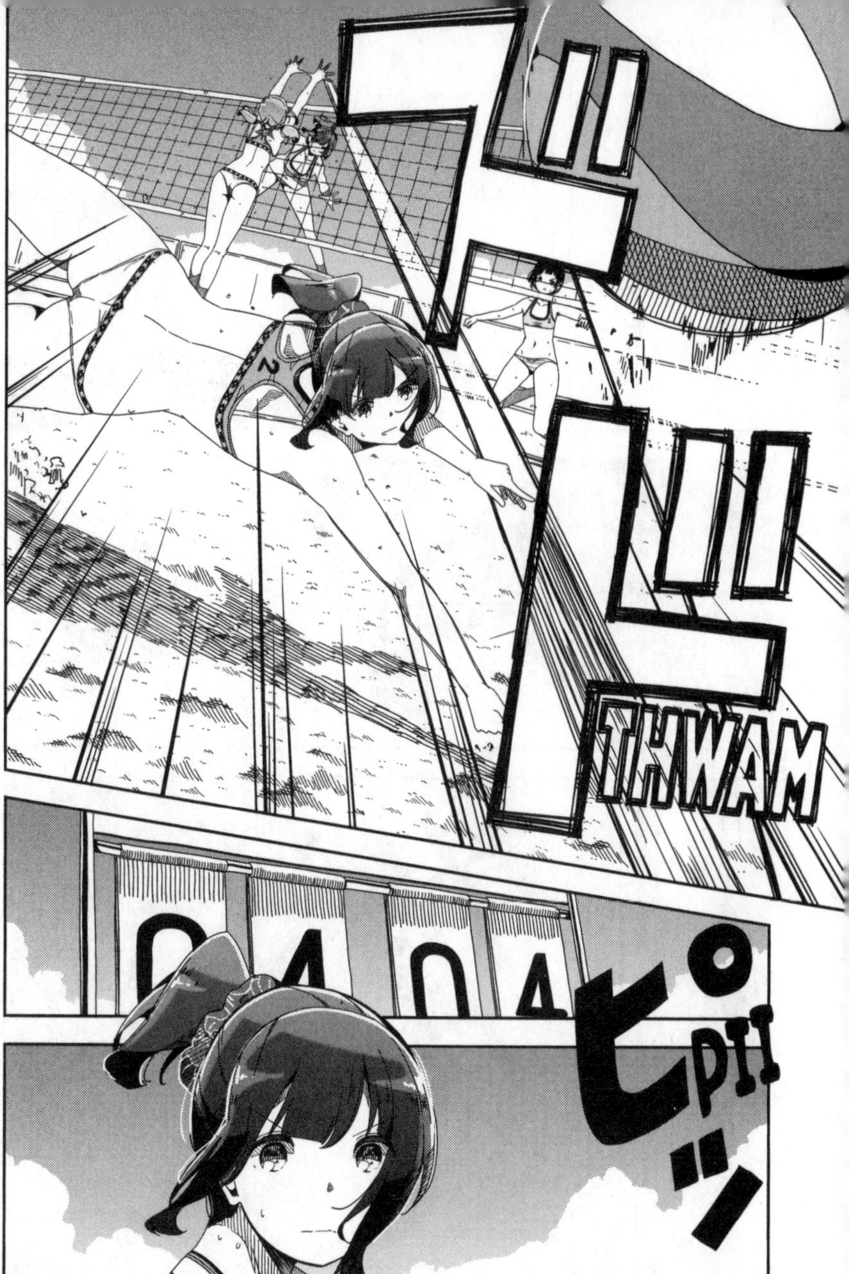
THWAM
PII

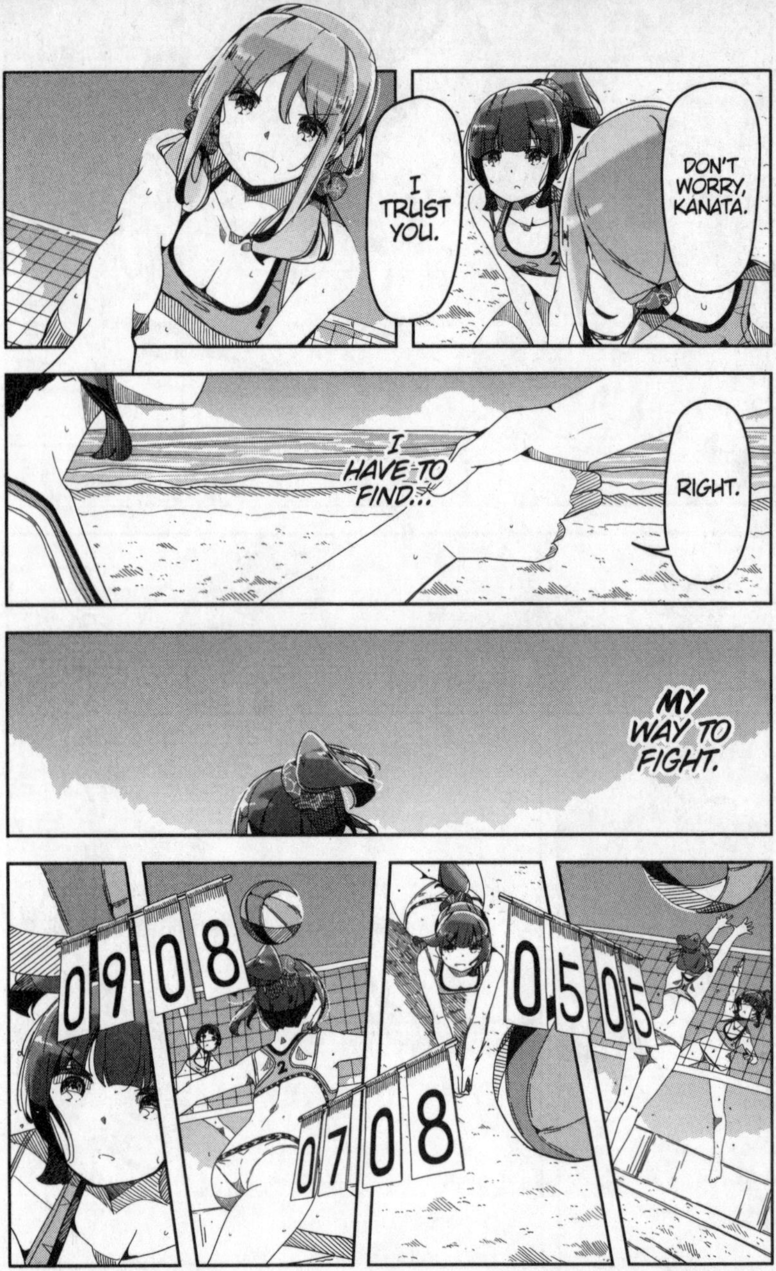
DON'T WORRY, KANATA.
I TRUST YOU.
RIGHT.
I HAVE TO FIND...
MY WAY TO FIGHT.
05 05
07 08
09 08

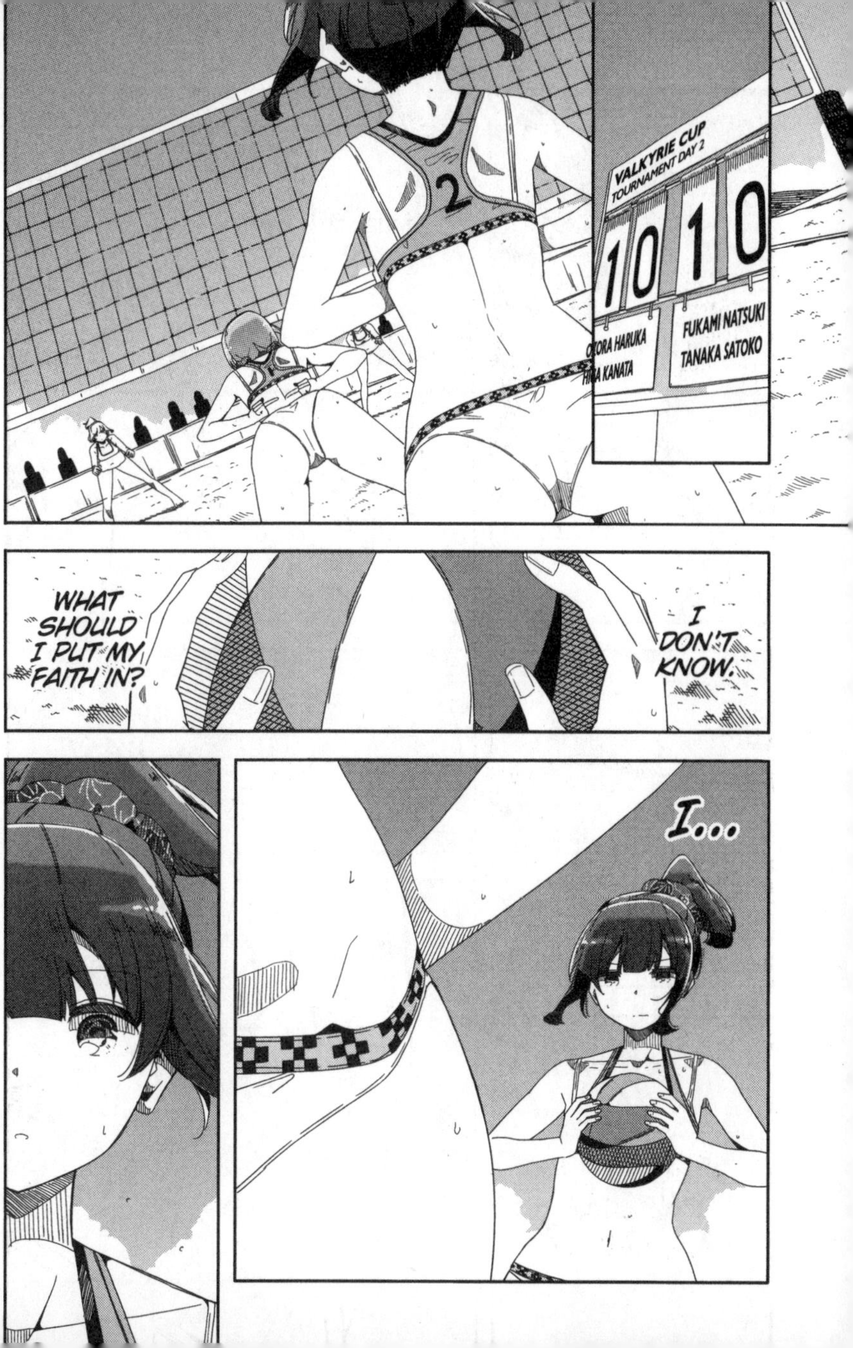
VALKYRIE CUP
TOURNAMENT DAY 2
10 10
OZORA HARUKA
HIGA KANATA
FUKAMI NATSUKI
TANAKA SATOKO
I DON'T KNOW.
WHAT SHOULD I PUT MY FAITH IN?
I...

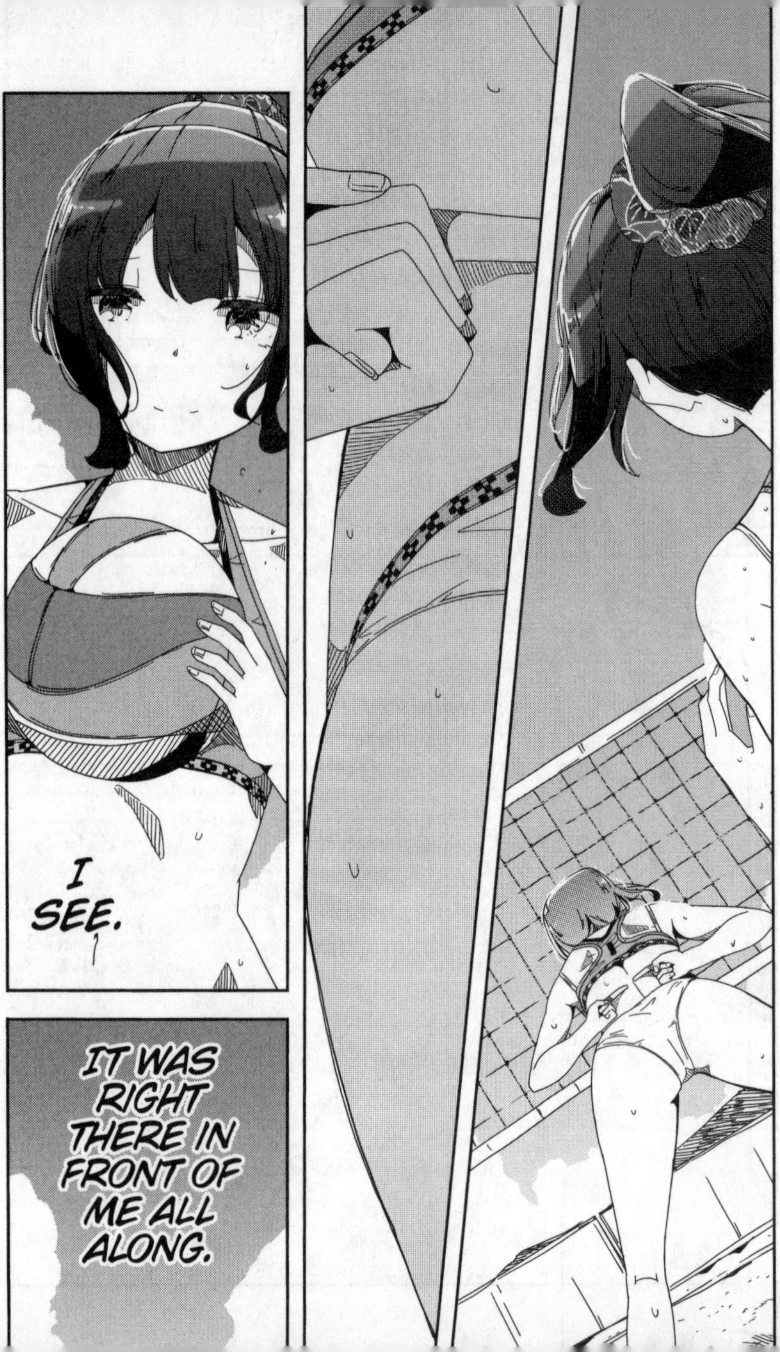
I SEE.
IT WAS RIGHT THERE IN FRONT OF ME ALL ALONG.

I'D LOST MY CONFIDENCE AGAIN.

SORRY, HARUKA.

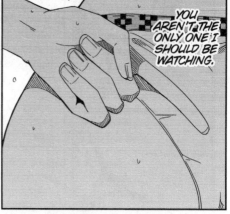

YOU AREN'T THE ONLY ONE I SHOULD BE WATCHING.

I REMEMBER WHAT I HAVE TO DO.

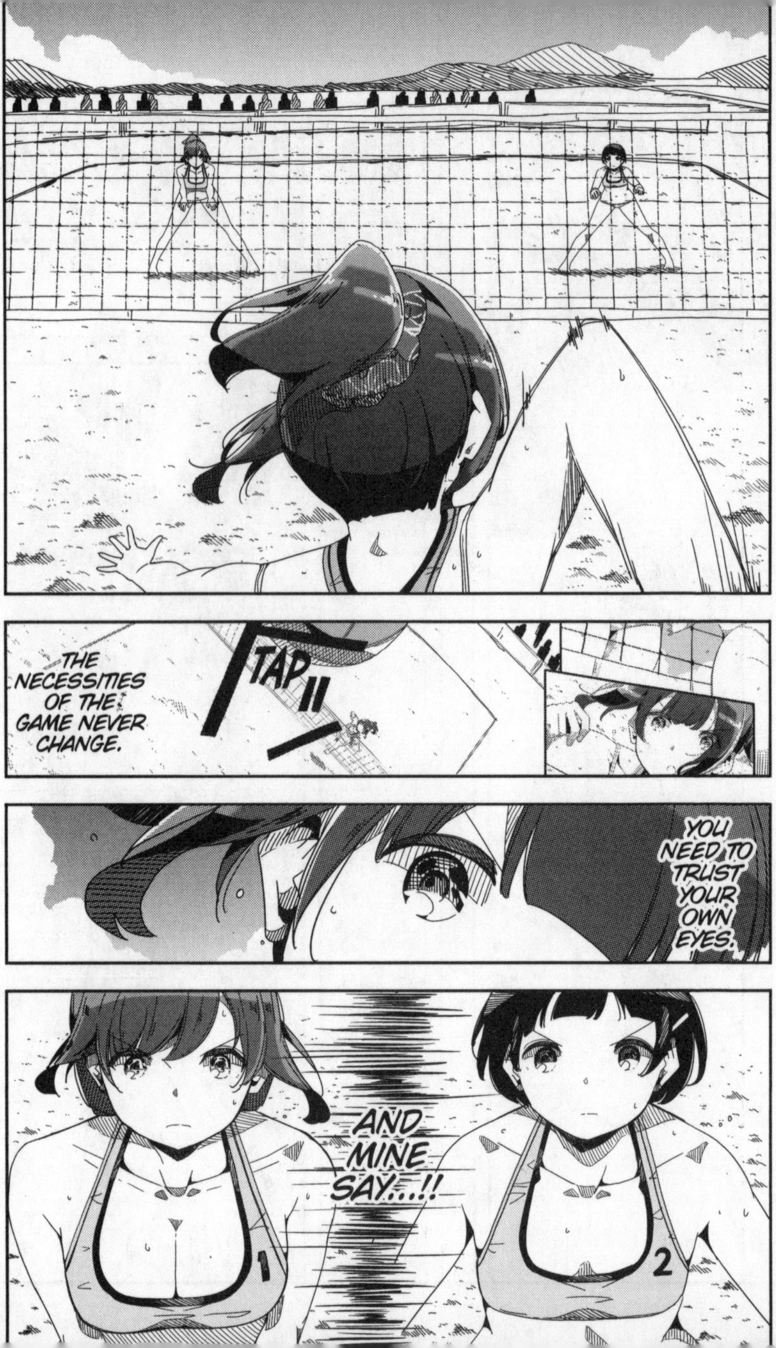
TAP
THE NECESSITIES OF THE GAME NEVER CHANGE.
YOU NEED TO TRUST YOUR OWN EYES.
AND MINE SAY...!!

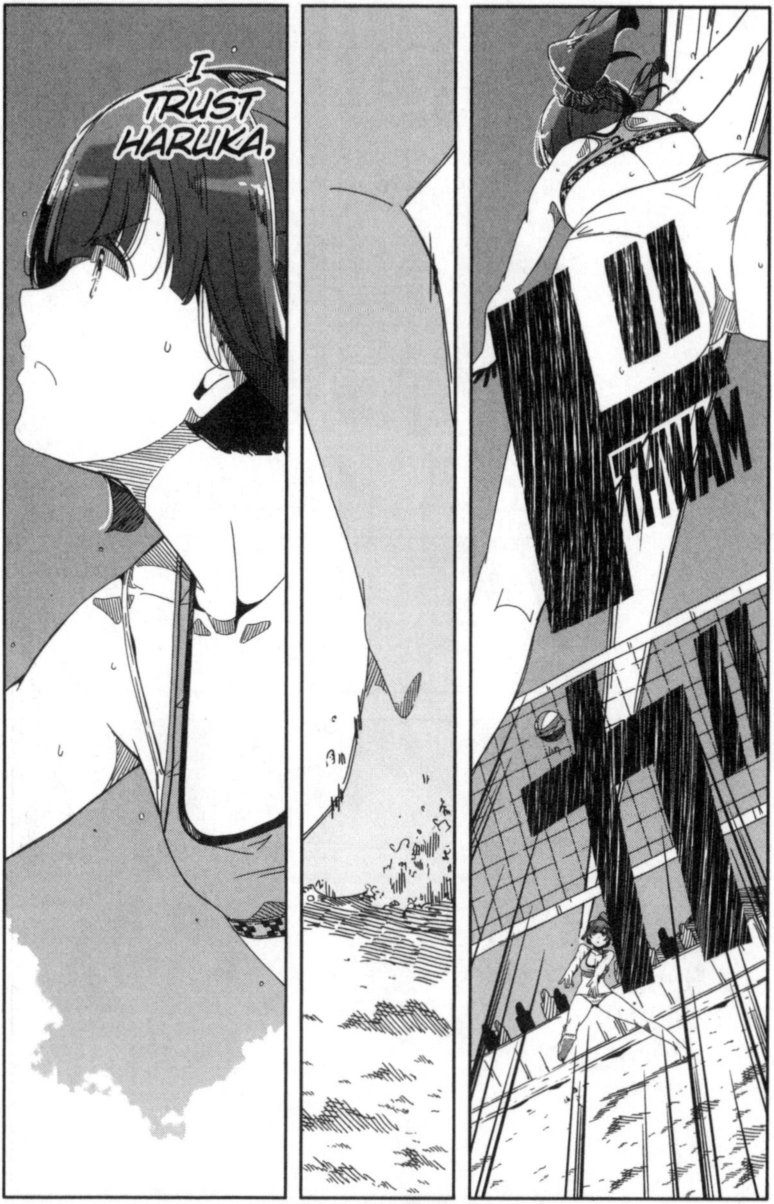
THWAM
I TRUST HARUKA.

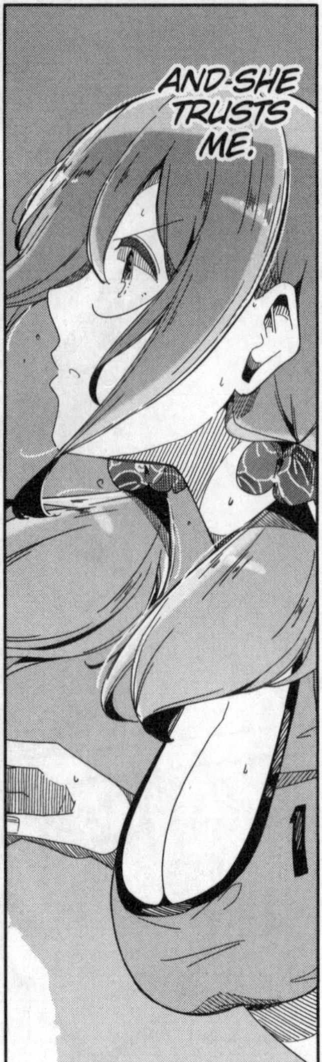
AND-SHE TRUSTS ME.

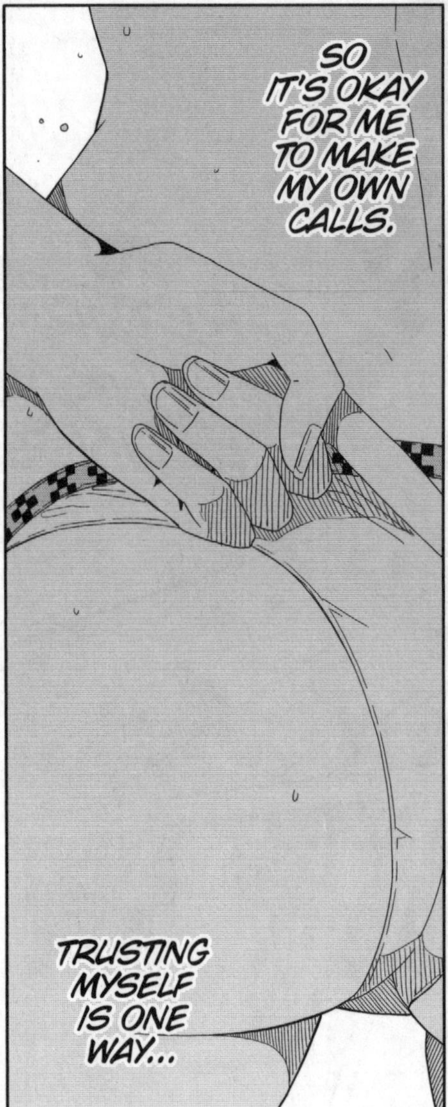
SO IT'S OKAY FOR ME TO MAKE MY OWN CALLS.
TRUSTING MYSELF IS ONE WAY...

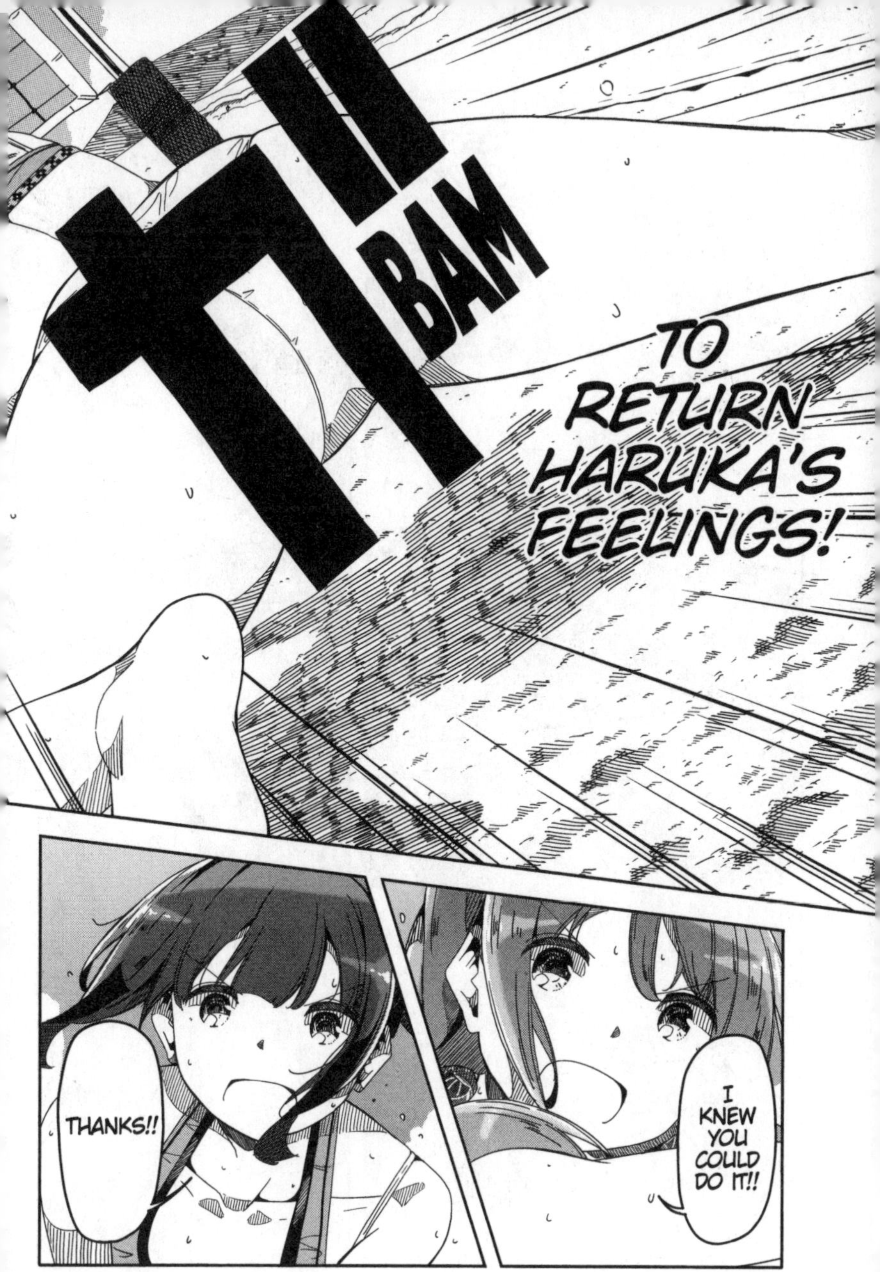
BAM
TO RETURN HARUKA'S FEELINGS!
I KNEW YOU COULD DO IT!!
THANKS!!

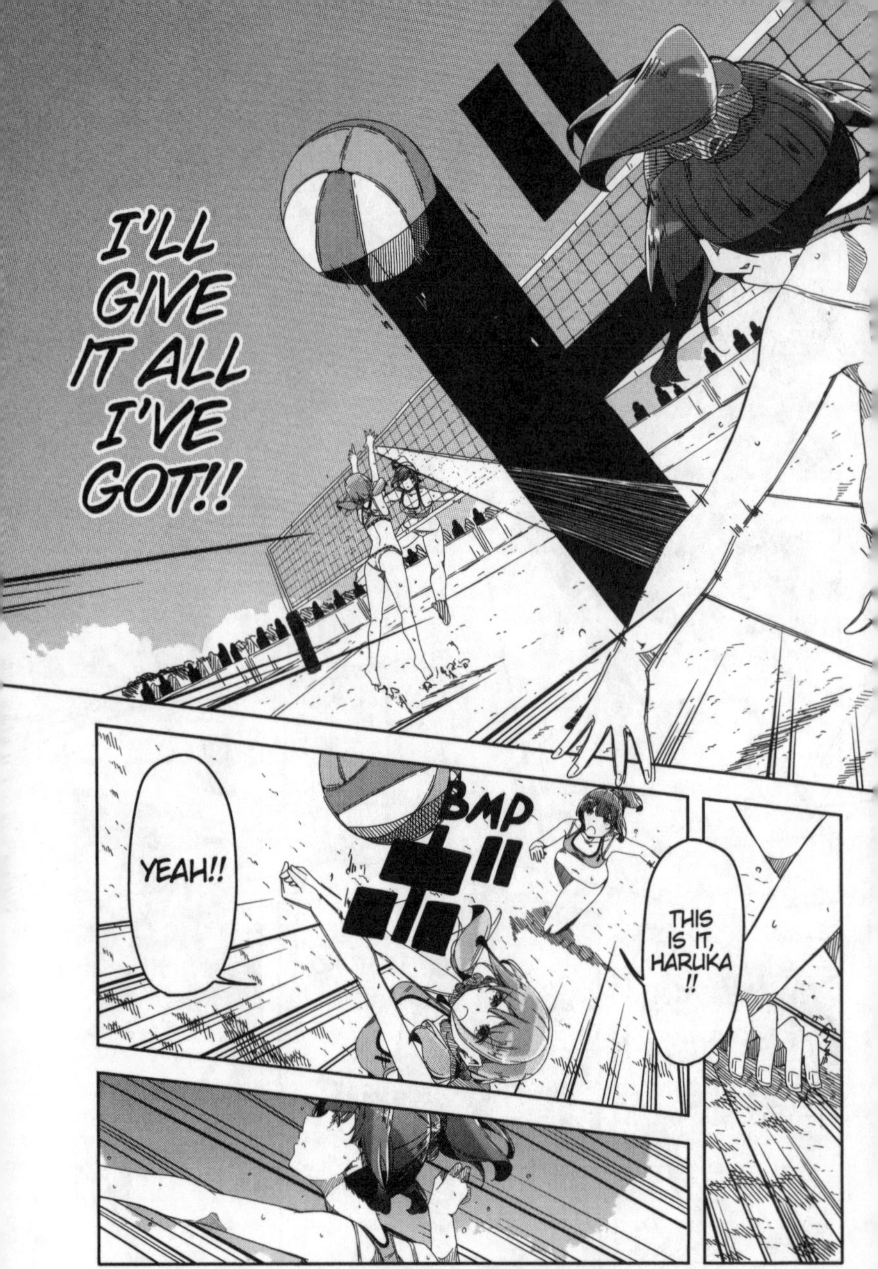
I'LL GIVE IT ALL I'VE GOT!!
THIS IS IT, HARUKA!!
BMP
YEAH!!

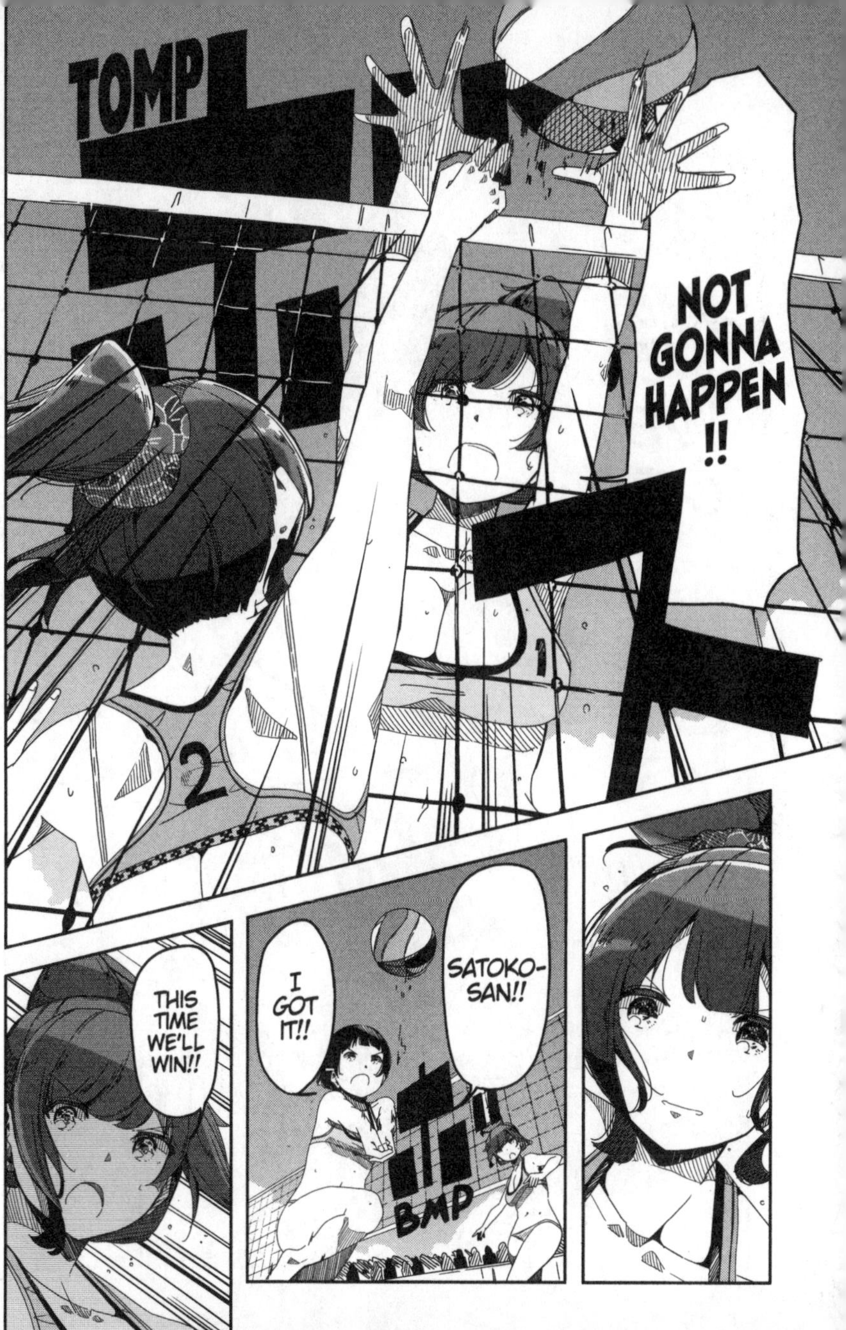
TOMP!
NOT GONNA HAPPEN!!
SATOKO-SAN!!
I GOT IT!!
BMP
THIS TIME WE'LL WIN!!

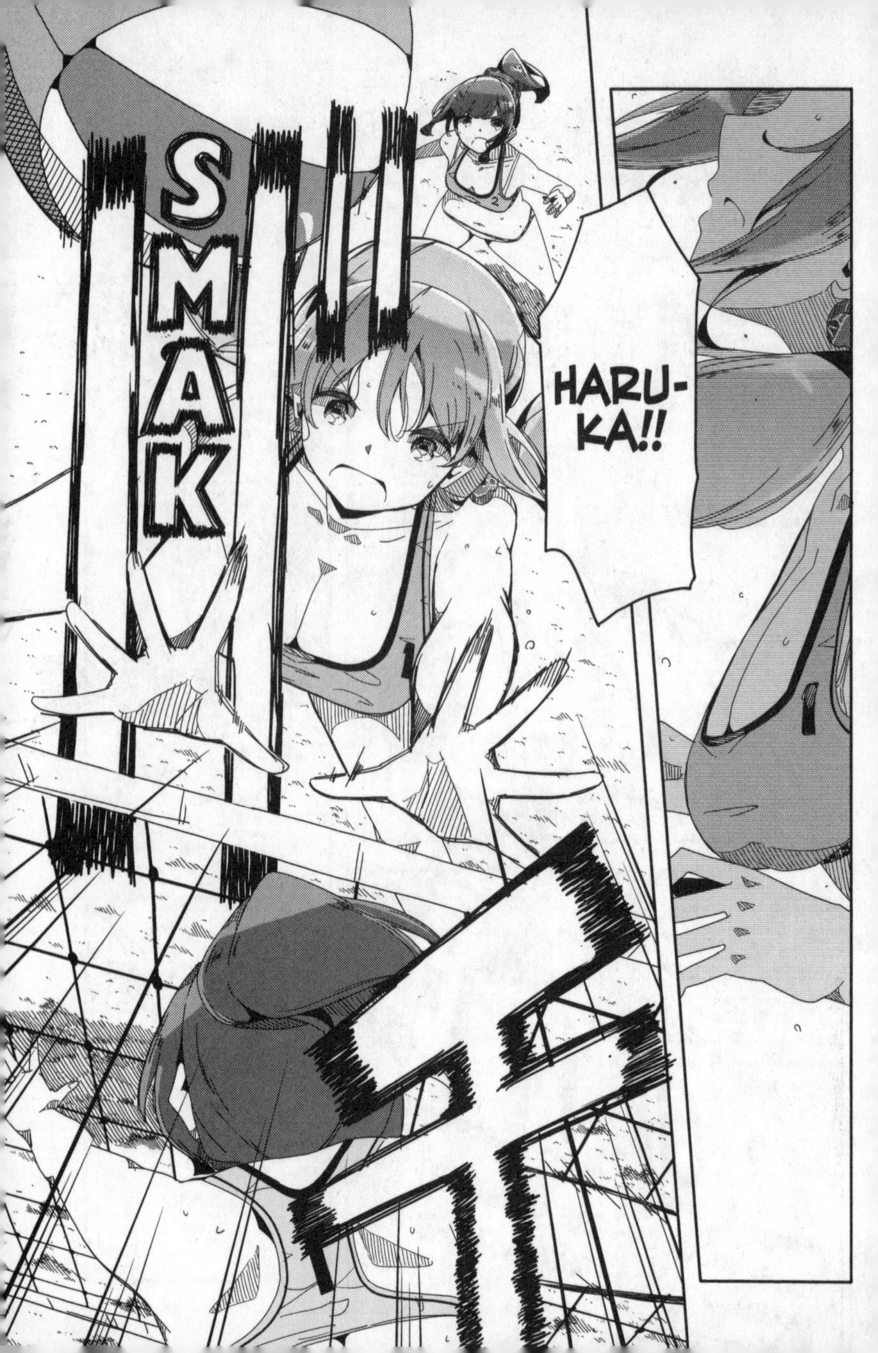
HARU-KA!!
SMAK

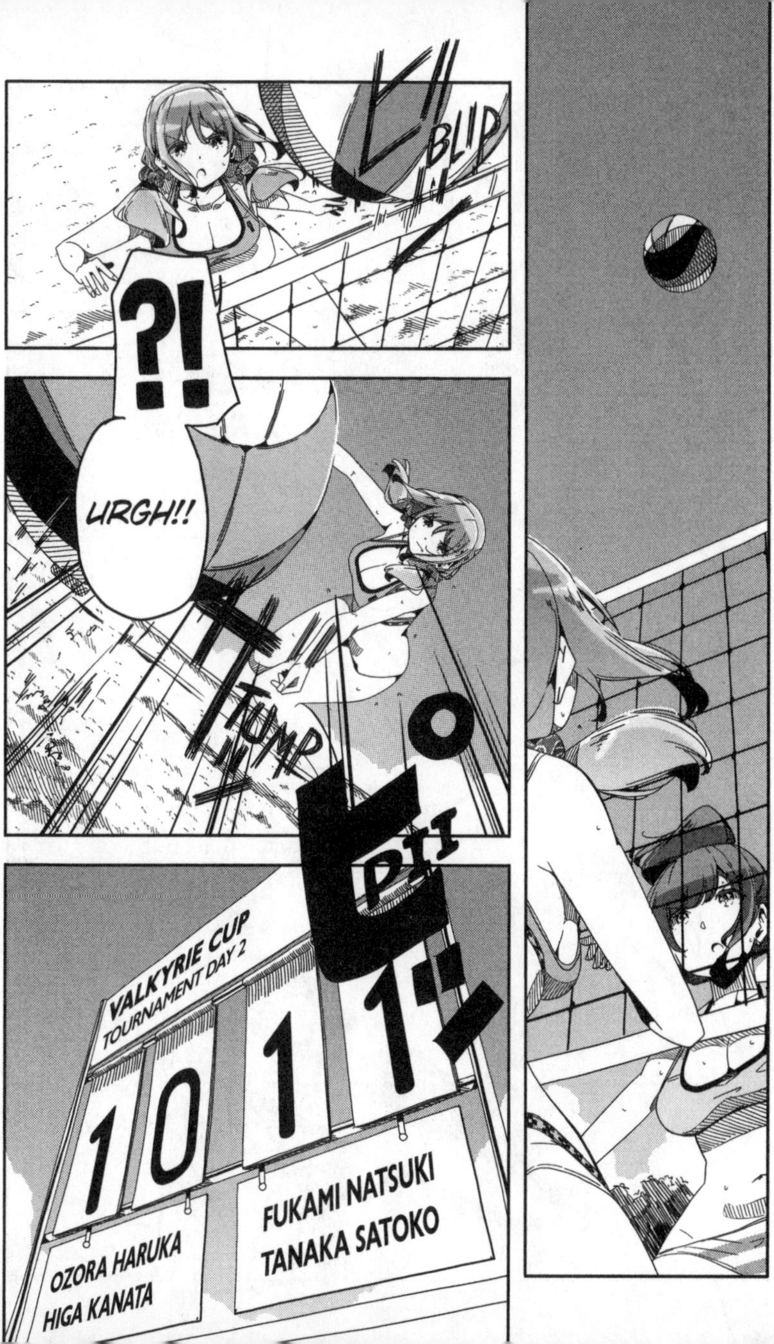
BLIP
?!
URGH!!
TUMP
PII
VALKYRIE CUP
TOURNAMENT DAY 2
11
10
FUKAMI NATSUKI
TANAKA SATOKO
OZORA HARUKA
HIGA KANATA

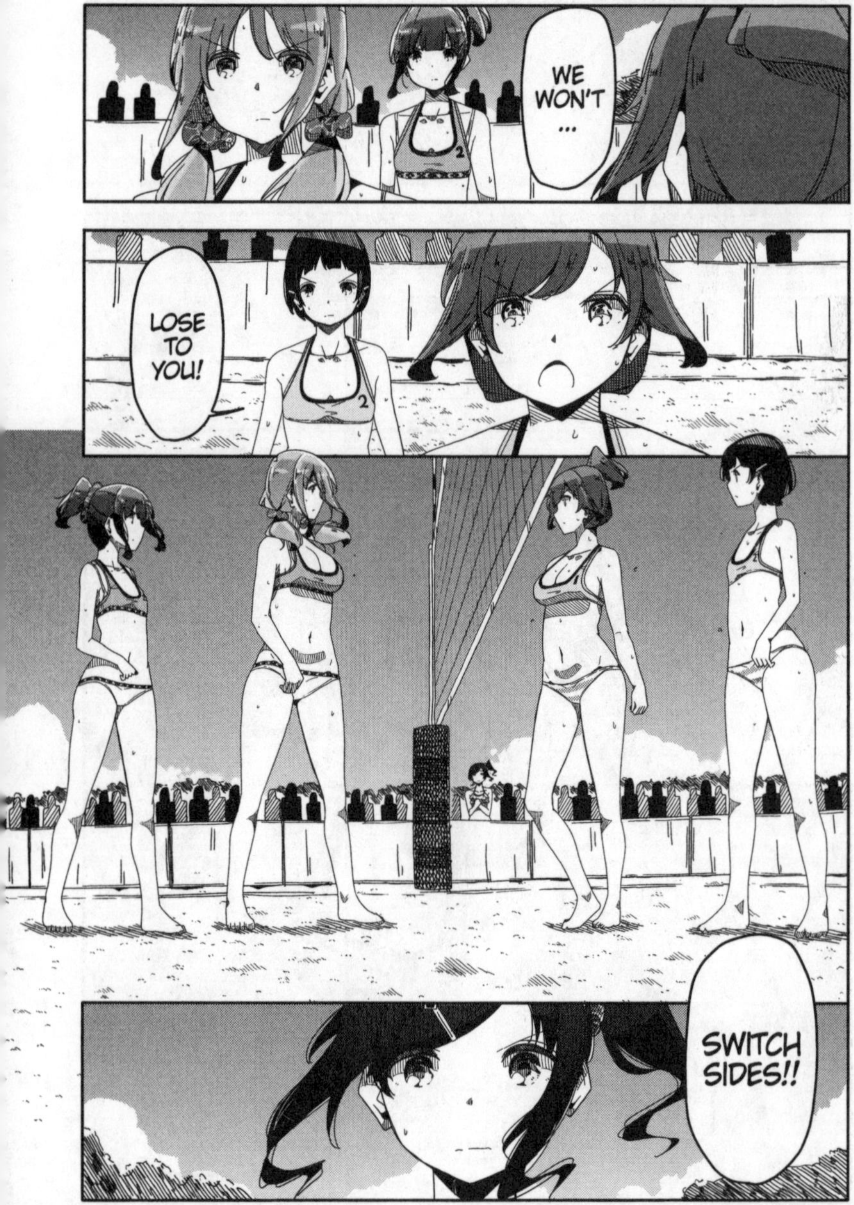
WE WON'T ...
LOSE TO YOU!
SWITCH SIDES!!

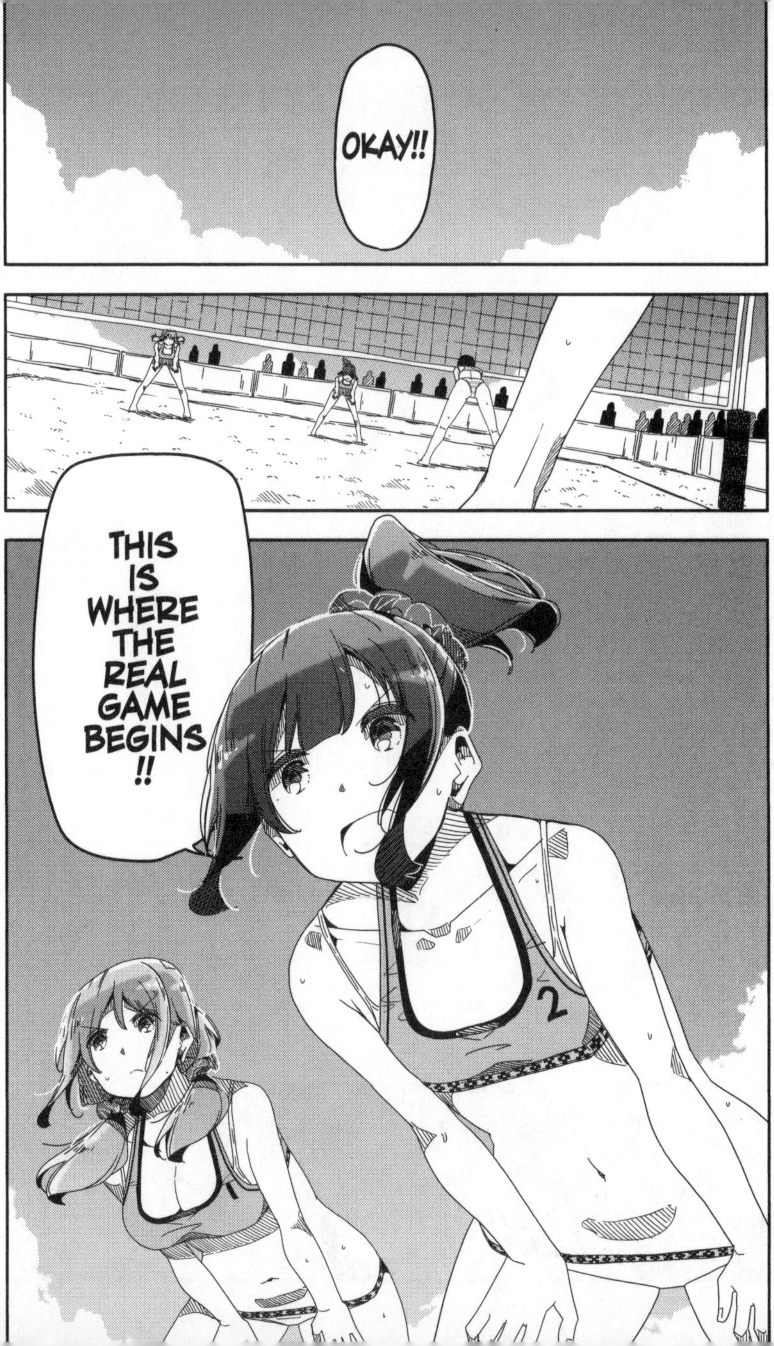
OKAY!!
THIS IS WHERE THE REAL GAME BEGINS!!

Harukana Receive

Presented by Nyoijizai

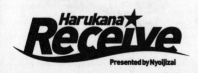

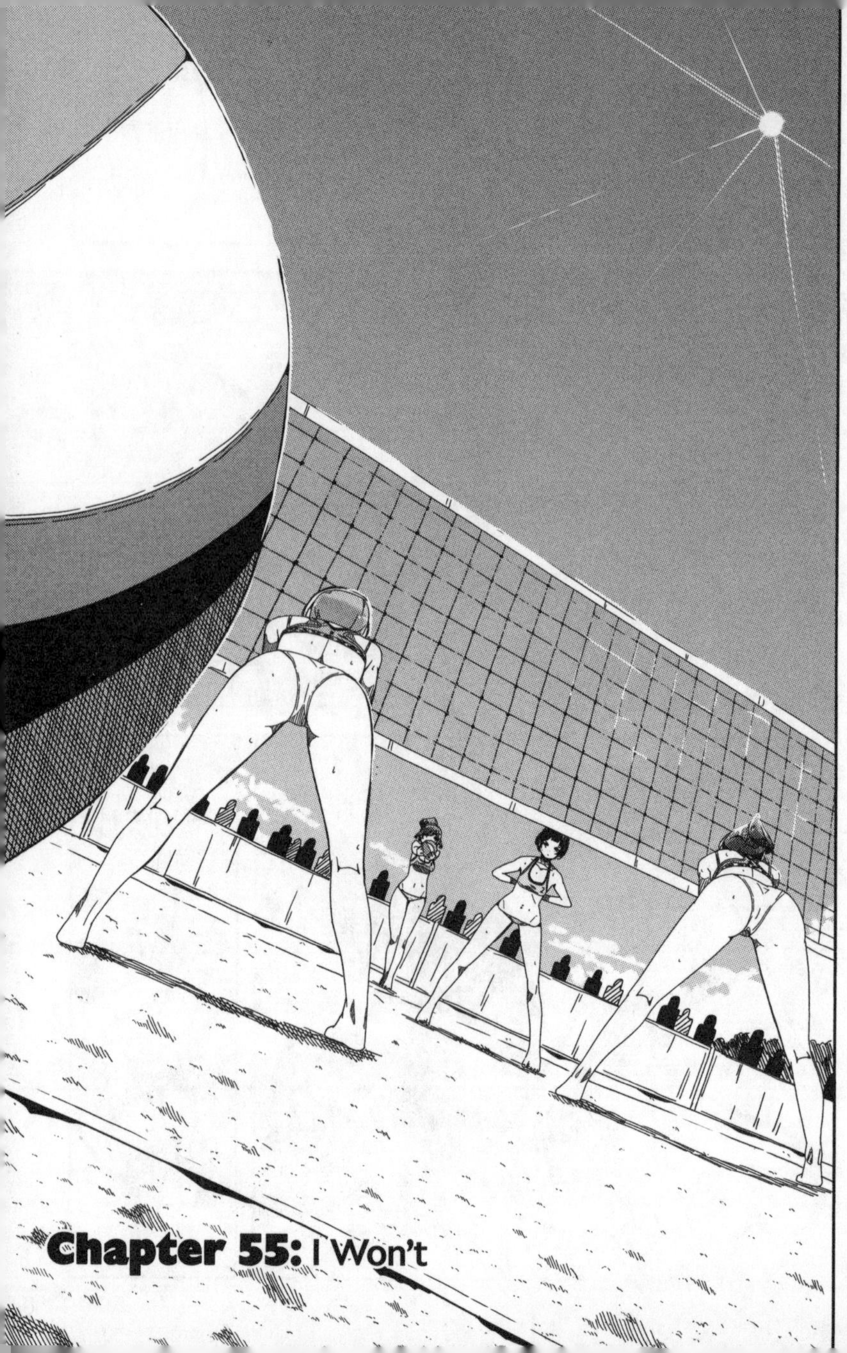

## Chapter 55: I Won't

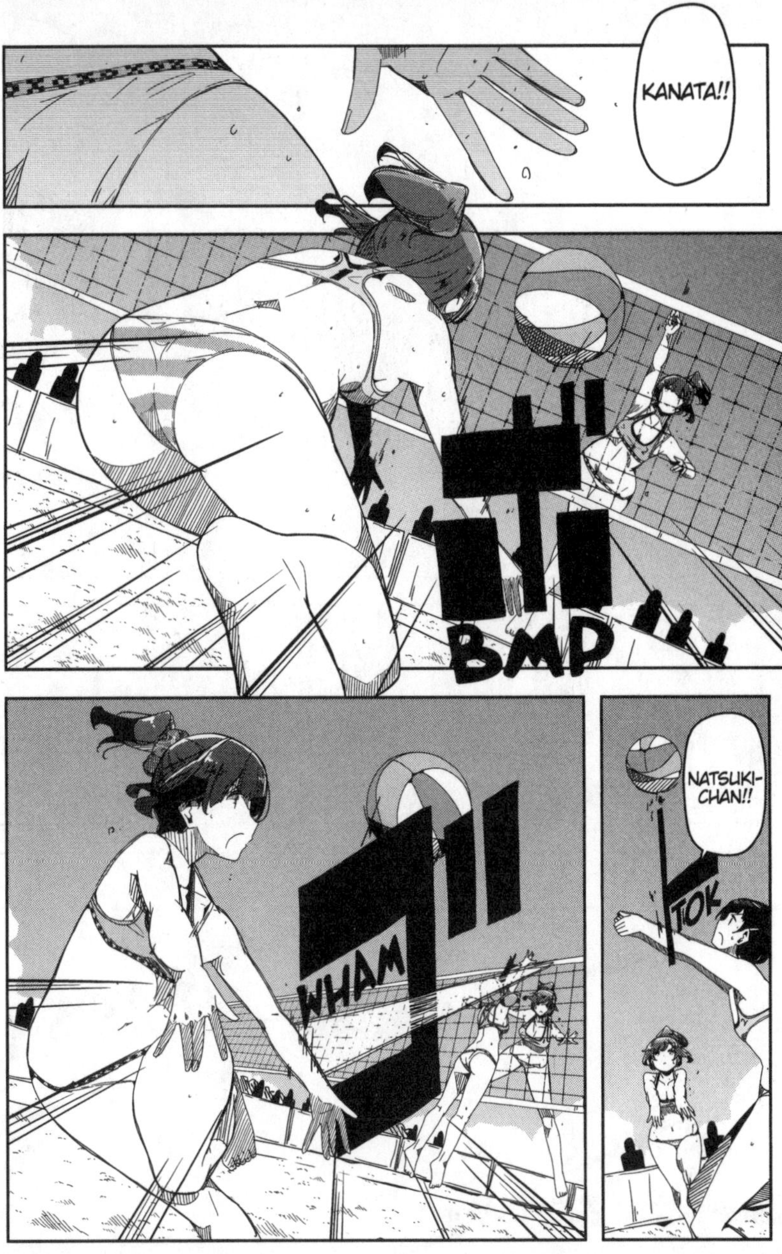
KANATA!!
BMP
NATSUKI-CHAN!!
TOK
WHAM

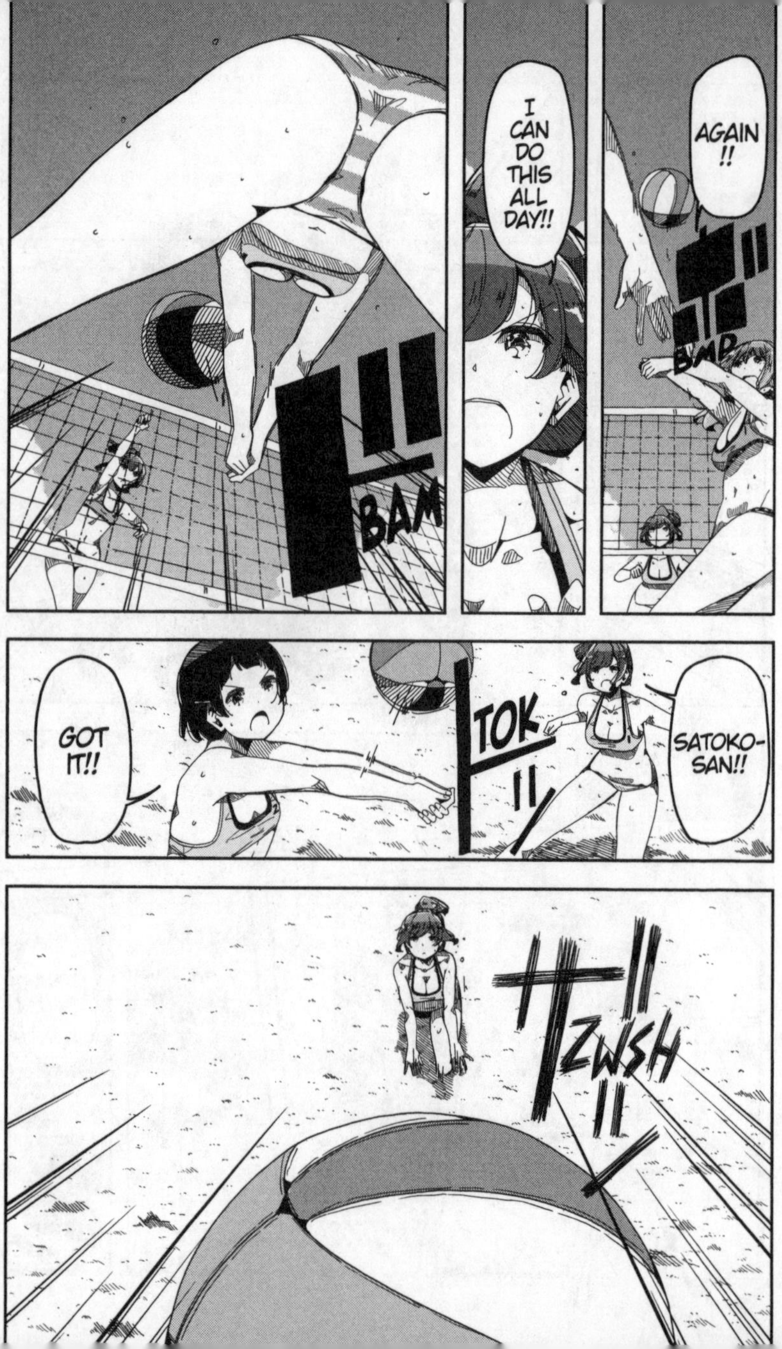
AGAIN!!
BMP
I CAN DO THIS ALL DAY!!
BAM
SATOKO-SAN!!
TOK
GOT IT!!
ZWSH

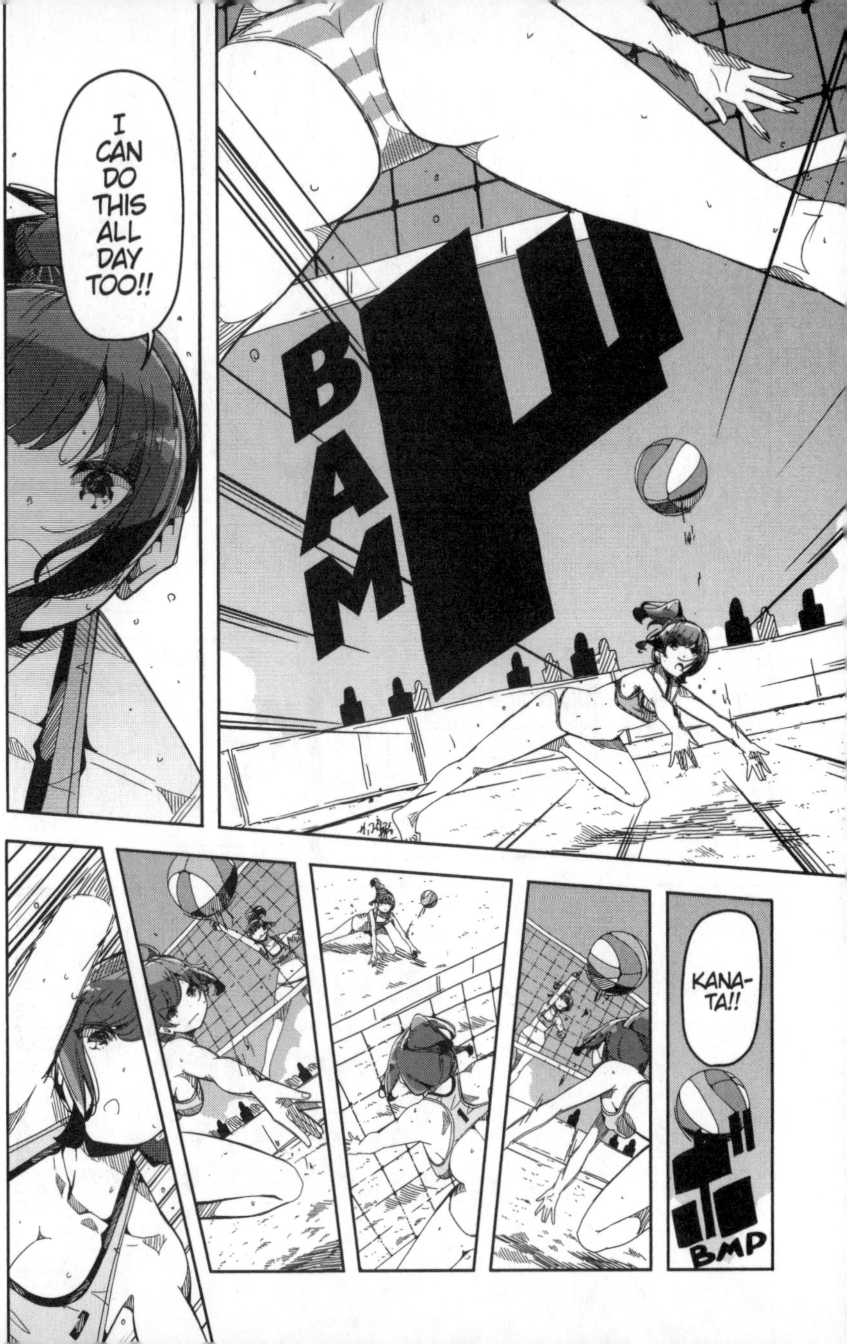
BAM
I CAN DO THIS ALL DAY TOO!!
KANA-TA!!
BMP

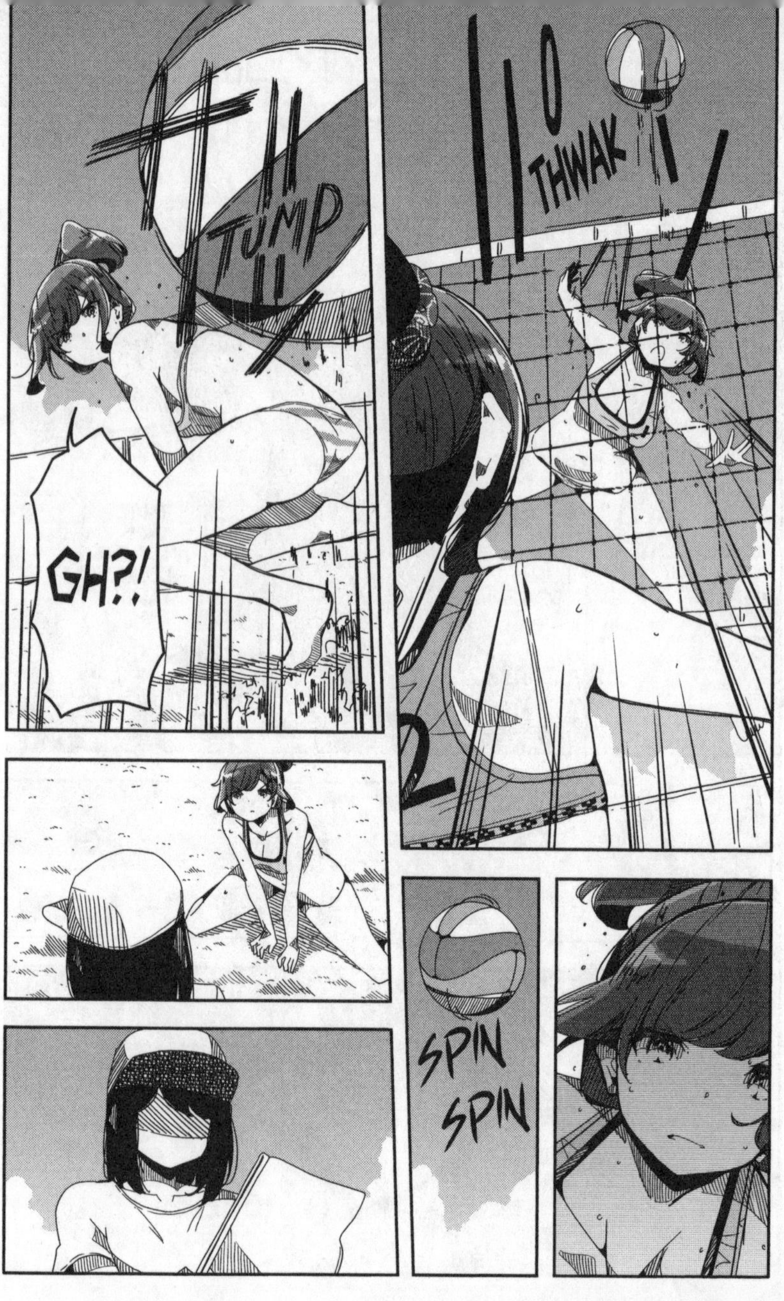
THWAK
TUMP
GH?!
SPIN
SPIN

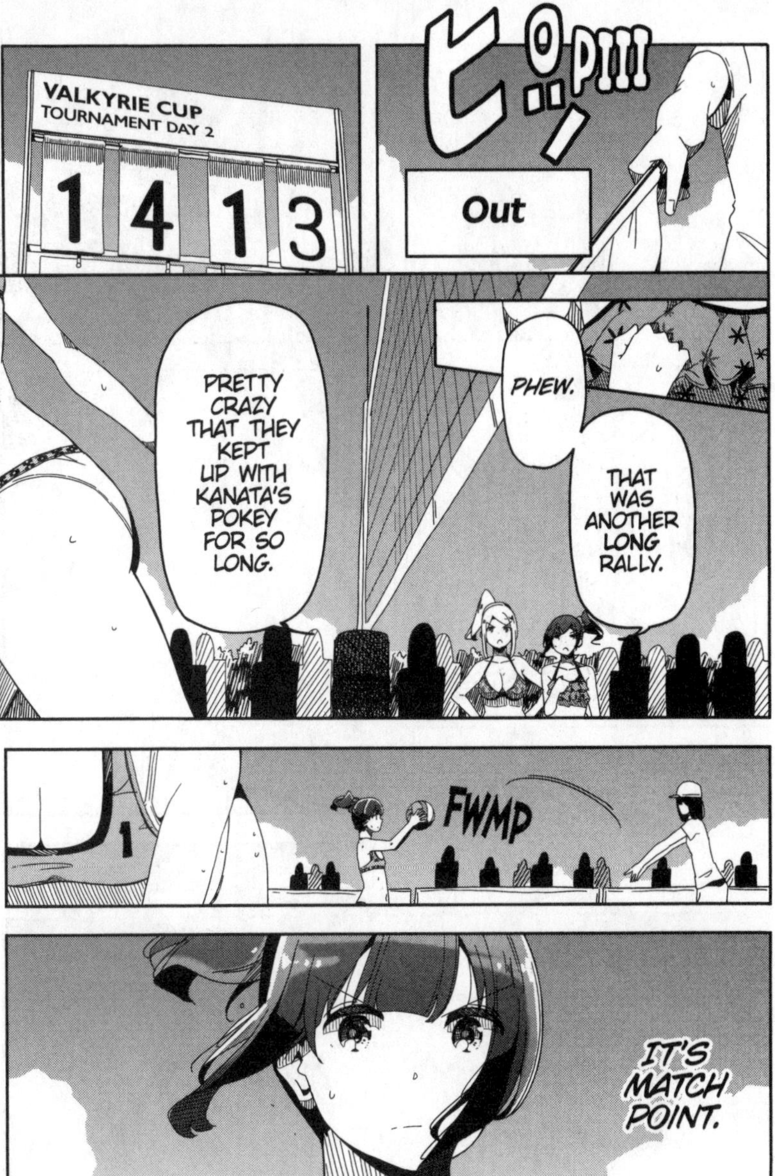
PIII
Out
VALKYRIE CUP
TOURNAMENT DAY 2
1 4 1 3
PHEW.
THAT WAS ANOTHER LONG RALLY.
PRETTY CRAZY THAT THEY KEPT UP WITH KANATA'S POKEY FOR SO LONG.
FWMP
IT'S MATCH POINT.

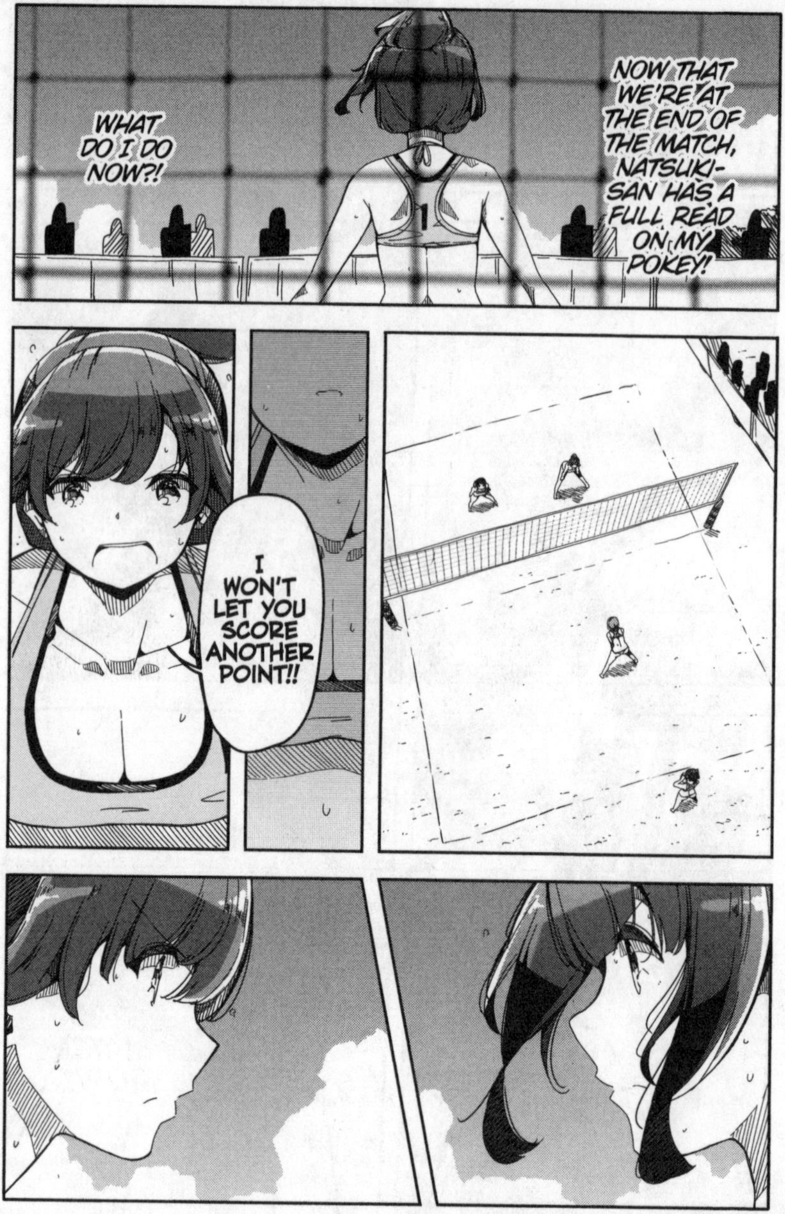
NOW THAT WE'RE AT THE END OF THE MATCH, NATSUKI-SAN HAS A FULL READ ON MY POKEY!
WHAT DO I DO NOW?!
I WON'T LET YOU SCORE ANOTHER POINT!!

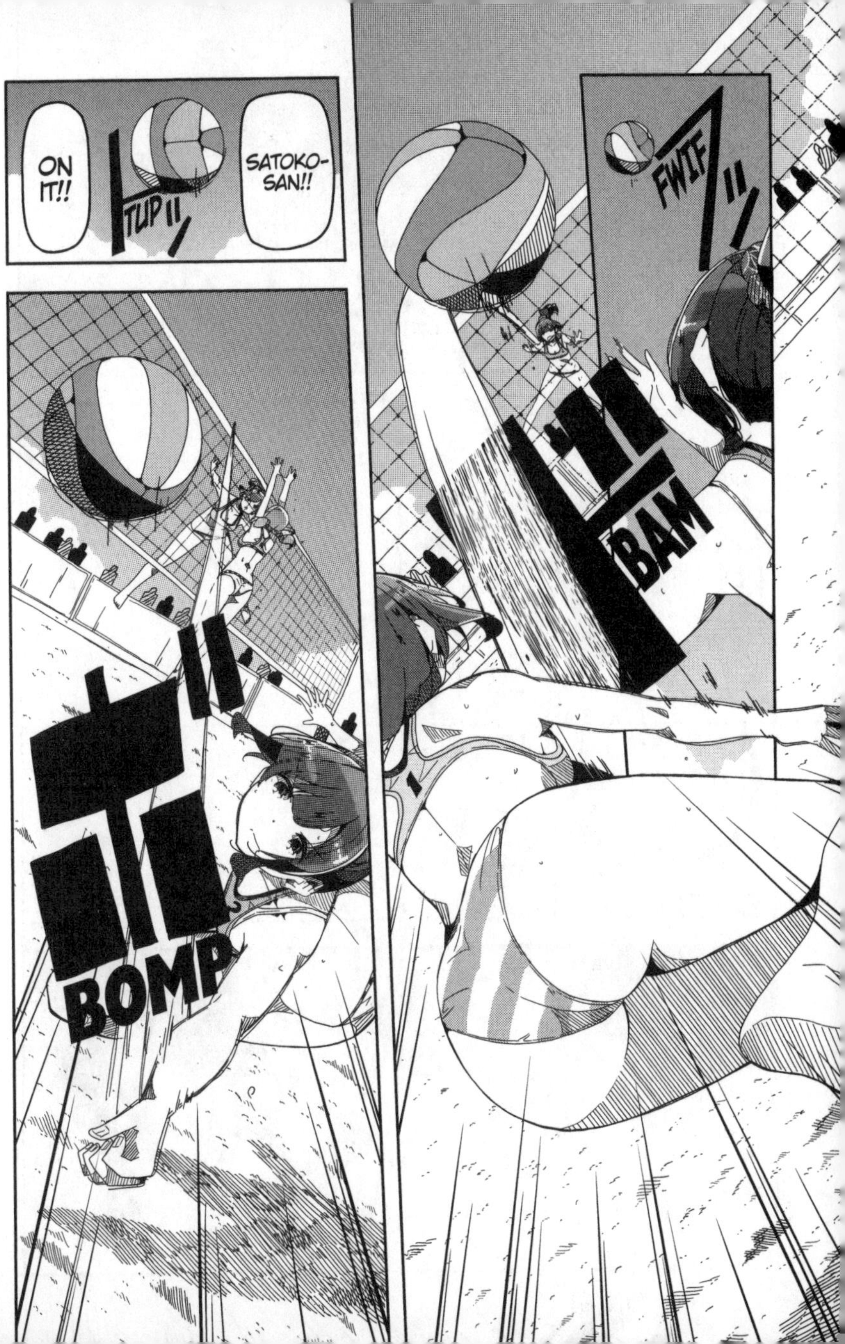
FWIF
BAM
SATOKO-SAN!!
TUP
ON IT!!
BOMP

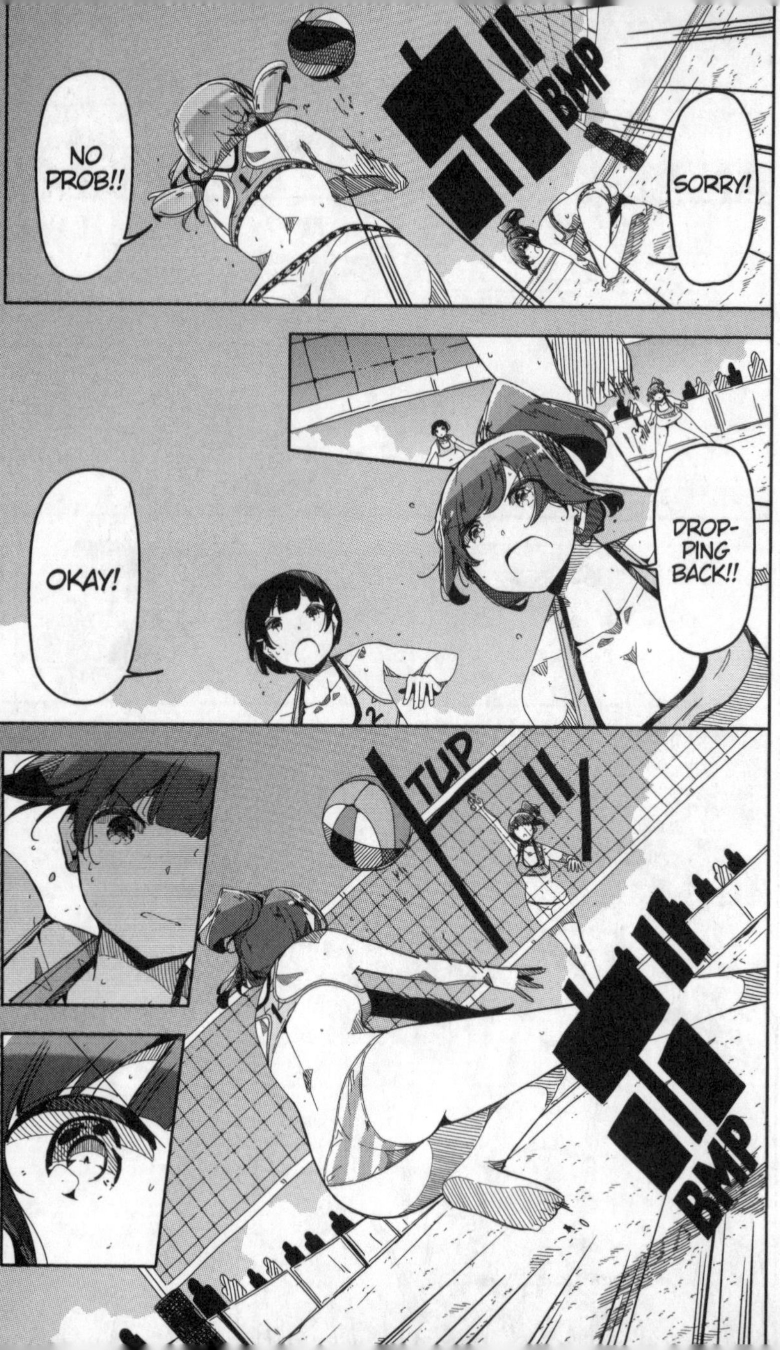
BMP
SORRY!
NO PROB!!
DROP-PING BACK!!
OKAY!
TUP
BMP

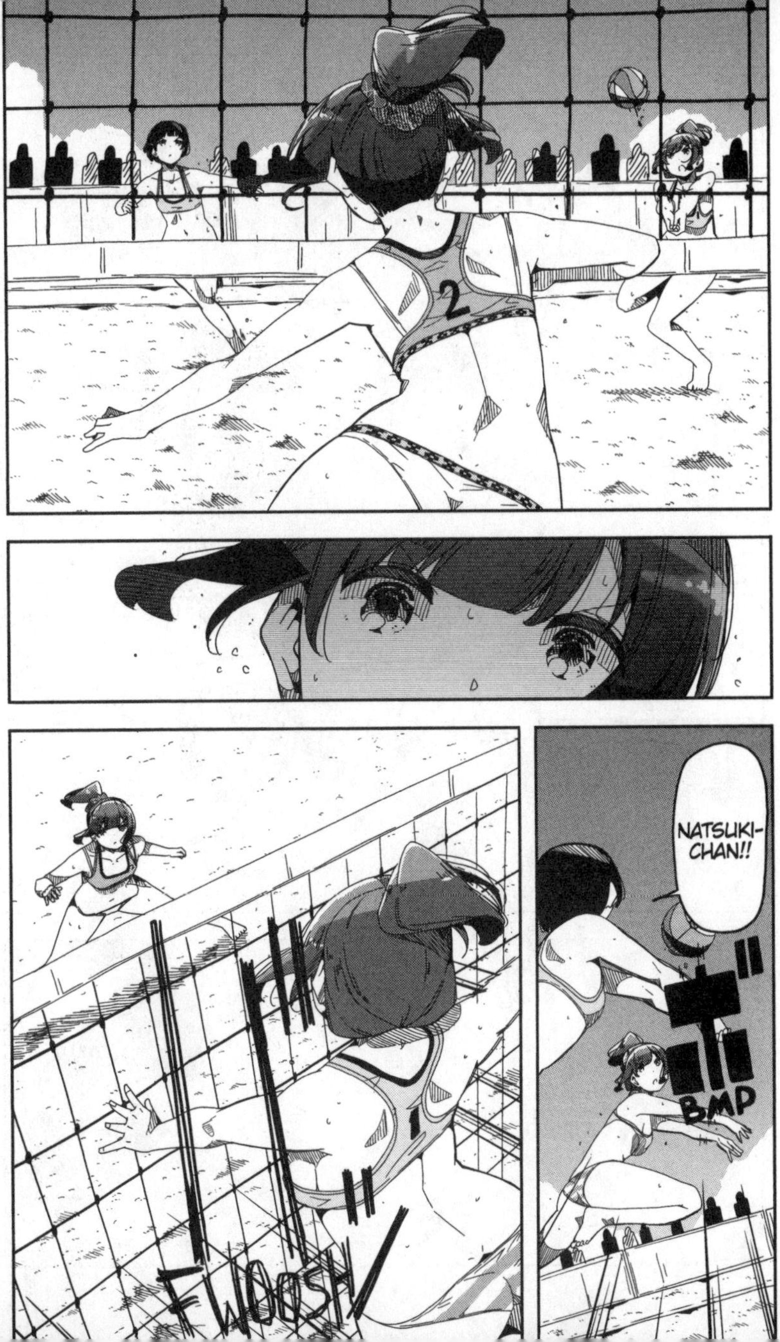
NATSUKI-CHAN!!
BMP
FWOOSH

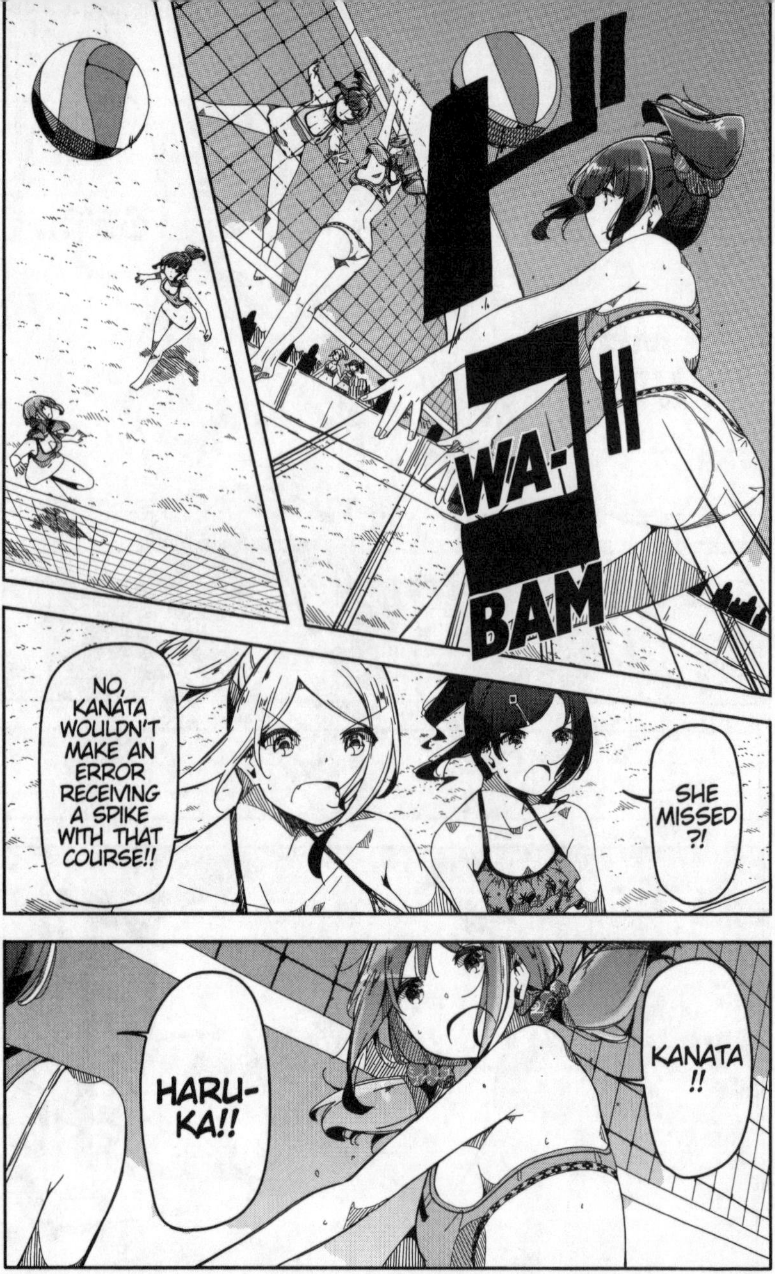
WA-
BAM
SHE MISSED ?!
NO, KANATA WOULDN'T MAKE AN ERROR RECEIVING A SPIKE WITH THAT COURSE!!
KANATA !!
HARU-KA!!

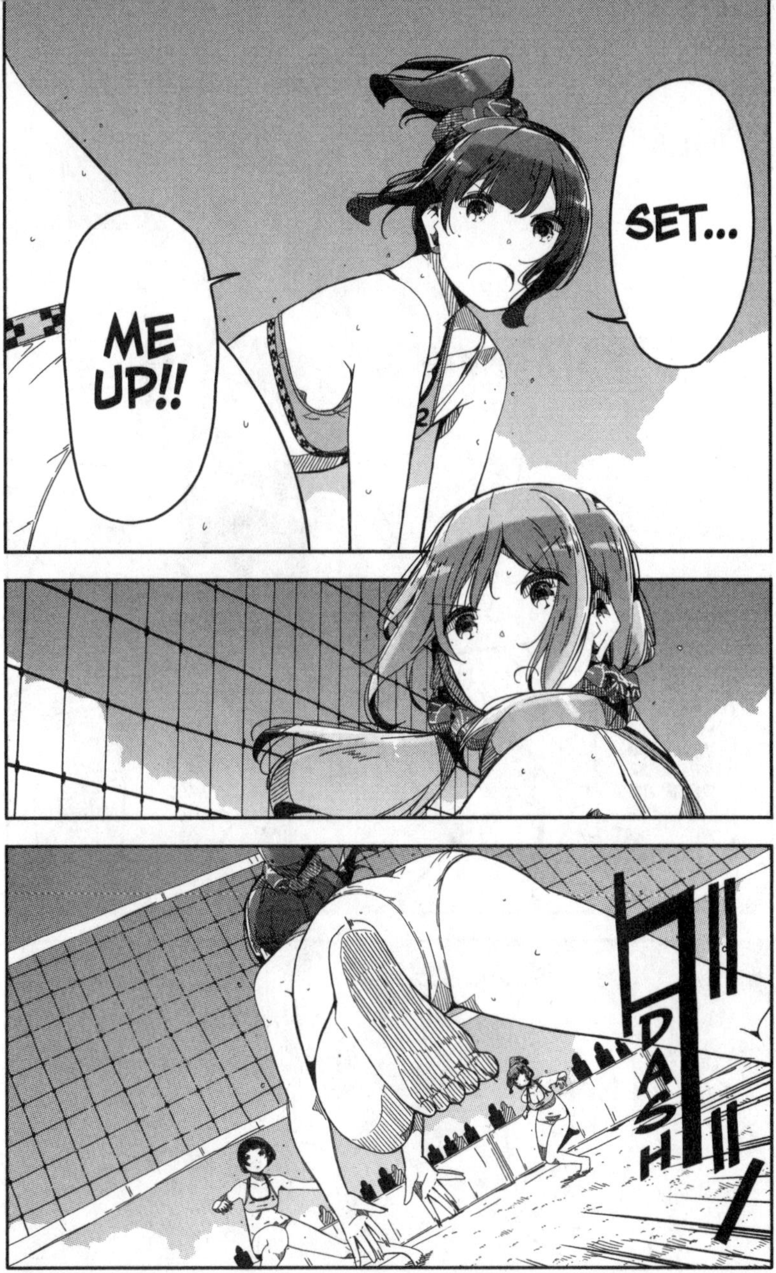
SET...
ME UP!!
DASH

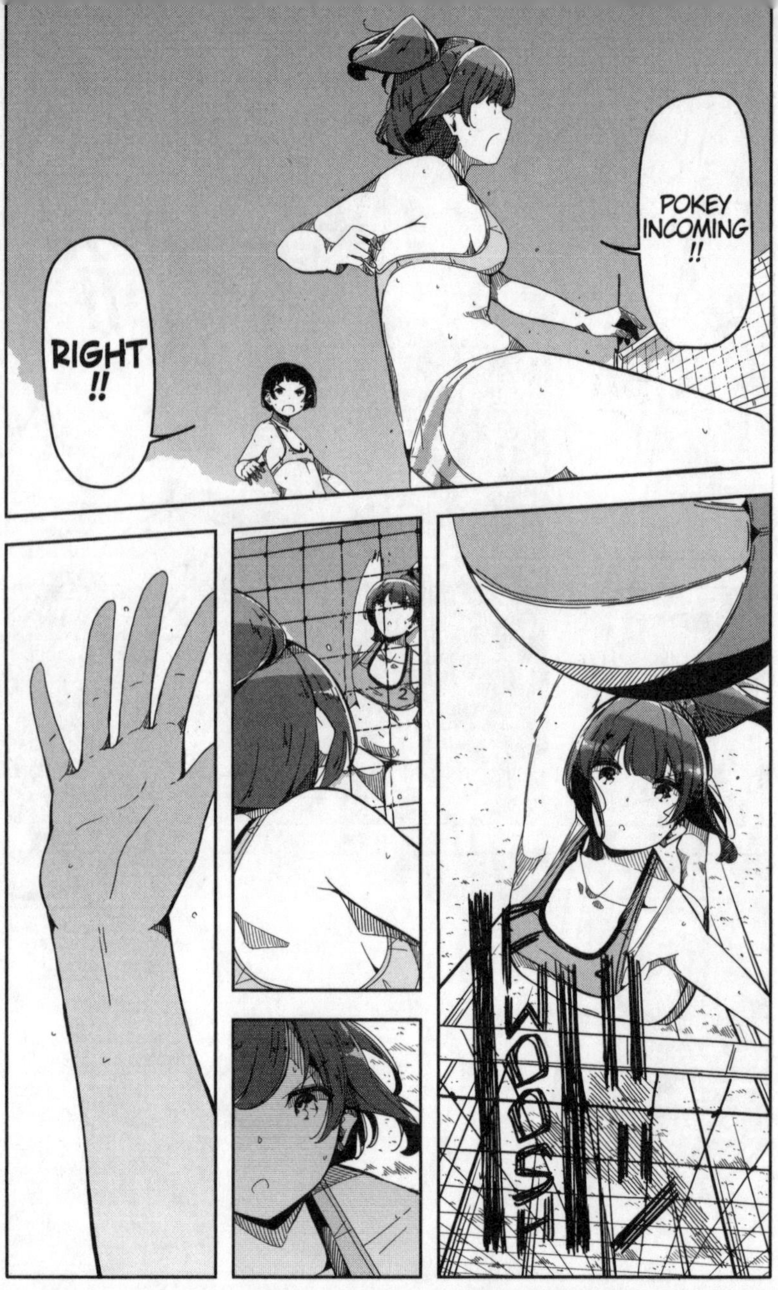
POKEY INCOMING !!
RIGHT !!
WOOSH

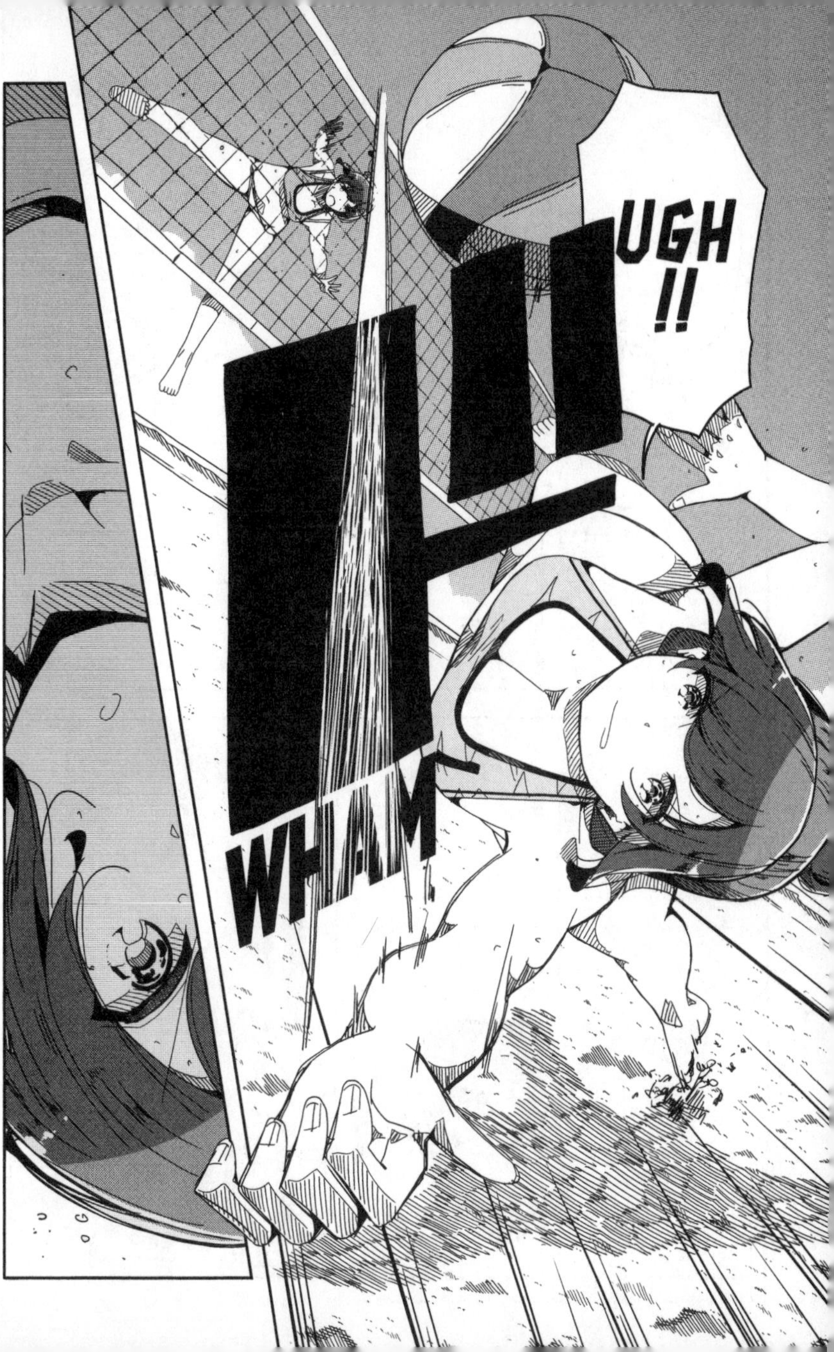
UGH !!
WHAM

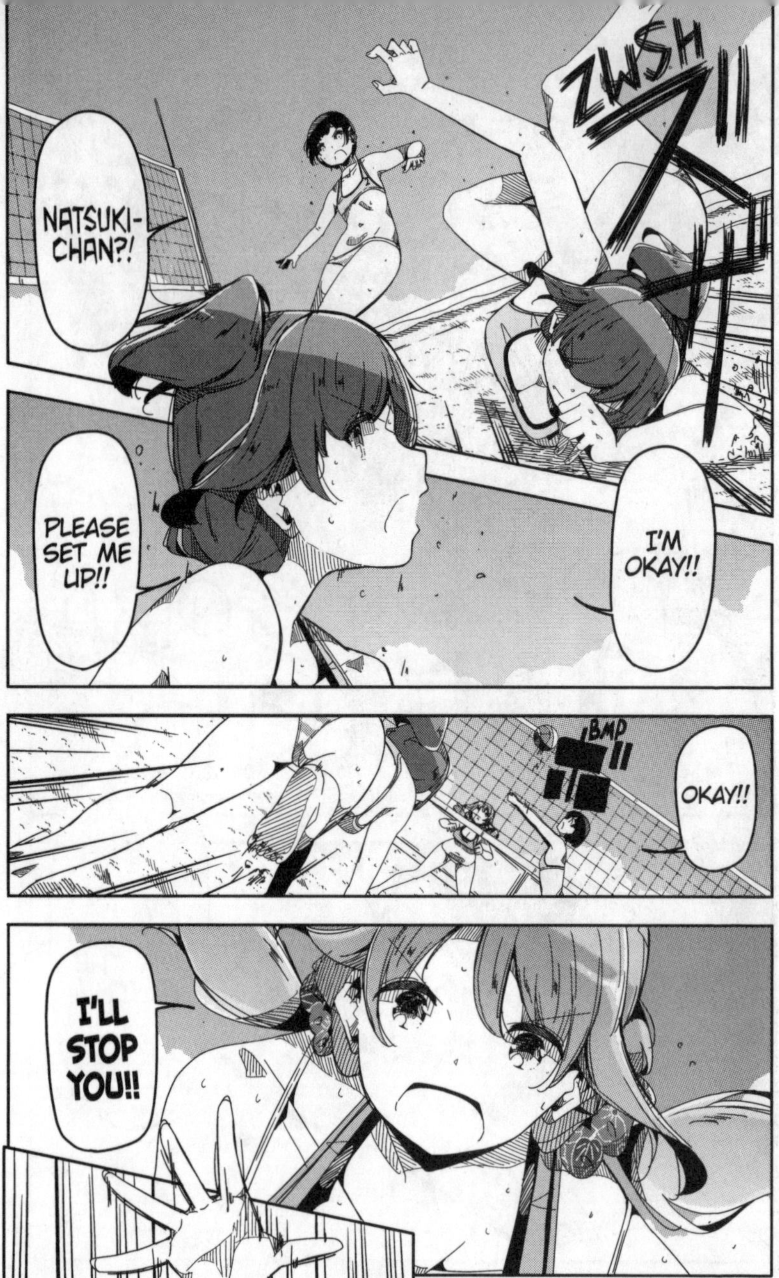
ZWSH
NATSUKI-CHAN?!
I'M OKAY!!
PLEASE SET ME UP!!
BMP
OKAY!!
I'LL STOP YOU!!

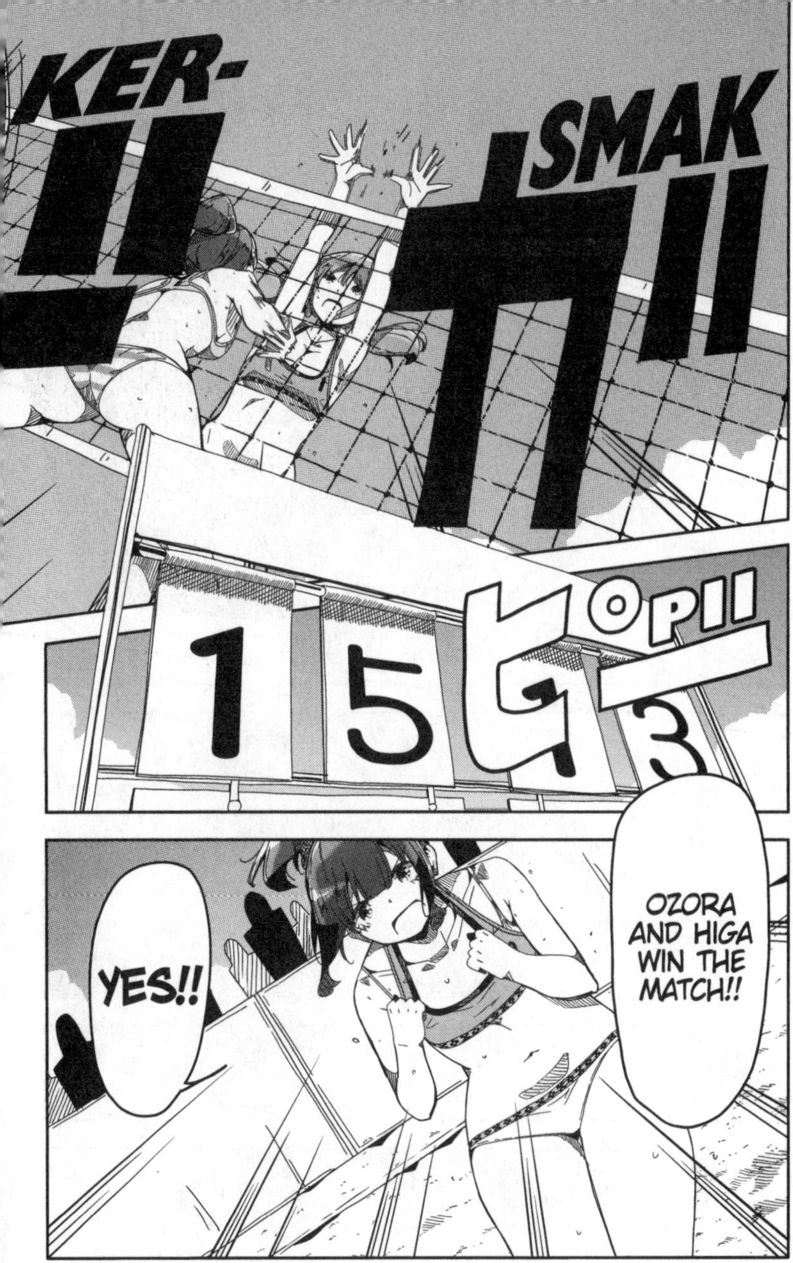
KER-
SMAK
15
3
PII
OZORA AND HIGA WIN THE MATCH!!
YES!!

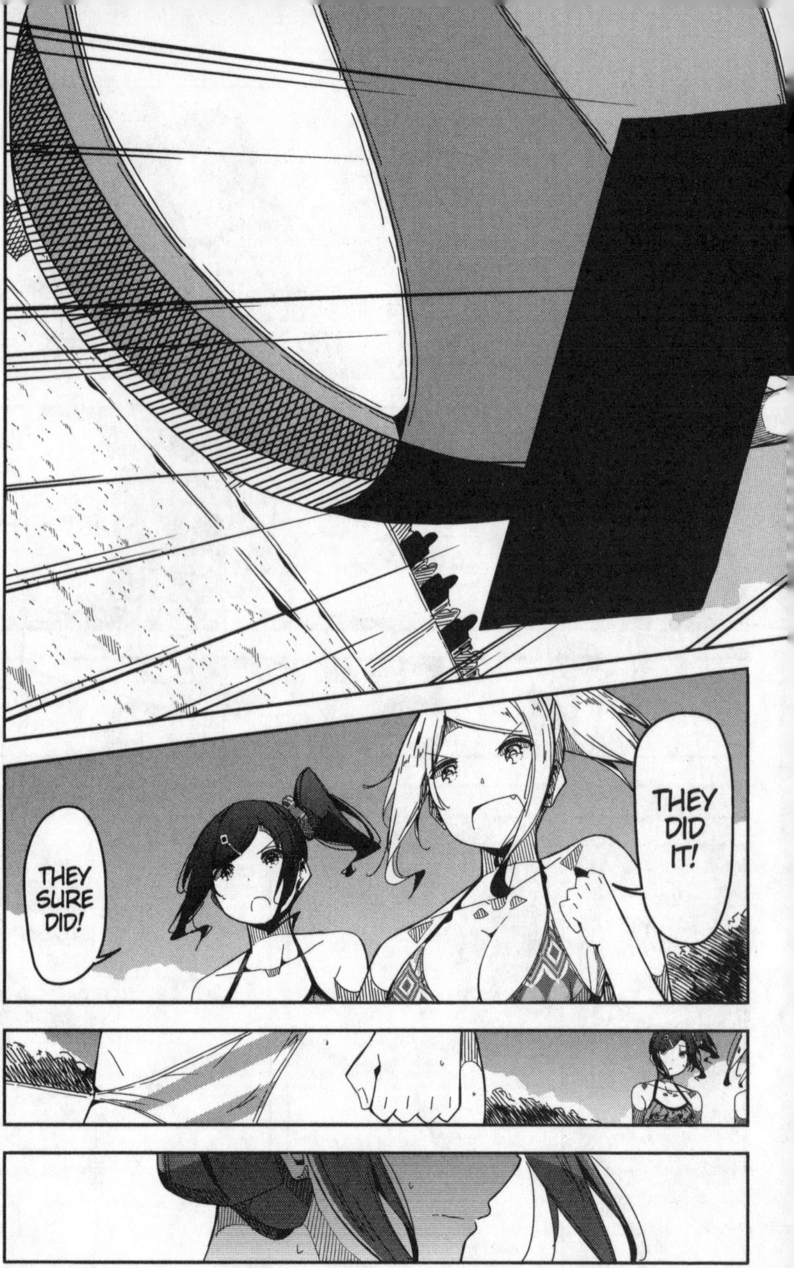
THEY DID IT!
THEY SURE DID!

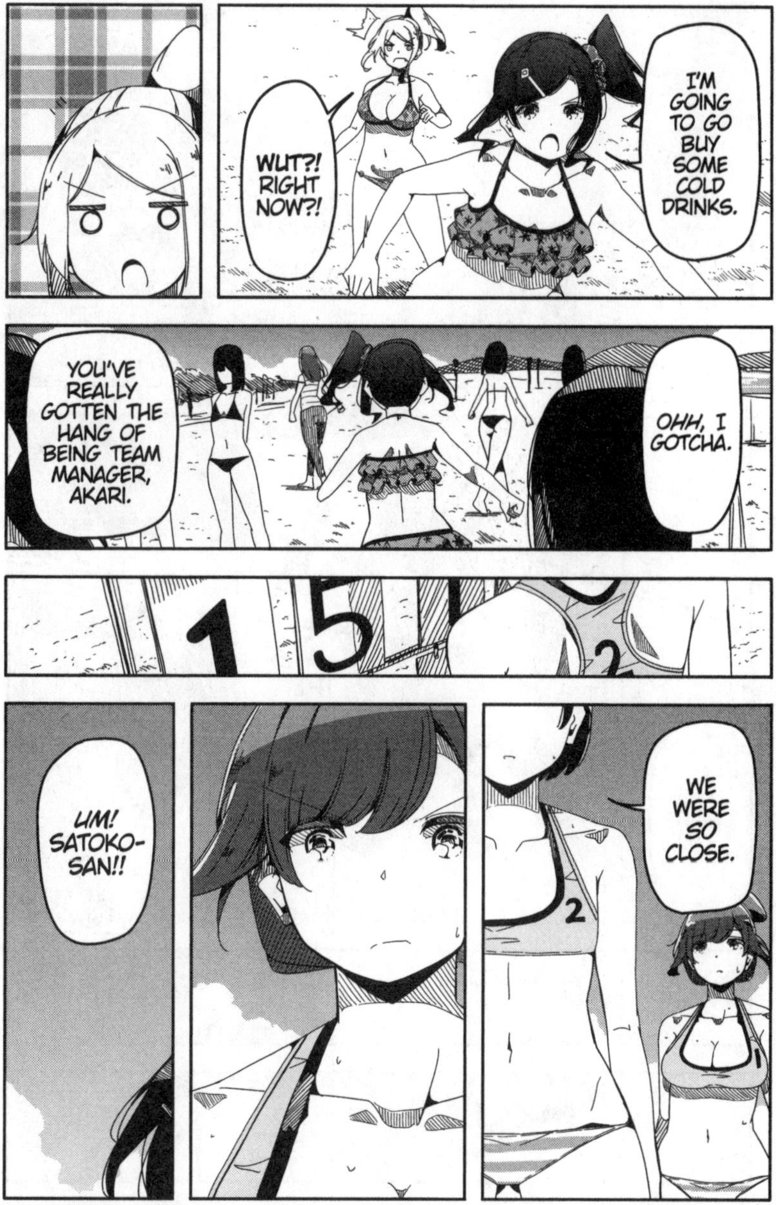
I'M GOING TO GO BUY SOME COLD DRINKS.
WUT?! RIGHT NOW?!
OHH, I GOTCHA.
YOU'VE REALLY GOTTEN THE HANG OF BEING TEAM MANAGER, AKARI.
WE WERE SO CLOSE.
UM! SATOKO-SAN!!

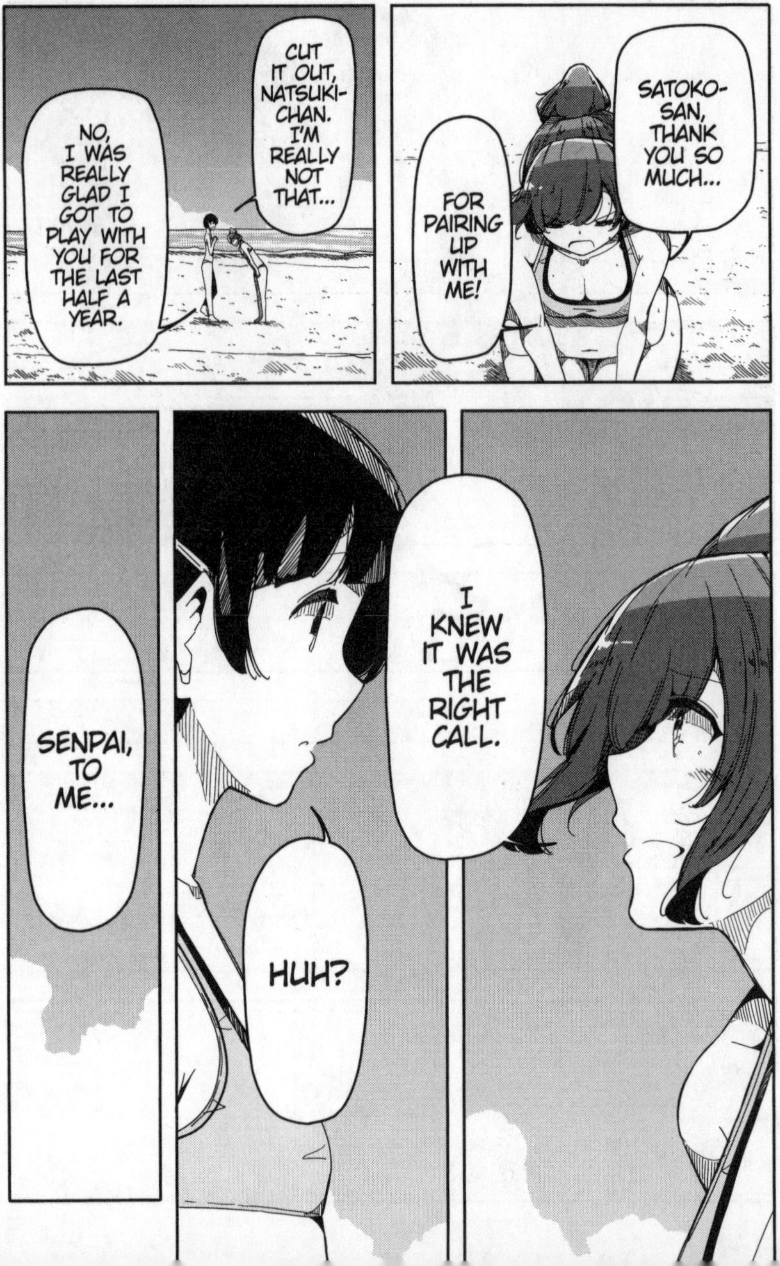
SATOKO-SAN, THANK YOU SO MUCH...
FOR PAIRING UP WITH ME!
CUT IT OUT, NATSUKI-CHAN. I'M REALLY NOT THAT...
NO, I WAS REALLY GLAD I GOT TO PLAY WITH YOU FOR THE LAST HALF A YEAR.
I KNEW IT WAS THE RIGHT CALL.
HUH?
SENPAI, TO ME...

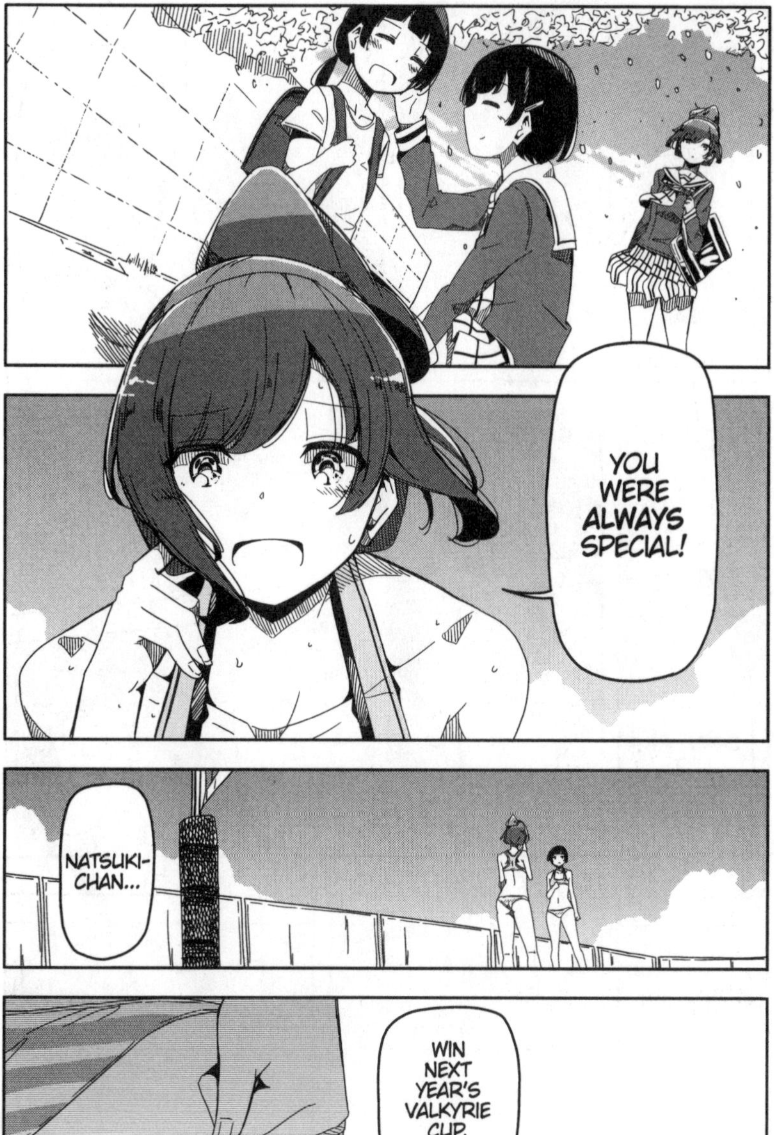
YOU WERE ALWAYS SPECIAL!
NATSUKI-CHAN...
WIN NEXT YEAR'S VALKYRIE CUP, OKAY?

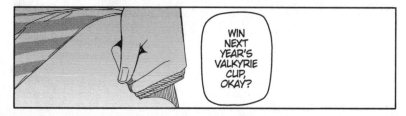

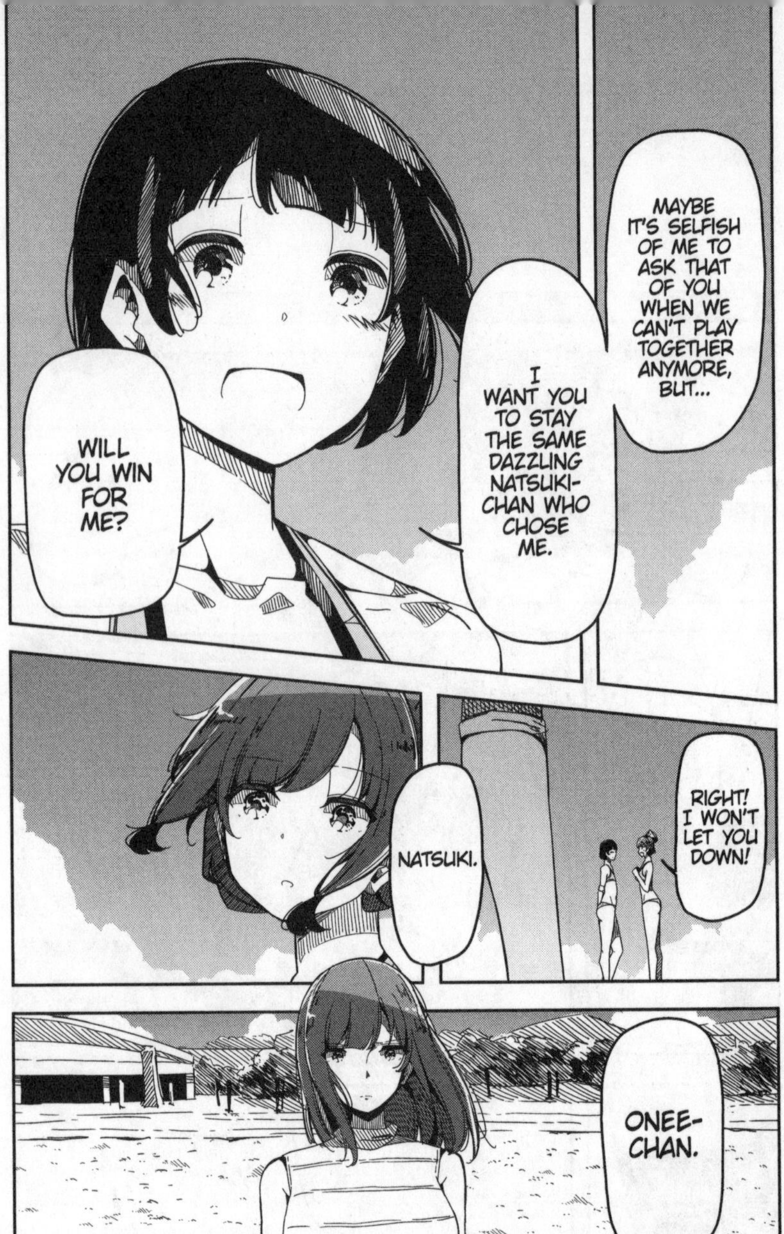
MAYBE IT'S SELFISH OF ME TO ASK THAT OF YOU WHEN WE CAN'T PLAY TOGETHER ANYMORE, BUT...
I WANT YOU TO STAY THE SAME DAZZLING NATSUKI-CHAN WHO CHOSE ME.
WILL YOU WIN FOR ME?
RIGHT! I WON'T LET YOU DOWN!
NATSUKI.
ONEE-CHAN.

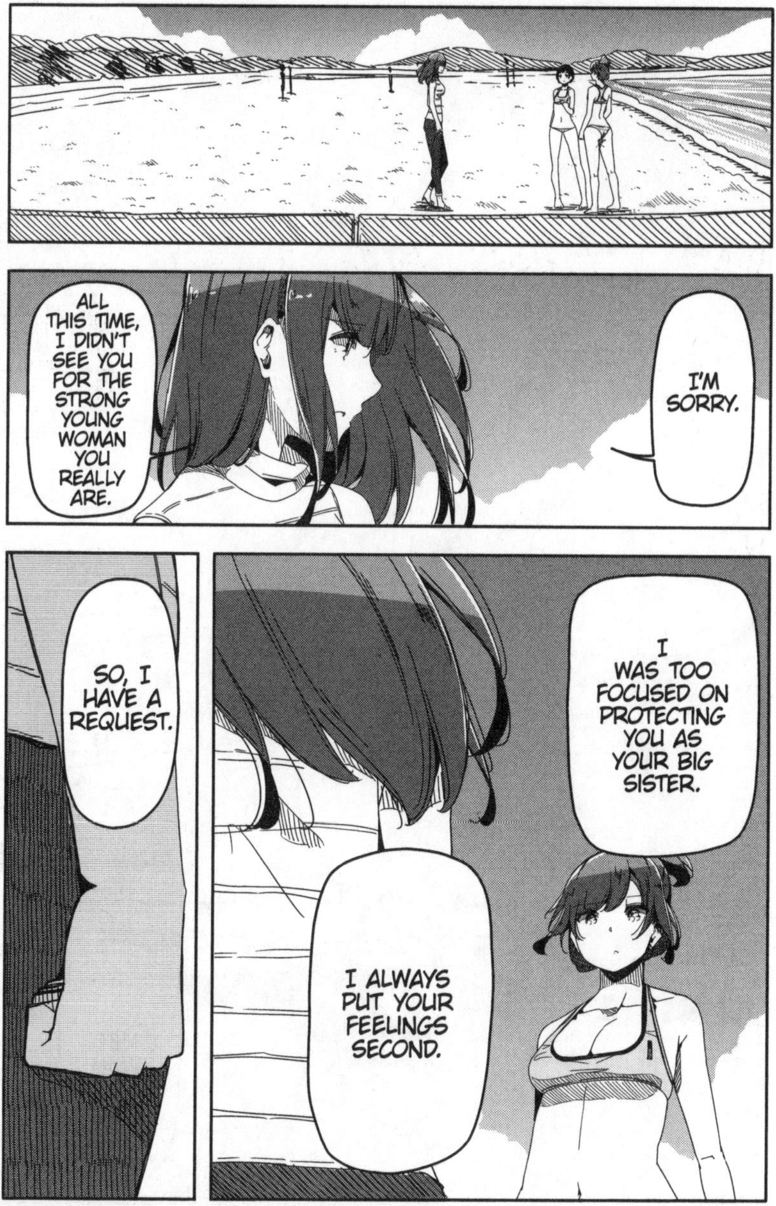
I'M SORRY.
ALL THIS TIME, I DIDN'T SEE YOU FOR THE STRONG YOUNG WOMAN YOU REALLY ARE.
I WAS TOO FOCUSED ON PROTECTING YOU AS YOUR BIG SISTER.
I ALWAYS PUT YOUR FEELINGS SECOND.
SO, I HAVE A REQUEST.

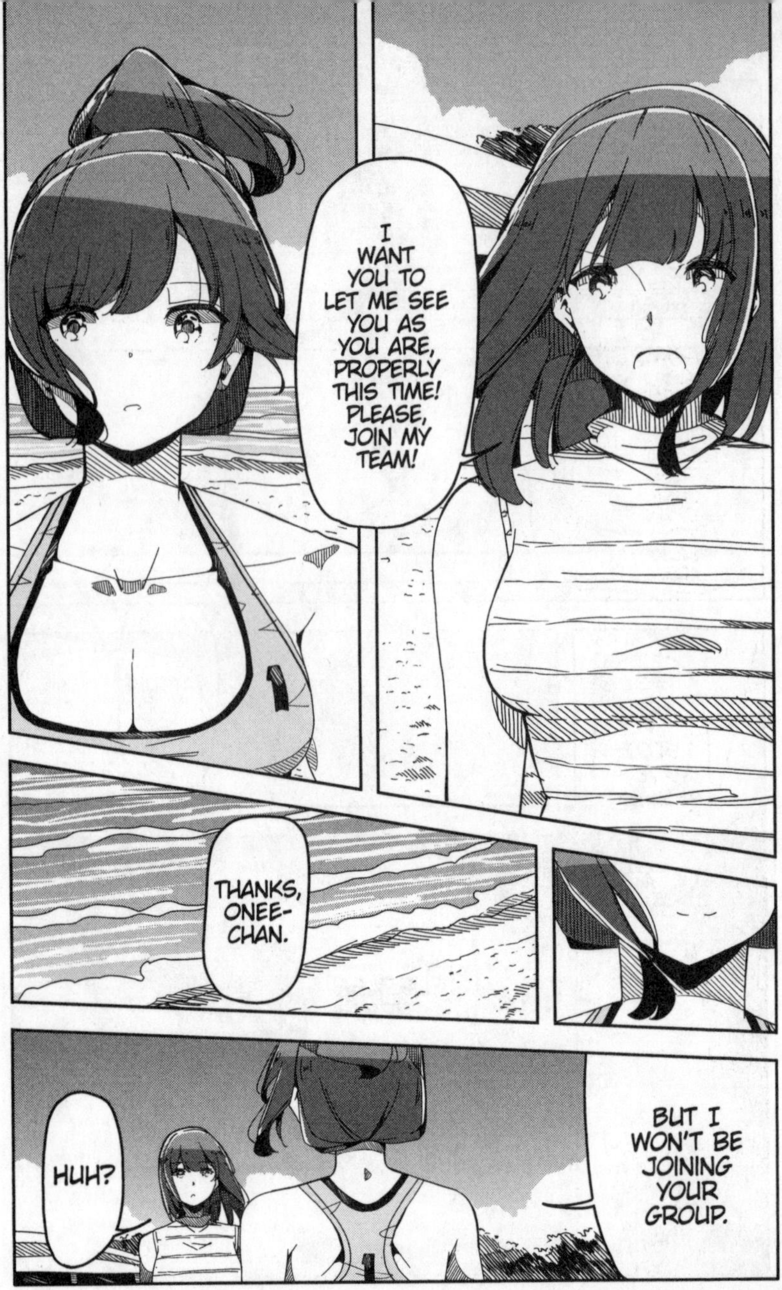
I WANT YOU TO LET ME SEE YOU AS YOU ARE, PROPERLY THIS TIME! PLEASE, JOIN MY TEAM!
THANKS, ONEE-CHAN.
BUT I WON'T BE JOINING YOUR GROUP.
HUH?

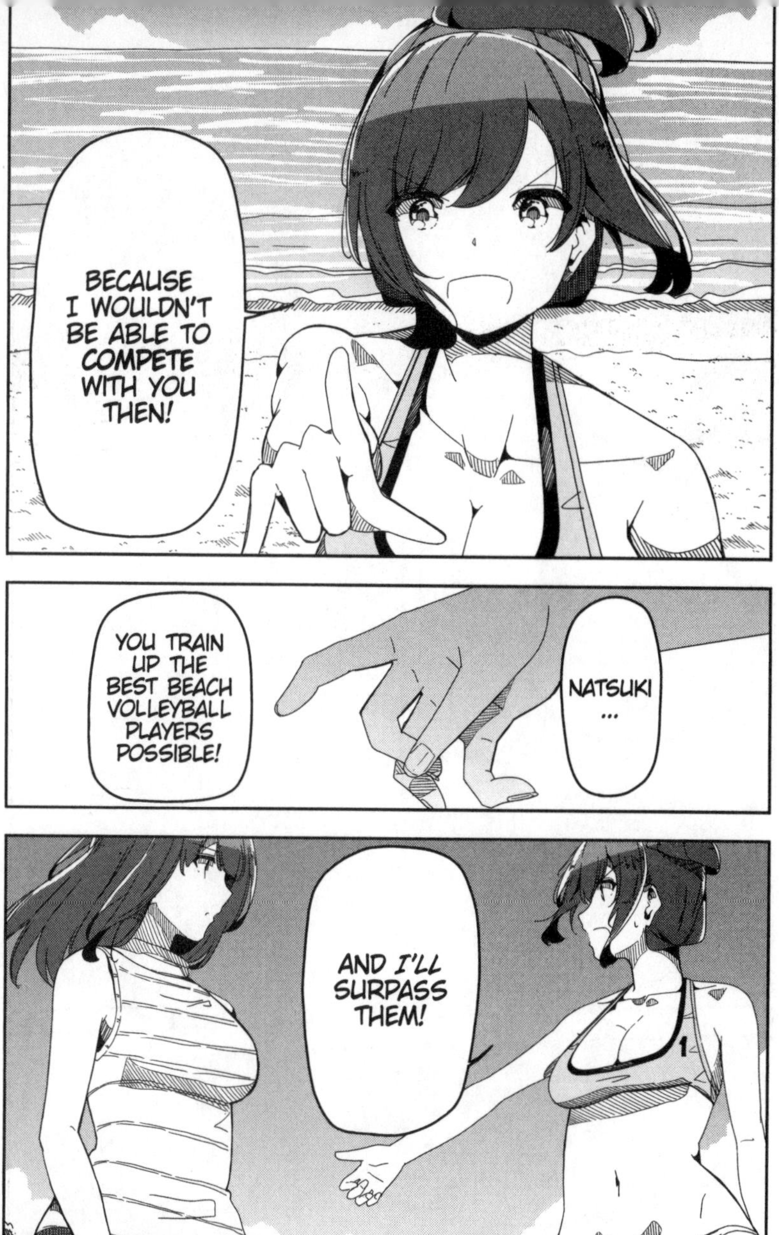
BECAUSE I WOULDN'T BE ABLE TO COMPETE WITH YOU THEN!
NATSUKI ...
YOU TRAIN UP THE BEST BEACH VOLLEYBALL PLAYERS POSSIBLE!
AND I'LL SURPASS THEM!

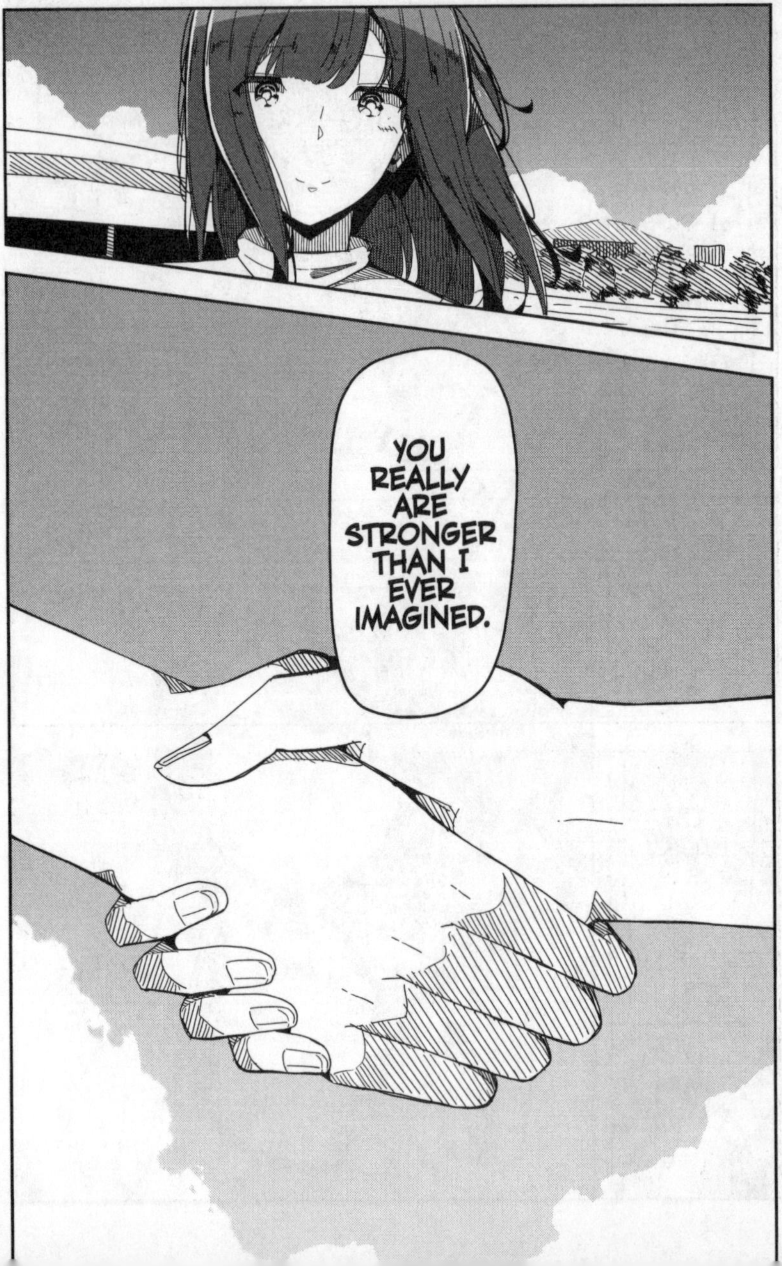
YOU REALLY ARE STRONGER THAN I EVER IMAGINED.

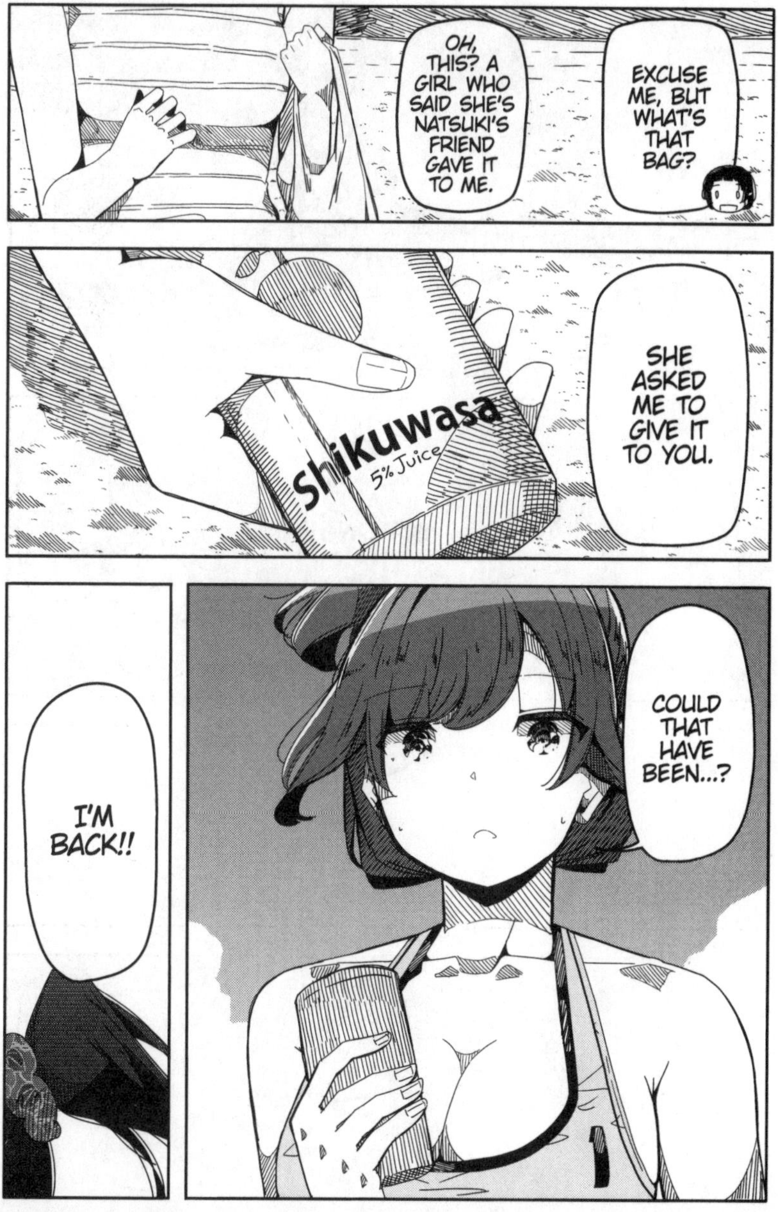
EXCUSE ME, BUT WHAT'S THAT BAG?
OH, THIS? A GIRL WHO SAID SHE'S NATSUKI'S FRIEND GAVE IT TO ME.
SHE ASKED ME TO GIVE IT TO YOU.
Shikuwasa
5% Juice
COULD THAT HAVE BEEN...?
I'M BACK!!

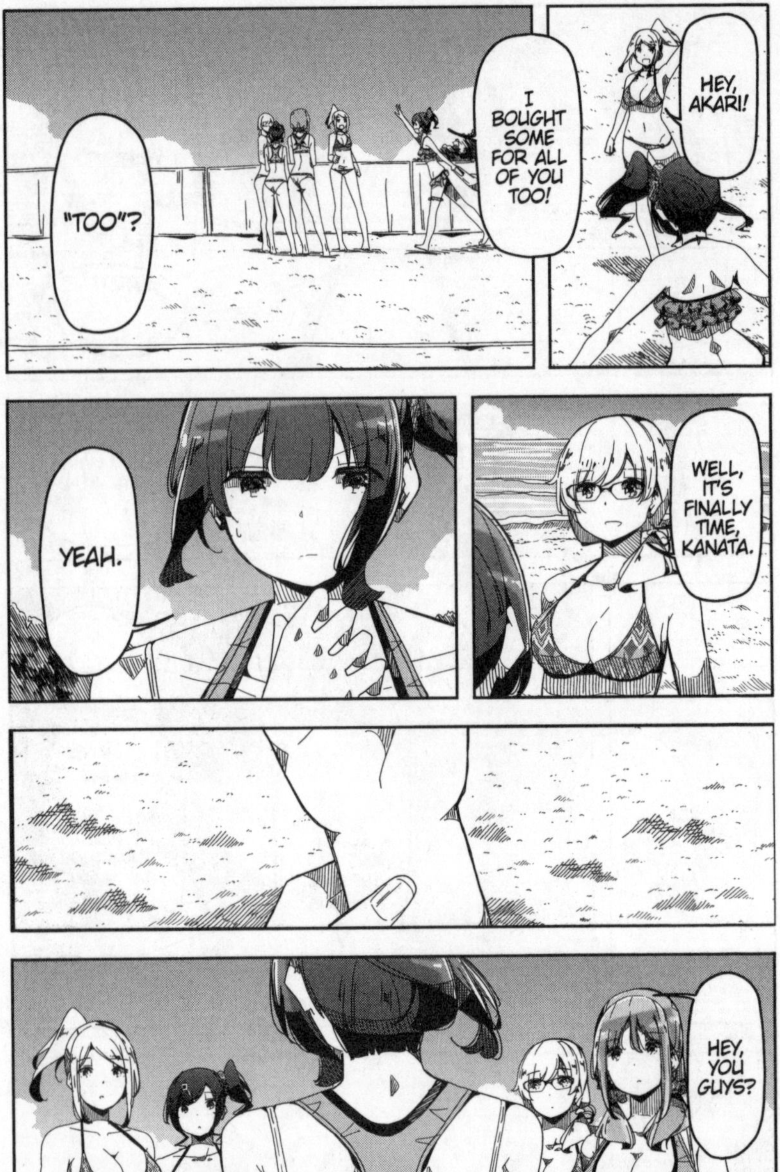
HEY, AKARI!
I BOUGHT SOME FOR ALL OF YOU TOO!
"TOO"?
WELL, IT'S FINALLY TIME, KANATA.
YEAH.
HEY, YOU GUYS?

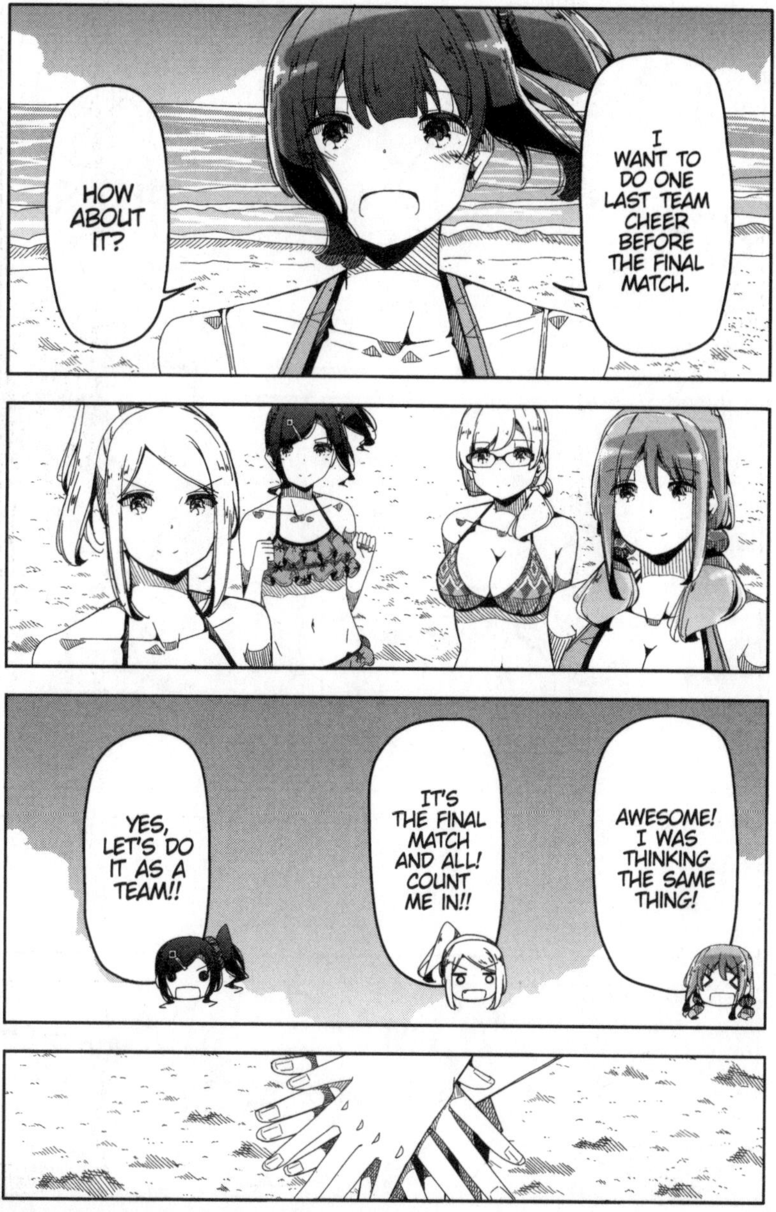
I WANT TO DO ONE LAST TEAM CHEER BEFORE THE FINAL MATCH.
HOW ABOUT IT?
AWESOME! I WAS THINKING THE SAME THING!
IT'S THE FINAL MATCH AND ALL! COUNT ME IN!!
YES, LET'S DO IT AS A TEAM!!

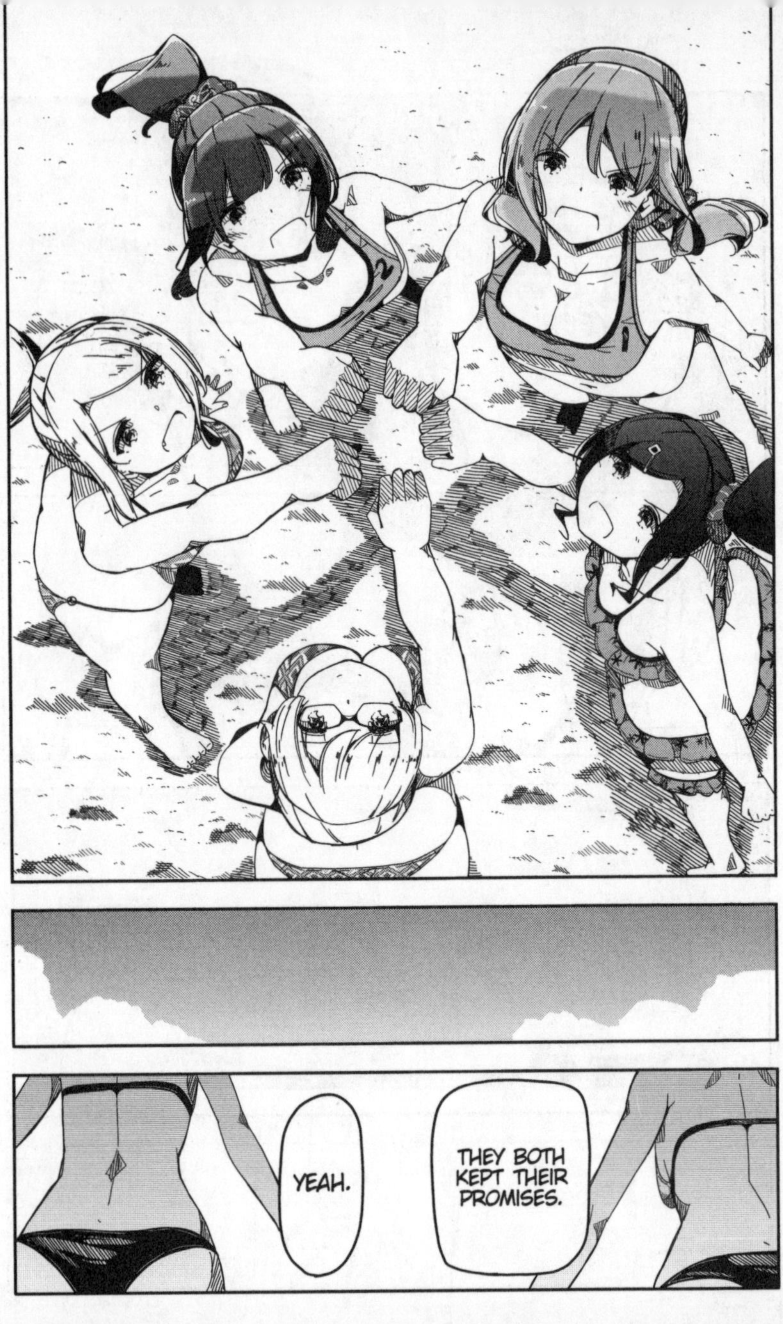
THEY BOTH KEPT THEIR PROMISES.
YEAH.

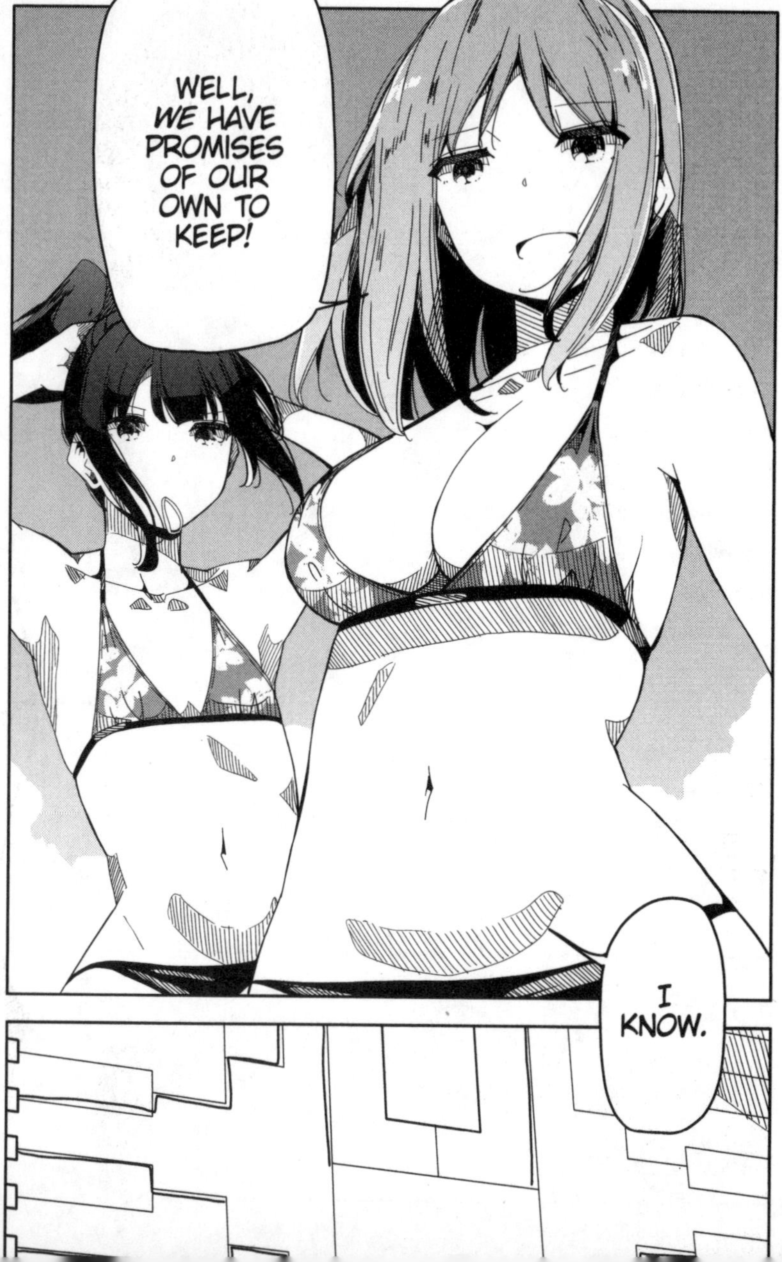
WELL, WE HAVE PROMISES OF OUR OWN TO KEEP!
I KNOW.

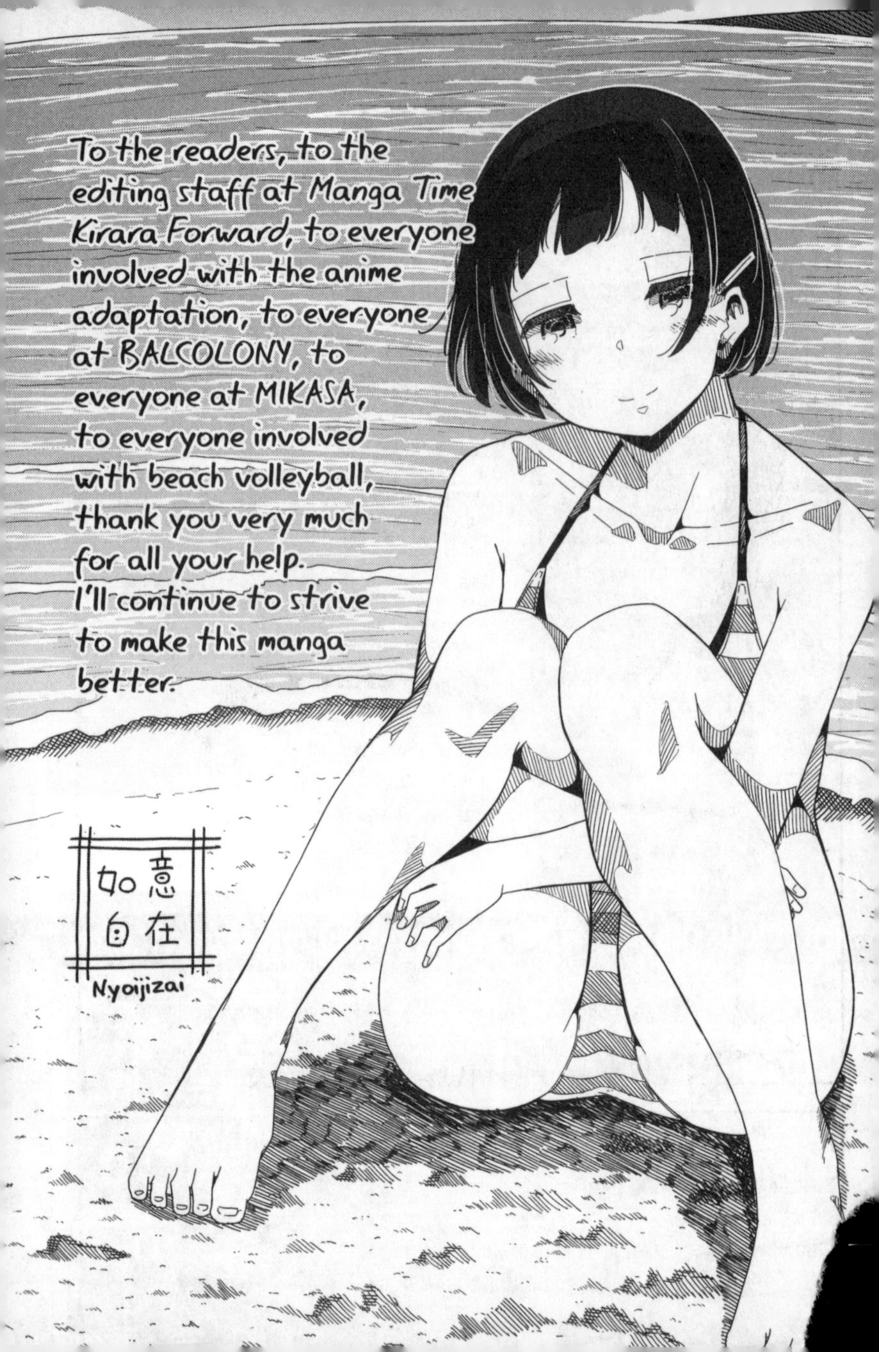
To the readers, to the editing staff at Manga Time Kirara Forward, to everyone involved with the anime adaptation, to everyone at BALCOLONY, to everyone at MIKASA, to everyone involved with beach volleyball, thank you very much for all your help. I'll continue to strive to make this manga better.
如意自在
Nyoijizai

# SEVEN SEAS ENTERTAIN

## Harukana Receive

**VOLUME 9**                    story and art by **NYOIJIZAI**

TRANSLATION
**Amanda Haley**

LETTERING AND RETOUCH
**Ray Steeves**

COVER DESIGN
**Kris Aubin**

PROOFREADER
**Krista Grandy**

EDITOR
**Shannon Fay**

PREPRESS TECHNICIAN
**Melanie Ujimori**

PRINT MANAGER
**Rhiannon Rasmussen-Silverstein**

PRODUCTION MANAGER
**Lissa Pattillo**

MANAGING EDITOR
**Julie Davis**

ASSOCIATE PUBLISHER
**Adam Arnold**

PUBLISHER
**Jason DeAngelis**

HARUKANARECEIVE Volume 9
© NYOIJIZAI 2020
Originally published in Japan in 2020 by HOUBUNSHA CO., LTD., Tokyo.
English translation rights arranged with HOUBUNSHA CO., LTD., Tokyo,
through TOHAN CORPORATION, Tokyo.

Seven Seas press and purchase enquiries can be sent to Marketing Manager
Lianne Sentar at press@gomanga.com. Information regarding the distribution
and purchase of digital editions is available from Digital Manager CK Russell
at digital@gomanga.com.

Seven Seas and the Seven Seas logo are trademarks of
Seven Seas Entertainment. All rights reserved.

ISBN: 978-1-64827-357-5

Printed in Canada

First Printing: January 2022

10 9 8 7 6 5 4 3 2 1

## FOLLOW US ONLINE: *www.sevenseasentertainment.com*

# READING DIRECTIONS

This book reads from *right to left*, Japanese style.
If this is your first time reading manga, you start
reading from the top right panel on each page and
take it from there. If you get lost, just follow the
numbered diagram here. It may seem backwards at
first, but you'll get the hang of it! Have fun!!

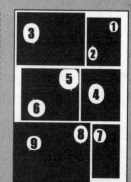